Living Together:
A Guide to the Law

by
*Anne Barlow, BA, Solicitor and Lecturer in Law
at the University College of Wales, Aberystwyth*

GW00336562

1992
Fourmat Publishing
London

ISBN 1 85190 151 5

First published 1992

Printed in Great Britain by
Billing & Sons Ltd, Worcester

© 1992 Anne Barlow
Published by Fourmat Publishing
133 Upper Street, London N1 1QP

Preface

The law relating to the unmarried family ranges over many disparate legal areas. There is at present no cohesive body of law which constitutes a "divorce law equivalent" for cohabitees and to a lesser extent their children. I have therefore attempted in this book to draw together the main areas of law which affect the unmarried family, firstly when living together as a unit, and secondly on relationship breakdown. As explained in Chapter 1, the term "unmarried family" is used to describe cohabitees of the same or different sexes, whether or not they have children. The book tends to concentrate on the position of those who are living, or who have lived, together in a fairly long term relationship, rather than on the single parent unmarried family. Given the breadth of the subject matter, it has not been possible to include every relevant topic. Child abduction, paternity tests and the position of children of unmarried families in care have not been covered, but are well documented elsewhere. The Children Act 1989 has comprehensively reformed the law relating to children. The important effects of these reforms upon parents and children of unmarried families are considered in context throughout the book, and particularly in Chapters 2 and 7. The significant procedural changes introduced by the new Rules, Regulations and Orders which accompany the Act are also discussed. Although the book is aimed primarily at the practitioner, it is hoped that it will also prove a useful source for teaching purposes. Finally, anyone attempting to write a book concerning the law has an uncomfortable feeling of swimming against the tide. The 1980s have seen major legislative reforms relating to children and housing law, both of which affect the unmarried family. The Child Support Act 1991 has now been passed, although it will not be implemented until 1993. Unfortunately as with all new legislation, many provisions are as yet untested in the courts, sometimes making speculation impossible to avoid. However, despite the wealth of recent legislation, the legal position of the unmarried family remains unsatisfactory and a small offering of suggested reforms can be found in the conclusion.

No book is written without support and encouragement from a number of sources and I have been exceptionally fortunate in this regard. I would therefore like to thank my colleagues at University College of Wales Aberystwyth for their patience and insight in their discussions with me. In particular I would like to thank Ann Sherlock and John Williams for reading draft chapters, Chris Rodgers for his valuable help in relation to the chapters on housing, Bill Hines and Indira Carr for explaining the mysteries of the mainframe computer to me and Barry Hough for taking more than his fair share of our joint administrative burdens. I would also like to thank my partners in practice Alan Edwards and Graham French as well as all my other colleagues there for their comments and assistance. Last but not least, I thank both Christine Morton and Mark Goodwin who have had the misfortune to live with me whilst in the throes of writing. I am grateful particularly to Mark, for providing me with both food and food for thought during this painful process!

Anne Barlow
January 1992

Contents

Table of Cases

page

page

PART I
LIVING TOGETHER

Chapter 1

The cohabitation relationship

1. Introduction

Perhaps the most difficult aspect of attempting to write a book about the "unmarried family" is the lack of satisfactory terms to describe both the family arrangement itself and the adult members of such a family unit. This task becomes more difficult where it is attempted, as here, to encompass the legal position of both heterosexual couples who are living together in a form of "quasi-marriage", and homosexual or "gay" couples living together as a joint unit in one household because of their relationship with each other.

The word "cohabitation" has come to denote the situation where two people live together as husband and wife in a family framework analogous to marriage, without actually having gone through a ceremony of marriage. The parties involved in such an arrangement are often described as "cohabitees", although the words mistress, common law husband/wife, *de facto* spouse and spouse equivalent are amongst a wealth of alternatives, none of which is completely satisfactory.

There is no formal definition of "living together as husband and wife" but the phrase, or variations of it, is often used in a legal context (see for example, the Domestic Violence and Matrimonial Proceedings Act 1976). The Law Commission in its Fourteenth Annual Report acknowledges that there are inconsistencies, but has not as yet addressed the problem:

"There is a growing tendency for the law to attach specific legal consequences to relationships outside marriage, but there is not as yet a wholly consistent approach in the different statutory provisions ... It may well be that there are valid policy reasons which dictate the use of different language in different statutes; nevertheless there is clearly a risk that difficulties of interpretation will occur." (Law Commission No. 97, para.2.32).

It seems to be assumed, at least by Parliamentary draftsmen, that where a phrase such as "living together as husband and wife" is used in statutes, such a situation is easily recognisable and thus not worthy of detailed definition. Whether or not such an assumption is justified is debatable, particularly as the definitions do vary from statute to statute. From a practitioner's point of view, each case has to be examined on its own facts in the context of the situation in which advice is sought. Thus for present purposes, attention is merely drawn to the fact that statutory definitions do vary and will be examined where appropriate in the ensuing chapters.

It is worthy of note here that the European Court of Justice has held that the definition of the term "spouse" does not include heterosexual cohabitees for the purposes of European Community Law (see *Netherlands State* v *Reed,* case 59/85). In addition, the European Commission on Human Rights has held that where homosexuals (that is, couples of the same sex) cohabit in a stable relationship, this does not fall within the scope of Article 8 of the Convention which protects the right to family life (see *X & Y* v *United Kingdom,* Application No. 9369/81, 32 Decisions and Reports 220). Furthermore, a decision that such a couple are not "living together as husband and wife" which in turn means that one is not able to succeed to the tenancy of the other on death, is not unjustifiably discriminatory within the meaning of Article 14 (*S* v *United Kingdom,* Application No. 11716/85, 47 Decisions and Reports 274, and see further Chapter 3).

Whilst the term "cohabitation" is usually applied in the context of couples comprising one man and one woman, it is a term equally appropriate to homosexual (or gay) couples who live together as a result of their relationship with each other. This raises the question of whether their respective situations display any common factors or problems which affect legal status. In both cases, each member of the couple, during the currency of the relationship, would normally regard the other member of the couple as their "next of kin" – the person whom they would wish to succeed to their estate or part of it if they were to die without leaving a Will, and the person to be notified in case of an accident or other emergency. Such couples organise themselves and live as one unit in society, which often involves purchasing or renting accommodation together and jointly purchasing household goods. It may be that no provision for contingencies such as the death of one of the parties or breakdown of the relationship is made. In addition, there are common misconceptions about the legal consequences of cohabiting or joint ownership, upon which couples may erroneously rely.

As is often the case, popular expectation and the true legal position of cohabitees may not coincide. For example, unless specific provision is made, the law does not as a rule allow people to appoint a person of their choosing as their next of kin for any purpose, whereas upon marriage a spouse automatically assumes this role.

This state of affairs means that unmarried cohabiting couples, be they heterosexual or not, are in much greater need than their married counterparts of legal advice on the consequences of joint enterprises undertaken or proposed by them. Certainly, where advice is sought on breakdown of the relationship or on death, the emotional effects and social consequences as well as the legal implications may be far more complex where the relationship involved cohabitation than otherwise would be the case. It is therefore crucial that advisors are aware of this, not only when instructed to advise at a time of crisis, but also when advising during the currency of the relationship, for example in the joint purchase of a house. If clear advice as to the legal implications is given at that stage, and a record kept or a document drawn up setting out the parties' respective shares, or at least the stated intentions as to their beneficial interests, this may avoid a dispute in the future. It may also be a good time to mention the possibility of making Wills and the unsatisfactory nature of the law on intestacy with regard to cohabitees, who are in effect the chosen next of kin of the other.

In some situations, legal rights or restrictions similar to those applicable to married couples have been extended to members of heterosexual cohabiting couples. Examples include the Domestic Violence and Matrimonial Proceedings Act 1976 and the provisions for claiming some welfare benefits. In other situations, the law totally ignores the cohabitation relationship, as is always the case with gay couples.

Thus there are many similarities in both the emotional and practical approaches taken by these two different types of cohabiting couple, and in their legal status. For these reasons, it is felt legitimate to consider the legal position of all cohabiting couples, with or without children, heterosexual or homosexual, as the subject of this book. It is therefore intended to use the words "cohabitation" and "cohabitee" in both the more common and the wider context, where appropriate, although the reader can assume that unless otherwise indicated, reference will be to cohabitation between a man and a woman. In addition, the term "partner" will be employed to describe the relationship of one of the parties to the other.

2. Social background

Marriage has always been society's preferred method of structuring family life and there is a great deal of social pressure to marry, including the tax incentive of the married allowance. Even so, cohabitation is continuing to increase.

In the case of homosexual couples, the reason is simple. They are unable to enter into a legal marriage in this country and any "marriage" is void (see s 11(c) Matrimonial Causes Act 1973). In Denmark this is no longer the case and marriages between homosexual couples are now recognised. Any comparable reform in this jurisdiction seems to be far off. Even where one member of a couple has undergone a sex change operation, it is not possible for them to enter into a marriage with a partner of their original sex (see *Corbett* v *Corbett* (orse. *Ashley) (No 2)* [1970] 2 WLR 1306 and *Corbett* v *Corbett* (orse.

Ashley) (No 3) [1970] 3 WLR 195). Such a decision has now twice been confirmed by the European Court of Human Rights not to be a violation of Article 12 of the European Convention on Human Rights which guarantees to men and women of marriageable age the right to marry and found a family (see *Rees* v *United Kingdom* 9 EHRR 56 and *Cossey* v *United Kingdom* 13 EHRR 622).

Some heterosexual couples cohabit rather than marry because one of them remains married to another person. Before the divorce law reforms in 1970, it was widely supposed that the reason for the fast increasing number of unmarried cohabiting couples was the fact that one or both partners were not free to marry, and that faster undefended divorce procedures would reduce the incidence of cohabitation. However, the statistics do not bear out these expectations. Despite the continuing increase in the divorce rate, cohabitation, in so far as it can be accurately measured, is also continuing to increase, notwithstanding the availability of easier divorce. This phenomenon requires an examination of the motives for cohabitation beyond inability to marry.

Certainly, a large proportion of people now cohabit before marriage, although the period of pre-marital cohabitation is variable. The *General Household Survey* 1988 (in table 3.9) shows that 26% of women under 50 who married for the first time under the age of 35 had cohabited with their husbands before marriage. In the case of second or subsequent marriages, this rose to 70% and the percentage for all marriages exceeds 50% (*Social Trends* 21). The proportion of women between the ages of 18-49 cohabiting has almost trebled in the period 1979 when it was 2.7%, to 1988 when it was 7.7%, or nearly 900,000 women. Another measure is the number of births outside marriage. In 1961 only 6% of children were registered as having been born outside marriage. In 1989, this figure had risen to over 25%. Of these, 70% were registered on the joint application of both parents, (which tends to suggest that they were cohabiting). In the same year, over half the unmarried parents making a joint registration stated that they shared the same address (*Population Trends* 63, Spring 1991).

Although little research has been conducted into the motives for cohabitation rather than marriage, other reasons proffered by commentators or based on small scale surveys are: an ideological objection to marriage by one or both of partners; a belief that a relationship is a private matter and not something which needs to be licensed by the state; a reluctance to marry following a previous failed marriage; a desire to avoid divorce on relationship breakdown and/or to avoid the legal consequences of divorce, such as payment of maintenance to a former partner; and freedom to vary the terms of a relationship without providing grounds for divorce.

For whatever reasons, there has been a marked increase in the number of couples who have decided to live together outside marriage and an increase in the number of children who live with parents who are not married. Whether or not the cohabitation is intended to endure in the short, medium or long term, such periods of cohabitation engender legal consequences about which lawyers are increasingly consulted, and in respect of which there is no neat body of law. Lawyers must search out disparate case law and be aware of which statutory provisions recognise the existence of cohabitees. They must, for example, distinguish those which include them in definitions as a member of their partner's family, from those which ignore the relationship and treat the partners as two unconnected individuals.

Statute in our jurisdiction has been slow to recognise cohabitation, unlike some of the other common law based countries such as Australia and Canada where some of the rights and obligations of married couples have been extended to cohabiting couples. Closer to home, the Scottish Law Commission has produced a discussion paper (No. 86) *The Effects of Cohabitation in Private Law*. It is currently considering whether there should be a legal response to the trend to increased cohabitation in the form of extending married couples' inheritance, property and aliment (maintenance) rights and obligations to cohabiting couples who fulfill certain criteria. The Law Commission for England and Wales has not yet been set such a task, indicating that major reform is not on the agenda here, at least for the time being.

3. Characteristics of the cohabitation relationship

The legal consequences of cohabitation can be far reaching, but unfortunately, cohabiting couples rarely seek direct legal advice about their situation until a crisis, commonly in the form of death, relationship breakdown or perhaps possession proceedings is upon them. There is a common misconception amongst cohabiting couples that rights are acquired after a certain period of cohabitation.

Although the precise legal consequences of the various aspects of cohabitation will be dealt with in detail in the following chapters, a few illustrations of the possible pitfalls of cohabitation are appropriate here. They also underline the advisability of prevention, in the form of agreements or contracts, Wills and declarations of trust in relation to property, rather than the only cure available – litigation.

It is common for people to enter into joint mortgages or other loans without realising the full implications of joint and several liability. This problem is not exclusive to cohabiting couples, but they are often faced with the consequences. There is no maintenance available to either partner of a formerly cohabiting couple, no matter how long the period of cohabitation. Maintenance is available only to any children of the relationship (see Chapter 8). Where a property has been bought jointly by a couple, unless there has been an express declaration of their respective beneficial interests in the conveyance, or in the form of a declaration of trust which sets out their shares, there is ample room for expensive litigation on relationship breakdown to resolve a dispute.

A cohabitee living in a property owned or rented in the sole name of his or her partner is in a precarious position should the relationship end either through breakdown of the relationship or death of the partner, unless provision has previously been made. Similarly, if Wills are not made, then on the death of one of the couple, all his or her property, including personal belongings and savings not jointly held, and in the absence of any children, will pass to an estranged spouse not yet divorced, a parent, brother or sister, rather than the partner, although in some limited circumstances an application may be made to the court for some provision to be made out of the estate (see Chapter 4).

Before looking at the possibility of cohabitation contracts as a means of providing for at least some of the contingencies which may arise during the course of or at the end of cohabitation, it is proposed to look at certain of the consequences of cohabitation which do not fall easily into the specific subjects covered in the following chapters and in relation to which advice is often sought.

(a) Changing names
There is nothing to prevent a cohabitee from changing his or her surname so as to be known by the same name as his or her partner.
Change of name by an adult can be achieved by means of a short
statutory declaration, declared pursuant to the provisions of the
Statutory Declarations Act 1835; or a deed setting out details of the
original name and the new name which must be substituted for all
purposes thereafter. It is advisable to have a deed witnessed by a
solicitor to ensure acceptance by all authorities. The original declaration or deed is then sufficient proof for banks, building societies, the
Passport Office and most other purposes, to ensure that official documentation is transferred into the new name.

It is possible to change one's name merely by common usage, and
some argue that this is the only way names are in fact changed, but for
official purposes evidence of the change is normally required and thus
a simple deed or declaration is advisable to avoid unnecessary complications and delay.

Names can also be changed by enrolled deed poll. The advantage
of this is that there is an official record of the change, as the change of
name is enrolled at the Filing Department of the Central Office of the
Supreme Court. However, the procedure is longer, including verifica-
tion of the person's identity by means of a declaration from a
Commonwealth citizen and householder resident in the UK who has
known that person for ten years, an advert in the *London Gazette* and
payment of both the advertisement costs and a fee to the Court. (For
guidance of the exact steps to be taken, and for precedents of the necessary forms, see Pearce, *Name-Changing: A Practical Guide* (1990),
Fourmat Publishing). It is also a procedure which is open only to citi-
zens of the UK, Commonwealth and the Republic of Ireland

There are still some purposes for which an enrolled deed poll is the
only acceptable option to effect a change of name. In particular, some
professional bodies such as the General Medical Council require
enrolment before the change of name will be accepted, and thus advisors should check whether the change needs to be registered with any
body likely to have such a requirement.

Changing a child's name may present more difficulty and the right, or lack of right, to do so is inextricably bound up with the law relating to children. Only where the parents of a child were never married to each other and no court order or recognised agreement has been made granting the father custody, parental rights or responsibility, can the mother safely change the child's surname, or indeed any of the child's names, without reference to the father. Where the conditions are fulfilled, the change can be achieved by an adapted form of statutory declaration or deed executed by the mother. Similarly, where one of the parents dies without appointing a testamentary guardian, and there has been no previous court order, a surviving parent *with parental responsibility* is free to change a child's names if he or she so wishes.

In any other situation, either parent with parental responsibility can now change a child's name. Yet it is advisable to obtain the other parent's consent, to prevent their reversing the name change. Where consent is not forthcoming, a specific issue order (s 8 Children Act 1989) may be sought; and where there is a residence order, leave of the court is required (s 13 CA 1989). This is discussed further in Chapter 2.

(b) Making wills

The position of cohabitees on intestacy renders them particularly vulnerable on their partner's death. As there is no blood or legal relationship between cohabitees, they do not come within any of the categories of person entitled to inherit on intestacy under s 46 Administration of Estates Act 1925. Thus, even where a cohabitee dies leaving no surviving relatives whatsoever, his or her estate will pass *bona vacantia* to the Crown rather than to the surviving partner. It is worthwhile noting that the Crown may be prepared to make an *ex gratia* payment to a cohabitee in such circumstances. Section 46(1)(vi) gives a discretion to make payments for dependants and "other persons for whom the intestate may have been expected to make provision". It is entirely discretionary but in fact may provide for a cohabitee who cannot make any other type of claim as they were not dependent upon their partner. As is detailed in Chapter 5, if the surviving partner was dependent upon the deceased and reasonable financial provision has not been made, then a claim under the Inheritance (Provision for Family and Dependants) Act 1975 for maintenance may be made. Such an application is not without difficulty. It is bound to be costly and may well be resisted by those who would otherwise inherit under the terms of a Will or on intestacy.

Thus cohabitees must be advised of the advantages of mutual Wills and the hazards of not making them. Mutual Wills, however, while avoiding the laws on intestacy, will not necessarily solve all cohabitees' problems, and much will depend on any responsibilities they have towards others. The following matters should be borne in mind when advising cohabitees in relation to Wills:

(i) Marriage always revokes a Will. Thus if mutual Wills have been made and the cohabiting partners marry each other, new Wills must be considered.

(ii) Wills can be revoked or changed at any time by a testator and it is not possible to bind a partner to the terms of a particular Will.

(iii) Without a Will, a partner will not be entitled to anything belonging to the other partner on his or her death, not even personal belongings. Only jointly owned property which has not been declared to be beneficially owned in specified shares will pass to the surviving joint owner. Thus, as discussed in Chapter 3, if property is owned jointly as tenants in common, a deceased's partner's beneficial interest will pass to the joint owner only if bequeathed to him or her by Will.

(iv) Where a partner has a former spouse and/or children who are still dependent upon him or her, they have a right to make a claim under the Inheritance Act 1975 that provision be made for them out of the estate. This will inevitably mean that the surviving cohabiting partner who is a beneficiary under the Will, is forced to concede or compromise the claim; or become involved in expensive litigation if advised to resist the claim, which would undoubtedly deplete the estate. Thought therefore needs to be given as to how best to balance these competing claims on the estate in a Will, in a way which would be held to be fair if challenged. Life assurance may well provide the answer in a situation where there may not be enough to provide for everyone adequately.

(v) It can be important correctly to identify a cohabitee beneficiary in a Will. A testator who refers in a Will to his or her cohabitee as their spouse, may unintentionally defeat the gift, although case law has tended to give effect to the testator's intentions where these are clear (see, for example, *Re Brown* [1910] 2 TLR 257 and *Re Lynch* [1943] 1 All ER 168).

(c) Life assurance

Where cohabitees enter into joint debts such as a mortgage, attention should be drawn to the implications of joint and several liability on the death of one of the partners. The financial difficulties that this causes can be circumvented by taking out a mortgage protection policy or an endowment mortgage, which would guarantee to pay off the debt in such a situation. Where one partner is financially dependent upon the other, life assurance is even more important to avoid the risk of losing the home on the death of the breadwinner. Strong advice should be given as to the consequences of failing to make appropriate provision, even where a Will has been made making the surviving dependent partner a beneficiary. Any life policy aiming to protect the surviving partner from sole or joint debts should either be assigned to the creditor such as the mortgagee or be written in trust for the other partner. The proceeds of the policy will not then form part of the estate of the deceased partner.

Similarly, where there are likely to be competing claims on an estate from other dependants, a life policy written in trust for a cohabitee, has the advantage of not forming part of the deceased's estate, and thus could not be made subject to a claim under the Inheritance (Provision for Family and Dependants) Act 1975. If, on the other hand, the benefit of any such policy is bequeathed by Will, it forms part of the estate and could be diverted to other dependants by virtue of the provisions of the 1975 Act.

4. Cohabitation contracts

Having examined some of the pitfalls of unmarried partnerships and families, what can be done to avoid the problems? Are cohabitation contracts detailing the agreed basis upon which the cohabitation is to operate the answer? It is popularly thought that such a contract would be binding upon the parties in the event of breakdown of the relationship, as is indeed the case in other jurisdictions. Unfortunately, in our jurisdiction, there is no certainty that the courts would enforce such a contract. In fact, as will be illustrated, such precedents as there are point in the other direction. However, the issue has yet to be decided in a contemporary context.

Contractual freedom is one of the boasts of the English legal system. In 1938 Lord Atkin endorsed the following statement made by Lord Jessel in 1875:

"If there is one thing more than another public policy requires it is that men of full age and competent understanding shall have the utmost liberty of contracting and that their contracts when entered into freely and voluntarily shall be held sacred and shall be enforced by the Court of Justice: therefore you have this paramount public policy to consider, that you are not lightly to interfere with their freedom to contract." (Lord Atkin in *Fender v St John Mildmay* [1938] AC 1 citing Lord Jessel in *Printing and Numerical Registering Co* v *Sampson* (1875) LR19 Eq 462 at 465)

However, due to other public policy considerations, it is presently unclear to what extent such freedom is available to cohabiting couples who, either before or during cohabitation, wish to encapsulate the terms of the cohabitation in an enforceable contract.

Whether or not a contract will be considered valid by the courts may depend on its contents as well as on a number of other factors. It is interesting to note that in 1988, the Council of Ministers of the European Community adopted the recommendation (no. R(88)3) that member states should not preclude cohabitation contracts dealing with property and money on the ground that the parties are not married to each other. Unlike the marriage contract, a cohabitation contract is a matter of a private rather than a public agreement, and thus the starting point is that the parties are free to agree the scope and nature of the terms themselves. Whether or not all or any of the terms of such a contract will be upheld by the courts may in any event not be the parties' only motive for having an agreement drawn up.

Couples are likely to want a cohabitation contract to cover their rights and obligations both during cohabitation and on breakdown of the relationship. Unlike their married counterparts who are thought to be prevented by public policy considerations from preparing for the contingency of breakdown, a cohabitation contract would not be void by reason of providing for such an eventuality. Interestingly, the Law Society's Family Law Committee has recently recommended that marriage contracts providing for the division of property on divorce should be enforceable where both parties have entered into them with the benefit of legal advice (see *Law Society's Gazette* 15 May 1991, page 2). As noted above, there is now a Council of Ministers' recommendation that cohabitation contracts dealing with property should be recognised. Both of these developments bode well for the likely enforceability of a cohabitation contract where it is limited to issues of property, but before discussing enforceability in detail, the range of matters which cohabiting couples may wish to included in their contracts is considered.

(a) Contents

The exact content of each cohabitation contract is obviously a matter for the couple concerned. The advantage of drawing up a contract is that it requires the partners to consider, before there is any dispute, their respective expectations, both during the relationship and, in so far as can be foreseen, on breakdown.

It is also possible to have a contract that deals only with the eventuality of breakdown, without regulating the terms of the relationship itself. Some couples may wish to commit to writing every aspect of the agreements between them, down to the minutiae of the washing up rota, whilst others may find this unnecessary yet see the value of discussing, agreeing and recording in advance their respective rights in relation to property, maintenance and any children. The more romantic may wish instead to trust their partner sufficiently to feel sure that in the event of breakdown, a satisfactory agreement would be reached. However, sadly, the bitterness that breakdown usually engenders often means that such trust is misplaced. This is as true for cohabiting homosexual couples as it is for heterosexuals.

Some argue that to ask or advise couples to agree such matters in a formal legal document may raise problems within a relationship that were not previously present, and that accordingly matters are best left undocumented. However, it is submitted that if such an exercise reveals different understandings about the implications of a couple's arrangements, then surely this is a matter which merits discussion during the currency of the relationship where possible, rather than on breakdown when compromise or re-evaluation of the position may be much more difficult.

What should be the main tenets of a cohabitation contract? As previously indicated, it is perfectly possible to include the agreed rules upon which the cohabitation is founded; these include whether or not other relationships are permitted; how the household chores should be shared; and the amount of leisure time the parties will spend together. However, no court would ever compensate a breach of any such terms with an order for specific performance, as is the general rule with contracts for personal services. It is unlikely that a court would compensate a breach of the rules of the relationship (as opposed to the terms contained in the contract relating to property division), with damages, as it may be felt that the parties did not intend to be legally bound by such rules other than to provide evidence of breakdown of the relationship. Their inclusion can never be more than a record of the parties' intentions in those areas and should only be expressed as such in the contract.

Providing the contract meets the general criteria for an enforceable contract as set out below, contract terms which detail how property which is brought into the relationship or subsequently purchased individually or jointly by the parties, is to be treated on breakdown, may well be enforceable. At the very least it will be strong evidence of the parties' intentions at the time of the contract and will be valuable in case of dispute. Similarly, if a property is bought for occupation by the couple as a family home, a clause indicating that it is property which is to be beneficially jointly owned in stated shares may negative any contrary indication on the title documents, providing the cohabitation contract is executed as a deed. Provision can also be made for giving notice under the agreement to terminate the relationship and to provide for the agreed division of property at that juncture. A clause to pay maintenance on breakdown of the relationship to a partner who would otherwise have no right to maintenance will also prove enforceable if the contract is executed as a deed. A fairly exhaustive list of relevant matters to be considered for inclusion in a cohabitation contract are set out by Barton (*Cohabitation Contracts*, Gower, 1985, pages 55-56) and reproduced here for reference:

"(a) statement of the purpose of the contract, for example to create an equal relationship;

(b) legality of the agreement, for example to be legally binding or merely a statement of expectations;

(c) the parties, for example, statement of ages, financial disclosures and health;

(d) aims of the parties, for example their collective and individual goals in the relationship;

(e) duration, for example, for lifetime, fixed period or until specified event;

(f) careers – employment, for example, do both want/are able to work, priorities;

(g) income and expenses, for example, how much, and how to be treated, whether or not to pool these and also savings;

(h) property held at inception, for example how to be treated;

(i) property acquired during cohabitation, for example whether to be treated as community property or not, who to manage. How gifts are to be treated and whether life insurance is to be taken out, how funded and who nominated as beneficiary. Similarly, whether nomination to be made to occupational pension fund;

(j) debts, for example, statement of what each currently owes and their attitude to credit;

(k) living arrangements, for example, who to choose location, whether town or country, policy as to guests;

(l) household tasks, for example, how divided;

(m) surname, for example, each to keep his or her own, one to adopt the other's, hyphenation, the position of children's surnames;

(n) sexual relations, for example, type, monogamy, rules for disclosure if not;

(o) personal behaviour, for example, smoking, hobbies, private area in house;

(p) relations with family and friends, for example any responsibility for children of previous relationship;

(q) children, whether or not to have any, how to bring them up;

(r) religion;

(s) health, for example private care, whether insurance to be taken out;

(t) inheritance and Wills, for example what if anything they will leave to each other;

(u) breaches of the agreement, for example liquidated damages, court proceedings, arbitration;

(v) resolving disagreements, for example professional conciliation or a named mutually agreed conciliator;

(w) variation or renewal of the contract;

(x) dissolution, for example when, notice, support, property, custody;

(y) conversion to marriage."

(b) Enforceability

The problems of enforcement have already been mentioned. The issues are raised by the law of contract, and are matters which courts must consider in relation to any contract the validity of which is challenged. There are are as many as five hurdles at which a cohabitation contract may fall:

(i)   it may be found illegal or void on grounds of public policy;

(ii) an intention to create legal relations may be absent;

(iii) it may be found void for uncertainty;

(iv) consideration may be absent; or

(v)   it may be found voidable where there is undue influence.

(i) Illegality on grounds of public policy: Contracts for immoral purposes, which of course include sexual immorality, are illegal and consequently unenforcable. Contracts deemed to be prejudicial to the marital state are also contrary to public policy and void. Despite the changing tide towards recognition of cohabitation in some statutes, these common law principles of the law of contract remain unchanged. Thus, although current thinking is that no court today would strike down a cohabitation contract entered into by a cohabit-

17

ing heterosexual couple on these grounds, this has not yet been tested in the courts. Accordingly the current legal position remains uncertain. The validity of a contract between a cohabiting gay couple may be significantly more vulnerable to an adverse finding that it promotes sexual immorality.

The case law dates back as far as the mid seventeenth century, and the most recent case which actually expressly considered the validity of such a contract was *Diwell* v *Farnes* [1959] 2 All ER 379. Given that no court has yet overruled them, these cases remain *prima facie* binding precedent. In *Diwell,* Ormerod LJ stated at p 384E: "... such joint venture must depend on a contract express or implied between the parties which being founded on an immoral consideration, would not be enforceable".

Many of the cases do not distinguish between parties in a long stable relationship, and a contract for the services of a prostitute.

Some ground rules can be elicited from the case law, and assist in assessing how to limit the possibility that a cohabitation contract will be held unenforceable. In *Walker* v *Perkins* (1764) 1 Wm Bl 517, a contract entered into before commencement of the cohabitation, and which provided for financial provision for the woman both during and on termination of the cohabitation period, was held to be void as it promoted sexual immorality. Yet an agreement entered into after cohabitation had ceased, making provision for the woman, and which was under seal, was held to be valid in *Annandale* v *Harris* (1727) 2 P Wms 432. Again in *Re Vallence, Vallence* v *Bladgeon* (1884) 26 Ch D 353, where the couple had lived together for more than thirty years, and six months before his death the man had given the woman a bond worth £6,000, a court refused to set aside the gift of the bond on the basis that it was bought with immoral consideration and consequently illegal, because it was past consideration and the short continued cohabitation could not be presumed to be the consideration for the gift of the bond. As this case concerned the gift of a bond, consideration was not of course needed. However, if immoral consideration was proved, it would have rendered the gift illegal.

Thus if the contract does not actually promote sexual immorality because the cohabitation has ceased or has already commenced, there is authority for saying that the contract is not void on this ground, although care needs to be taken that there is sufficient other consideration or that the agreement is executed as a deed.

Thus advisors should always ensure, when drafting a cohabitation agreement, that any reference to the parties' agreement to cohabit is put in the past tense, and is not drafted in such a way as to imply that the consideration for the terms of the agreement is future cohabitation.

Of course if a modern test case were to find a cohabitation contract void on the sexual immorality ground, it would not be possible to sever this part of the contract and preserve the rest of the terms as severance is not available where there is an illegal contract.

Even if the prevailing view, that no court would hold a contract illegal for promoting sexual immorality given that cohabitation is now so socially accepted and even affords parties statutory protection in some areas, is correct, would a cohabitation contract be found void on the grounds that it is prejudicial to the institution of marriage?

As Barton (see page 16) suggests, such a contract may be deemed by the court to fetter the ability to marry third parties where a defined period of intended cohabitation is included, or could be found to further prejudice an existing marriage if one of the parties to the contract remains married to another. Thus there is scope for a court to find a cohabitation contract void. However, this aspect of the public policy principle has not been extended to a finding that all cohabitation contracts are prejudicial to the institution of marriage, so that at least where two single people are parties to the contract, it seems extremely unlikely that a court would be persuaded to hold the contract void. An assertion that a cohabitation contract is prejudicial to the marital state would be difficult to support, where, for example, the contract makes it clear that the cohabitation is viewed as a trial marriage. Even where parties are married to others, given the existence of divorce, it seems highly unlikely that the contract itself could be deemed prejudicial, particularly where it was entered into after separation of the spouses and after cohabitation between the cohabitees had commenced.

In a cohabitation contract between homosexual partners, the argument is perhaps open that neither party would in any event ever wish to marry a person of the opposite sex, and therefore the contract of itself is not prejudicial to the state of marriage.

Accordingly, it seems most unlikely that cohabitation contracts would be unenforceable on this ground alone, and in any event, unlike contracts found to be illegal for promoting sexual immorality, it would be possible to sever the offending part of the contract leaving the remainder of the terms, those, for example, dealing with jointly owned property, intact and enforceable.

A more positive view regarding the enforceability of cohabitation contracts despite the lack of modern judicial authority on the point, is given weight by recent decisions which will be more fully discussed in Chapters 3 and 10 in relation to housing and property. In these cases the courts have enforced promises made to "mistresses" by their partners. Promises to continue to provide accommodation on breakdown of the relationship have been enforced by imputing a licence for life (see *Tanner* v *Tanner* [1975] 1 WLR 1345 and *Chandler* v *Kerley* [1978] 1 WLR 693). The courts have also found resulting and constructive trusts where cohabitees have purchased a property in the sole name of one of them, but their actions showed it was clearly intended as a joint venture (see for example *Eves* v *Eves* [1975] 1 WLR 1338 and *Cooke* v *Head* [1972] 1 WLR 518). In none of these cases has there been any mention that such agreements may be illegal or void on public policy grounds, although in cases relying on trusts, such a consideration is irrelevant as the courts apply the law of trusts rather than the law of contract. However, the recommendation of the Council of Ministers made in 1988 (no. R(88)3; see page 13) does specifically deal with contracts between cohabitees and recommends that member states should give effect to these where they relate to money and property.

Where there is a child of an unmarried relationship, the courts have endorsed the making of binding agreements for maintenance for mother and child. It was said in *Horrocks* v *Forray* [1976] 1 WLR 230, at p 239 "when an illegitimate child has been born, there is certainly nothing contrary to public policy in the parents coming to an agreement which they intend to be binding in law, for the maintenance of mother and child."

Of course where there are children, it is not possible to oust the jurisdiction of the court with regard to maintenance, but certainly a clause providing maintenance for one or other of the partners on relationship breakdown would seem to be enforceable providing the other ingredients for a valid contract are not wanting.

(ii) Absence of intention to create legal relations: There is a rebuttable presumption that parties to an agreement regarding domestic arrangements do not intend to be legally bound. The principle was set out in the case of *Balfour* v *Balfour* [1919] 2 KB 571 where a promise by a husband who worked abroad, to his wife who had to stay behind on medical grounds, that he would pay her £30 per month was held to be unenforceable both because she had provided no consideration and also because the domestic nature of the agreement showed that there was no intention to create legal relations. Atkin LJ at page 578 said:

"Those agreements, or many of them, do not result in contracts at all ... even though there may be what as between other parties would constitute consideration for the agreement ... They are not contracts ... because the parties did not intend that they should be attended by legal consequences."

However, where there is a written agreement, especially if it has been drawn up by a legal advisor, this should be enough to rebut the presumption, as parties do not have agreements drawn up unless there is an intention that they should be legally binding (see *Meritt* v *Merritt* [1970] 1 WLR 1211).

The case of *Layton* v *Martin* [1986] 2 FLR 277 provides a word of warning to cohabitees who indicate that they wish to draw up their own agreements without taking legal advice. In that case, the man wrote to the woman asking her to live with him and offering her "financial security during my life – and on my death". A few months later she went to live with him; they stayed together for eight years, although they separated two years before his death. However, the court refused to enforce the alleged contract against his estate and Scott at page 239 underlined the difficulty faced:

"In family or quasi family situations there is always the question whether the parties intended to create a legal binding contract between them. The more general and less precise the language of the so-called contract, the more difficult it will be to infer that intention."

The content of a contract may also influence the court's view. Thus the less domestic detail that is contained, and the more terms there are relating to more legalistic matters, such as a statement of respective interests in jointly owned property, the more likely a court would be to infer the requisite intention

In any event, this is a hurdle easily overcome by cohabitees who do wish to create a binding contract; an advisor drafting a contract can, to ensure the intention is unambiguous, specifically recite the intention to be bound.

(iii) Contract void for uncertainty: As with any contract, if the terms are so vague and uncertain that they are incapable of enforcement, then this will either be a term which the court ignores, or, if the uncertainty comprises terms which are fundamental to the operation of the contract, may vitiate the whole contract. Thus a term agreeing to make financial provision without any indication of the nature or extent or the rules according to which such provision could be ascertained would be void for uncertainty. Thus advisors drafting a cohabitation contract should have this potential problem in mind.

(iv) Absence of consideration: As with any contract, there must be consideration for a cohabitation agreement to be enforceable. In the case of cohabitation agreements, the consideration for one party's agreeing to make financial provision for the other may be the act of cohabiting with the other party; this risks being deemed immoral consideration, consequently rendering the contract illegal. There is a simple answer; if the agreement is in the form of a deed, no consideration for the bargain is necessary. Advisors should therefore recommend a deed be executed. With the introduction of the provisions of the Law of Property (Miscellaneous Provisions) Act 1989, even the mystery of the seal has been dispensed with, and, apart from the requirements that it be in writing and dated, a document merely needs to record that it is being signed as a deed in the presence of independent witnesses to the signatures.

(v) Contract voidable for undue influence: A finding of undue influence exercised by one party over the other inducing that person to enter into the contract will vitiate the contract in its entirety. If the

terms of a contract are heavily weighted in favour of one of the parties, it may be susceptible to such a finding. In contracts between spouses, there is no presumption of undue influence; to defeat a contract, it must be proved. In contrast, where a contract between an engaged couple substantially favours one party, there is a rebuttable presumption of undue influence and it must be proved that no such influence induced the less favoured party to enter into the bargain (see *Zamet* v *Hayman* [1961] 1 WLR 1442).

Whether or not there is a presumption of undue influence between cohabitees is unknown. As advisors may advise only one party to a contract (to avoid potential conflict of interest), it is obviously desirable, where there is any hint of inequality of bargaining power, to ensure that the less favoured party is urged to seek independent legal advice.

(c) Cohabitation contracts in other jurisdictions
Given that the situation in our own jurisdiction is still uncertain, it is helpful to consider the position in other common law jurisdictions to which the court could be referred.

In the case of *Marvin* v *Marvin* 18 Cal 3d. 660 involving the actor Lee Marvin and his former cohabitee, the Supreme Court of California explicitly rejected the contention that a cohabitation contract entered into by cohabitees living in a stable relationship is unenforceable on immoral purposes ground. It said, at page 669, "A contract between non-marital partners is unenforceable only to the extent it explicitly rests upon the immoral and illicit consideration of meretricious sexual services."

This has been followed in some seventeen other States in the USA, and a similar finding was reached in the Australian case of *Andrews* v *Parker* [1973] Qd R93.

In *Marvin*, the court also found that the performance of household services in a relationship between cohabitees should not be presumed to be a gift, and may thus provide sufficient consideration for a share in property owned by the other partner. It is of course by no means certain that an English court would follow this line of development. Their tendency, at least in the past, to look for constructive and resulting trusts and licences for life in the absence of any written agreement between parties, is, it is submitted, a useful barometer of the likely judicial approach to such an issue, although it is admitted that more recent cases have drawn back from this approach (see *Lloyds Bank PLC* v *Rossett* [1990] 2 FLR 155 and Chapter 10). Parliament, on the other hand, could follow some other jurisdictions and actively encourage cohabitation agreements. This, it is submitted, would be a worthy course to adopt given the increasing number of people who choose to live together outside marriage. As noted above, there is already a recommendation passed by the Council of Ministers that effect should be given to cohabitation contracts concerned with money and property.

In Minnesota, USA, a statute Minn. Stat. 513.076 (Cum. Supp. 1980) excludes, as being contrary to public policy, any claim based on cohabitation unless the parties have previously executed a contract which complies with the provisions of the statute. It must be in writing, signed by the parties and enforceable only when the relationship has ceased.

In Canada, five Provinces have legislated on the issue. The most comprehensive reforms are found in Ontario (Family Law Reform Act 1980), Prince Edward Island (Family Law Reform Act 1978), New Brunswick (Marital Property Act 1980) and Newfoundland (Matrimonial Property Act 1979). These allow cohabitees to enter into agreements governing matters both during and after their relationships in so far as they deal with property ownership, support obligations; education and moral training of their children (although custody and access can be dealt with only in a separation agreement); and any other matter. The legislation provides for severance of a void term and will not enforce terms relating to children in so far as they are not in the best interests of the child. Such agreements must be in writing, signed and witnessed.

In Newfoundland, cohabitees are permitted to opt into matrimonial property legislation and once they do, are treated as if they were spouses.

To date, there do not appear to have been any cases where cohabitation contracts between homosexual couples have been enforced. However, in another Californian decision, *Jones* v *Daley* 122 Cal App 3d 500 1981, the court refused to uphold the contract only on the narrow ground that it was unable to sever an express term about sexual services contained in their agreement and which accordingly fell foul of the rule established in *Marvin* v *Marvin* (above). In California at least, therefore, it seems possible to draft valid cohabitation contracts for both homosexual and heterosexual couples.

5. Conclusion

What are the advantages and disadvantages of entering into a cohabitation agreement, and how should clients be advised? It seems clear that where there are children, subject to not ousting the jurisdiction of the court, agreements between parents are welcomed. Furthermore, as long as the provision of sexual services is not explicit consideration, the contract is executed as a deed and the other requirements for a valid contract discussed above are met, there seems a strong chance that the English courts would enforce a contract which contemplates the division of property and financial support on relationship breakdown. Not to do so would fly in the face of the recommendation of the Council of Ministers made in 1988 that member states should recognise such contracts. In any event, if there is an agreement between parties, regardless of whether or not one would in fact seek to enforce it against the other on breakdown, it must be evidence of the parties' intentions at the time of the agreement. As such, at the very least, it provides the starting point either on separation, or on death, when there is a risk of a dispute with relatives.

An agreement may confer on a party rights he or she could not otherwise acquire; from the other party's point of view, this binds them to something they did not have to concede, yet in happier times actually wanted to give to their partner. Advisors of course need to point out the possible future disadvantages.

Presumably, a cohabitation contract could attempt to opt in to matrimonial legislation by virtue of a term stating the parties agree to make such financial provision for the other as they would be required to do by the court had they married each other on the date cohabitation commenced. However, such a term on its own could provoke an unfavourable decision from an English court, either on public policy grounds, or even perhaps by virtue of the uncertainty of the provisions being contemplated. Thus any such terms should be in addition and without prejudice to such definitive provision as the parties can agree at the date of the contract.

Other disadvantages of entering into a cohabitation contact include the fact that it is of course impossible to cover every eventuality – an argument for, in appropriate cases, attempting to opt in to matrimonial legislation as a provision of last resort. A comprehensive agreement with some omissions may imply that their absence means they were deliberately excluded and so are not to be implied by a court.

This again underlines the need either to make the contract clear in its limitations, for example, by confining it to maintenance and without prejudice to any other claims against property; or to be as comprehensive as possible. The best result may be achieved by a series of separate agreements dealing individually with maintenance and property during the relationship and on breakdown. These could then be amended as circumstances changed.

It is important to remember that most cases concerning relationship breakdown are settled out of court. A cohabitation agreement will always provide a starting point, or provide for conciliation through a professional agency before resorting to court proceedings.

In this sense, providing the potential conflict of interest between the parties is kept firmly in mind by advisors at the drafting stage, there is much to be said for encouraging cohabitees to set down their affairs in an agreement, despite the doubts surrounding its legal enforceability. As is always the case when advising a client about a Will, advisors must emphasise the need to keep the situation under review, and to vary the contract from time top time as circumstances change.

Chapter 2

The status of children

1. Parental status

As was illustrated in Chapter 1, there has been a steep increase over the last thirty years in the number of children registered as having been born outside marriage. In 1989, more than twenty five per cent of all children born were born to parents who were not married to each other. There has also been a significant increase in the number of births registered by both parents. In 1971, this accounted for forty five per cent of such births but by 1989 the figure had risen to seventy per cent (see *Social Trends* 21). More than half of these parents gave the same address, and it is reasonable to conclude from such statistics that a significant number of children begin their lives in an unmarried family.

The legal disadvantages to which a child was traditionally subjected as a consequence of having been born outside marriage have largely been swept away by various reforms, culminating in the provisions of the Family Law Reform Act 1987 ("FLRA 1987"). Affiliation orders have been abolished, and many of the distinctions between legitimate and illegitimate children made in different enactments,

27

such as those concerning inheritance rights on intestacy, have been dispensed with. The old provisions may still be significant for some time to come, as where an affiliation order was made in the past, or under a Will made before the coming into force of the relevant provisions of the 1987 Act. Public attention now rarely focuses on the parental position, but the father of a child born outside marriage still starts from a very much disadvantaged position in terms of legal status. This is as true for a father of a child born in a stable relationship between cohabitees as it is for the father of a child born of a more casual encounter. Perhaps surprisingly, the Children Act 1989 ("CA 1989") does nothing to alter the position of the unmarried father on the birth of his child.

Before the CA 1989, when a child was born to parents who were not married, by virtue of s 85(7) Children Act 1975 ("CA 1975"), all the legal rights relating to the child vested solely in the mother. Affiliation orders, whilst proving paternity, did not bestow any parental rights on the father, merely the obligation to pay maintenance. Although affiliation orders were abolished, the situation was not altered by the FLRA 87, although it did by s 4 introduce "parental rights orders". This enabled an unmarried father, for the first time, to obtain a court order granting him shared parental rights and duties with the mother. As discussed below, s 4 CA 1989 replaces parental rights orders with "parental responsibility orders". Alternatively, the mother and father can agree to share parental responsibility for the child and avoid the need for a court order, providing the agreement is recorded in a document in the prescribed form and registered in accordance with the regulations made under the Act. Yet the unmarried father's status at the time of the child's birth remains unaffected, whatever the nature of the relationship between the parents, even by this most recent reform. There is not even a presumption of paternity where unmarried parents were living together at the date of a child's conception, as exists in some other jurisdictions. Thus if both parents wish the father to have legal recognition, then various steps have to be taken. These will be considered in the following sections.

2. Registering the birth

The birth of any child must be registered within forty-two days. Unfortunately, where the parents are not married and both wish to be recorded as parents on the birth certificate, the procedure is not as simple as for married parents. Strictly, in the absence of an order or formal agreement granting the father joint parental rights or responsibility, the choice of name to be registered for the child lies with the mother. However, there is nothing to prevent her from registering the child with the father's surname if she wishes, or indeed with any other surname.

Sections 24 and 25 FLRA 1987 amended the Births and Deaths Registration Act 1953 ("the 1953 Act") by adding new ss 10 and 10A which set out the procedure to be followed. Paragraph 6 to Sch 12 CA 1989 has made further consequential amendments. The unmarried father is under no *duty* to register the birth, but now has the status of a qualified informant which *entitles* him to register the birth. However, this right does not automatically allow him to be recorded as the child's father on the register even if his surname is being given to the child. A record of the father's identity on the register can only be achieved in one of the following ways. Firstly, and most simply, a joint request by the mother and father (who must both attend in person) that the father's name be recorded will be sufficient. If this is not possible, then the identity of the father can be recorded by either the mother or father alone if they each make and supply a statutory declaration as to the child's paternity. Otherwise, the father's name can be recorded on the written request of either the mother or the father, providing one of the following documents is produced: a parental responsibility agreement made between the parents in proper form; or a court order made in proceedings between them for affiliation, custody, financial provision, parental rights or parental responsibility. In addition a declaration that the order or agreement is still subsisting is needed. It is also possible, by virtue of s 10A of the 1953 Act, to re-register the birth at a later stage to include the father's name. The requirements and procedure remain exactly the same and thus any of the methods described will achieve this end. However, once the child has reached the age of sixteen, their consent to the re-registration is also needed. Registration of the identity of the father of a child of unmarried parents on the birth certificate, is *prima facie* evidence of paternity and shifts the burden of proof onto the father if he later wishes to dispute it. Registration of the father's identity on the birth certificate does not of itself, however, confer any rights or duties upon the father.

3. Parental rights and duties and parental responsibility

(a) The general position

The law relating to parental rights and duties has just undergone a radical conceptual change, the precise effect of which will only be seen over time. Thus, the CA 1989 has replaced the concept of "parental rights and duties" with the notion of "parental responsibility". This is defined in s 3(1) as: " ... all the rights, duties, powers, responsibilities and authority which by law a parent of a child has in relation to the child and his property".

The CA 1989 repeals the whole of the Guardianship of Minors Acts 1971 and 1973, as well as (*inter alia*) the Children Act 1975. The old concepts of custody and access have also disappeared and are broadly replaced with residence and contact orders on relationship breakdown. However, in the same way that custody used to vest in an unmarried mother alone, only the mother in an unmarried family automatically acquires parental responsibility on the birth of a child (s 2(2) CA 1989), leaving unchanged the unmarried father's position of initial disadvantage. Questions of residence, contact and parental responsibility following breakdown of an unmarried relationship will be explored in Part II (see Chapter 7), and will not therefore be discussed in this chapter.

Unmarried parents can now agree to share parental responsibility, but even where no order or agreement has been made, some minimum standards are imposed upon the unmarried father. Where the father (or indeed any person) lives with a child, limited duties are found in s 1 Children and Young Persons Act 1933 to ensure the child receives an education and is not neglected or maltreated. Section 3(5) CA 1989 provides that any person who does not have parental responsibility but who has care of the child may do what is reasonable in all the circumstances of the case for the purpose of safeguarding or promoting the child's welfare. This new provision enhances the position under the old law of the cohabiting unmarried father with regard to, for example, consenting to medical treatment for the child.

In addition, as with married parents, where one or both unmarried parents have acquired parental rights and duties or parental responsibility, all parental rights which exist only for the child's protection diminish as the child increases in age and understanding as was decided in the case of *Gillick* v *West Norfolk and Wisbech Health Authority* [1986] AC 112.

By virtue of s 4 FLRA 1987, unmarried parents who wished to share parental rights, duties and responsibilities were able to do so for the first time, although before s 4 CA 1989, it was still necessary to issue court proceedings to achieve this. Even s 4 CA 1989 requires an agreement between parents to share parental responsibility to be in prescribed form and recorded in a prescribed way. Thus parents who become aware of the possibility of sharing parental responsibility for their child are likely to need legal advice. How many unmarried parents will become aware of the new provision remains to be seen. It is feared that the majority will remain ignorant of the procedure, and many others may not consider that the effort required to obtain the order, or even a formal agreement, is a worthwhile exercise. Just how great a deterrent the formalities will prove is not yet known, but the new agreement procedure discussed below will certainly encourage those who had previously only been deterred by the thought of having to participate in court proceedings.

(b) Advantages and disadvantages of sharing parental responsibility
Before considering the procedure, it must be pointed out that a mother who agrees to share parental responsibility pursuant to s 4 CA 1989 is giving up her right to sole parental responsibility of the child unless and until another court order is made restoring it. Once parental responsibility is conferred on the father, it cannot be unilaterally withdrawn by the mother. Thus a decision to share parental responsibility at an early stage in the child's life may have important ramifications if the relationship later breaks down and the arrangements for the child

or children cannot be agreed between the parents. The existence of a parental responsibility agreement or order will be a factor to be taken into account on making orders relating to the child on breakdown, and may influence how the court views the father's role in the child's life. Any mother agreeing to share parental responsibility should accordingly be advised that, in effect, she is placing herself in a position much more akin to that of a married mother vis-à-vis her rights over her child. In a stable relationship, she may well be happy to take such a step, but should know at the outset the possible ramifications. These considerations also reveal a possible conflict of interest between the parents, and separate advice is most desirable where the father seeks an agreement or intends to apply for an order.

How much real difference a parental responsibility order or agreement will make in practice to unmarried cohabiting parents who later separate is debatable. Wherever there is a dispute, the child's interests are paramount, and thus it is likely to be the degree of parental involvement and the respective circumstances of the parents which will be critical. An unmarried father who has joint parental responsibility, but who has otherwise shown little interest in the child, will not succeed in a dispute on breakdown to any greater degree than a comparable father without parental responsibility. However, it is conceivable that an unmarried father who has had the major role in bringing up a child may find it easier to obtain an order that the child reside with him on breakdown (a residence order) if the mother has legally acknowledged joint parental responsibility. This is of course unconfirmed by the courts yet, but courts have tended in the past to have a certain mistrust of unmarried fathers in custody disputes, and a commitment to joint parental responsibility by the father may tip the balance away from the mother and towards the father to the extent of placing him in the same position as a married father. Certainly, a mother must be advised that she is in effect giving up her sole control over the child, although as an unmarried father can in any event apply to the court for a residence order (and could previously apply for custody on breakdown), the making of a s 4 order may not in practice prove to be that significant. Section 4(3) also gives the court power to discharge a parental responsibility order or agreement in appropriate circumstances.

Given this procedure is new, and replaces the similar s 4 FLRA 1987 parental rights order provision, which itself was in force for barely three years, it is not yet possible to assess the impact of such orders in subsequent disputes relating to children on breakdown. The advantage from the mother's point of view is that a parental responsibility order extends parental duties, as well as rights, to the father. Before s 4 FLRA 1987, although the court could award custody of the child to the father if appropriate, no order for joint custody was available to unmarried parents whatever the circumstances. An order also means that should the mother die, the father automatically becomes the child's guardian, as happens where a child's parents are married. However, without a s 4 order, unless the mother has appointed the father (or some other person) testamentary guardian in accordance with the provisions of s 5(3) and (5) CA 1989 (see page 37), the child will be left without a legal guardian. The father who wanted to be responsible for his child would have to apply to the court for a s 4 order at that stage, or for a s 8 residence order, or for an order appointing him guardian pursuant to s 5(1) CA 1989.

Conversely, where a s 4 order exists, s 5(7) provides that any appointment by the mother of a testamentary guardian other than the father does not take effect until after the death of the father with parental responsibility, unless there was a residence order in favour of the mother at the date of her death. Thus, from the mother's point of view, a s 4 order will mean that the father will automatically become the child's guardian on her death even if this is against her wishes.

A s 4 agreement or order is also recognition by the father of paternity and of his duties towards his child, including the duty to maintain even in the absence of a maintenance order. It enables a father to consent to medical treatment and jointly take decisions about, for example, schooling, or change of surname, which are otherwise in law the sole province of the unmarried mother. It should be noted that even where there is no s 4 agreement or order, subss 2(9) and (10) CA 1989 enable a person who has parental responsibility to arrange for some or all of it to be met by one or more persons acting on his or her behalf, although parental responsibility cannot be surrendered or transferred to another person. This gives much greater flexibility than under the old law, and could be of assistance to unmarried parents who wish to share the care of their child, but do not wish to enter into a s 4 agreement.

It is thought that where parents are cohabiting in a stable relationship, they may both wish to place themselves as nearly as possible in the position of married parents and this is the intention and effect of a s 4 agreement. Nonetheless, some distinctions, although not necessarily disadvantages, remain. The citizenship of a child of unmarried parents is still transmitted through the mother rather than the father, and a child will acquire his or her domicile of origin from the mother not the father. Although it is important for both parties to understand the consequences of a s 4 agreement or order, unless breakdown or irreconcilable differences relating to the child are foreseen, such an agreement or order will enable parenthood to be shared in the same way as it is by married parents and be proof that both parents are keen to share with the other the associated rights and duties.

(c) Orders and agreements for joint parental responsibility

It was not until the introduction of s 4 FLRA 1987 that unmarried parents were able to share parental rights, duties and responsibilities. The section provided that: "where the father and mother of a child were not married to each other at the time of the birth, the court may on the father's application, order that he shall have all the parental rights and duties with respect to the child".

Thus only the father could make the application and this is still the position with the new applications under s 4 CA 1989. However, the latter section also enables parental responsibility to be shared by virtue of a written agreement between the parents, which was not possible before. Under the 1987 Act, the magistrates' court, the county court and the High Court all had jurisdiction to hear applications. This is also the case with applications for parental responsibility orders under s 4 CA 1989, although the need to apply for an order seems likely to arise only upon breakdown or, perhaps, on the death of the mother, as there should be no need to issue proceedings if the parents agree. The parties can achieve the same end by entering into an agreement as discussed below. Unlike the position under the 1987 Act, where a parental responsibility order is sought, the procedure is now the same whichever venue is chosen, since the CA 1989 harmonised the procedure in all three courts. Applications are made by the father's completing form CHA 1. This is then issued by the court and the applicant must serve copies on the mother and on any other person prescribed by the court rules (see below). No supporting affidavits are now required. Written supporting evidence takes the form of signed statements containing a declaration that the maker believes them to be true. The application form, together with the exact procedural steps are set out in the Family Proceedings Courts (Children Act 1989) Regulations 1991 for the magistrates' courts, and in the Family Proceedings Rules 1991 for the county court and High Court. Section 4 CA 1989 has of course repealed s 4 FLRA 1987, but any old style parental rights orders made under the 1987 Act will be treated as if they were parental responsibility orders made pursuant to s 4 CA 1989 (para 4, Sch 14 CA 1989). Although there is great similarity between the old and new s 4 orders, there are also some important differences. The 1989 Act has changed the vocabulary in that it talks of parental responsibility (defined by s 3(1) – see above) rather than rights and duties, although in this context the concept remains broadly the same. In addition the starting point for the court when asked to make a s 4 order is that it must not make any order under the Act unless it considers that to do so would be better for the child than making no order at all (s 1(5)).

As has been noted above, s 4 CA 1989 introduces a new method by which unmarried fathers may share parental responsibility with the mother. Section 4(1) provides:

"Where a child's father and mother were not married to each other at the time of his birth–
(a) the court may, on the application of the father, order that he shall have parental responsibility for the child; or
(b) the father and mother may by agreement ('a parental responsibility agreement') provide for the father to have parental responsibility for the child."

Thus an unmarried father may make an application to court for a s 4 order. He will have to show that it is better to make the order than to make no order at all and the child's welfare will be the court's paramount consideration (s1(1)) rather than being the "first and paramount consideration" as it was under s 1 Guardianship of Minors

Act 1971 ("GMA 1971"). It is not thought that the omission of the word "first" will greatly affect the approach taken by the courts. There have now been some cases giving guidance on when parental rights orders under s 4 FLRA 1987 should be granted, and these will remain pertinent to applications under s 4 CA 1989. In *Re H (Illegitimate Children: Father: Parental Rights) (No 2)* [1991] 1 FLR 214, Balcombe LJ set out some of the factors to be considered by the court when asked to make a s 4 order. These include the degree of commitment shown by the father to the children; the degree of attachment between the father and the children; and the father's reasons for applying for an order. In this case, although the children were in care and the subject of an application that they be freed for adoption, a parental rights order was made giving him *locus standi* in the application. In *Re C (Minors: Parental Rights)* [1992] 1 FLR 1, this approach was followed and a parental rights order was made despite the fact that all the rights were not immediately enforceable. The important question was whether the association between the parties was sufficiently enduring and whether the father, by his conduct during and since the application, showed sufficient commitment to the children to justify giving him a legal status equivalent to that of a married father, due attention being paid to the fact that a number of the parental rights conferred would be unenforceable (see Mustill LJ at p 2). In *D v Hereford and Worcestershire County Council* [1991] 1 FLR 205, Ward J expanded on the test in *Re H* (above) and suggested that the test should be, has the father, or will he, "behave with parental responsibility for the child". Here again the child was in care.

The 1989 Act breaks new ground in that, for the first time, unmarried parents can agree to share parental responsibility without going to court, or even asking the court to approve a consent order. However, s 4(2) stipulates that a parental responsibility agreement must be made in the form prescribed by the Parental Responsibility Regulations 1991 (SI 1478). The agreement needs to be completed and signed by both the mother and father in the presence of a witness, and a separate form is needed for each child. The agreement will not take effect until it has been filed (together with two copies) with the Principal Registry of the Family Division at the High Court, Somerset House, Strand, London WC2 1LP.

Where a new s 4 order or agreement has been made, s 2(7) CA 1989 provides that each person who has parental responsibility may act alone without the other in meeting that responsibility. There is no longer a right of veto where the other person with parental responsibility disagrees with an action to be taken in relation to the child, although either parent is entitled to apply for a "specific issue order" under s 8(1) CA 1989 (see pages 146 and 151-152) to determine a specific question which has arisen in relation to any aspect of parental responsibility. The only limits on the independent exercise of parental responsibility provided by the Act are that nothing incompatible with any order made under the provisions of the Act must be done; and the right of independent action does not override the need to obtain the consent of another person if this is required by statute, such as for the purposes of adoption.

Only a court can bring a parental responsibility order or agreement to an end. The application may be by one of the persons who has parental responsibility; or, with leave of the court, by the child providing he or she has sufficient understanding to make the application (subss 4(3) and (4)).

The Law Commission has predicted that s 4 orders and agreements would be used mainly by unmarried parents cohabiting in a stable relationship who do not wish to marry, yet wish to share parental responsibility. An order or agreement can be seen to be particularly helpful, providing it coincides with the mother's wishes and the welfare of the child, in the tragic event of the child's mother dying without having appointed a guardian. However as stated above, there is nothing to prevent the father from applying for a s 4 order at that time, or indeed from applying under s 5 to be appointed by the court as the child's guardian. However, it is possible at that stage that another individual will apply to be appointed guardian, whereas if a s 4 order or agreement had previously been made, then the father would automatically become the child's guardian.

The same result can be achieved if the mother appoints the child's father (who does not have parental responsibility) as testamentary guardian in accordance with s 5(5). It is now possible to appoint a testamentary guardian other than by Will. This can be done by any parent who has parental responsibility, and will have effect, providing it is in writing, dated and signed by the person making the appointment. It will still be valid if it is signed at the direction of the appointor in his or her presence and in the presence of two witnesses who attest the signature. Testamentary guardians can still be appointed by Will, but the new procedure is simpler and can be used to vary any appointment previously made by Will. As mentioned above, where there is a surviving parent with parental responsibility, the appointment of a testamentary guardian takes effect only on the death of the surviving parent.

To summarise, if unmarried cohabiting parents wish to share parental responsibility this can be done by means of a parental responsibility agreement which meets the requirements of s 4 CA 1989. Where there is no agreement, the father can still apply to the court for an order and must show that to make an order is better for the child than making no order at all. This may be difficult is the mother does not agree but is the child's prime carer. Where cohabitees have children, careful consideration should be given to the question of the benefits and possible disadvantages of parental responsibility agreements and orders. Even more important perhaps, is the need for the parent or parents with parental responsibility to appoint a testamentary guardian for their children and such appointments should be kept under review and amended if circumstances change.

(d) Children of previous relationships
Many unmarried families include children of one of the parties by another relationship. Where the adults of a new family marry each other, their children are recognised as children of the family (s 52 Matrimonial Causes Act 1973 ("MCA")). Generally, no duty to maintain them will arise and their legal status will be governed solely by the position of their natural parents and any orders made in proceedings between these parents.

Section 2(9) CA 1989 provides that any person who has care of a child may do what is reasonable to safeguard or promote the child's welfare, and accordingly where a child of a previous relationship lives with cohabiting adults, this provision covers the relationship between a child and the adult who is not the child's parent. The natural parent's cohabitee will not normally be able to acquire parental responsibility under the Act, unless he or she successfully applies for a residence order, which will be discussed below, or unless he or she is appointed the child's guardian. The cohabitee may be appointed by the natural parent as the child's testamentary guardian (as outlined above); and upon the death of the natural parent, if the deceased parent had a residence order in his or her favour, the testamentary appointment of a guardian will take effect even though the other natural parent still retains parental responsibility (s 5(7)). The surviving natural parent could however apply to the court to be appointed a guardian and such an appointment would take effect jointly with the testamentary guardian. Similarly, if the child's other parent does not have parental responsibility, which will arise in the case of unmarried fathers only, then the mother could appoint her cohabitee as guardian and this will take effect on her death.

Where no testamentary guardian was appointed but there was a residence order in favour of the deceased natural parent, the cohabitee could apply to the court to be made the child's guardian whether or not the surviving parent has retained parental responsibility. The surviving natural parent can make a similar application (see s 5(1) CA 1989). Where there was no residence order, and the surviving parent has retained parental responsibility, the deceased parent's cohabitee will not be able to apply to be appointed guardian by the court, and any testamentary appointment is postponed until the death of the surviving parent with parental responsibility. If the child's father never had parental responsibility, the mother's cohabitee, as well as the child's father, could apply to the court to be appointed guardian, in the absence of an appointment by the mother before her death.

This again highlights the importance of making arrangements for children. Another change brought about by the CA 1989 (which has of course abolished the little used option of custodianship), which may be of assistance in relation to children of previous relationships, is found in subss 10(2) and (5). The former enables *any* person, with leave of the court, to apply for a s 8 order. Section 8 orders will be discussed in Chapter 7, but include residence and contact orders. Thus a non-parent cohabitee who has built up a good relationship with their partner's child could apply for leave on breakdown or on the death of the partner. Where the child has lived with the non-parent for three years or more, or where the applicant has the consent of the parent with a residence order or both parents with parental responsibility, then s 10(5) gives them a right to apply for a s 8 order. This right can be exercised at any time, not only in the context of breakdown or death. Thus a non-parent cohabitee living with the child and one of his or her natural parents could in theory apply for a residence order jointly with the resident natural parent. Section 12(2) then provides that if a residence order is made in favour of a non-parent, the court must make an order giving that person parental responsibility for the duration of the residence order. However, s 1(5) of course provides that in addition to applying the welfare principle, the court should not make any order unless to do so is better for the child than making no order at all. If such an order is likely to make the child's relationship with their other natural parent difficult, the court may well fall back on the "no order" presumption.

4. Change of name

As discussed in Chapter 1, the right to change the name of a child of unmarried parents rests with the mother alone, unless a court order affecting her parental rights has been made. Before the CA 1989, an unmarried father could obtain legal and actual custody of his child pursuant to s 9 GMA 1971, but it is debatable whether the right to change the child's name was thereby transferred. It is arguable that if there is no order extending parental rights/responsibility to both parents jointly under s 4 FLRA 87 or s 4 CA 1989, then the right to choose a child's name remains with the mother notwithstanding the custody order. This is because only rights "relating to a child's person" could be transferred when a custody order was made, and it is questionable that the right to change a child's name relates to the person. However, an unmarried father who has been granted custody and subsequently wants to change the child's name, may now do so, as the transitional provisions of the CA 1989 deem all such fathers to have a parental responsibility order under s 4 CA 1989. Further, where a residence order is made in favour of an unmarried father on relationship breakdown pursuant to s 8, s 12(1) CA 1989 specifically requires a court making a residence order in favour of a father without parental responsibility to make a s 4 order. Generally though, unmarried fathers will be unable to change their child's name unless they have parental responsibility by virtue of s 4 CA 1989. Where parental responsibility is shared, either parent can exercise it independently of the other and thus it seems it will be quite legitimate for one parent to change the child's name without the other's knowledge, and any dispute could only be finally settled either by a specific issue order or by the making of a residence order. A specific issue order can be sought by either parent to resolve a change of name dispute, providing no residence order to determine with whom the child should live has been made or is being applied for.

Where a residence order has been made, then s 13 of the 1989 Act provides that a child's surname cannot be changed without the written consent of every person who has parental responsibility, or leave of the court. Thus leave will have to be sought, but not in the guise of a specific issue order. As we have seen, the Act generally provides that no order should be made unless it would be better for the child than making no order at all. In addition, it specifically provides, in relation to contested s 8 applications, for the child's wishes and feelings, in the light of his age and understanding, to be taken into account. This makes it imperative to apply to change a child's name only if the child agrees, or is not of an age to express his or her feelings. It is worthy of note that residence orders can be made as between unmarried parents, and thus the restriction on changing a child's surname following the making of a residence order will apply as much to unmarried families as to married parents where the parent with whom the child does not reside retains parental responsibility following breakdown.

Some children who come to form part of an unmarried family may be the children of one of the cohabitees born during a marriage, and thus cohabitees may also seek advice if they wish to change these children's surnames. On divorce, a custody order would previously state that a child's surname should not to be changed without the consent of the other parent in writing or by leave of the court (r 92(8) Matrimonial Causes Rules 1977). Section 8 orders, deciding issues of residence and contact, will now be made on divorce and will contain a similar caveat. Section 13 CA 1989 always applies to changing the names of children of married parents where a residence order is made, as married parents each have and will retain parental responsibility.

5. Adoption and infertility treatment

The Adoption Act 1976 ("AA 1976") does not permit adoption by cohabiting couples; only married couples or single people may apply to adopt a child (see ss 14 and 15 AA 1976). Thus if a couple wishes to adopt jointly, so that they share parental responsibility, they must be married. It is possible for one of a cohabiting couple to apply to adopt but of course detailed investigations are carried out by the local authority in relation to all members of the prospective adopter's household before a child is placed for adoption. Some local authorities may not be prepared to recommend adoption by a single person who is cohabiting, although there is nothing in the Act or the Regulations which prevent this course of action. The investigation procedure is very thorough and the initial placement of a child can take place only if the local authority or approved adoption society recommends the placement. If a woman cohabitee successfully adopts a child, it is not open for her male partner to obtain parental responsibility by virtue of a s 4 agreement or order. Section 10 CA 1989 does, as was discussed above, enable a person, with the consent of all the persons with parental responsibility or with whom the child has lived for at least three years, to apply for a residence order. As a residence order can be made in favour of more than one person, it is possible that the court would agree to the making of a joint residence order in this situation as it may be the only way a cohabiting couple could share parental responsibility. Section 12(2) CA 1989 directs the court, on making a residence order in favour of a non-parent, to make an order giving that person parental responsibility for as long as the order remains in force.

The same difficulties would arise for a cohabiting gay couple wanting to adopt, as no adoption order can be made on the application of more than one person other than a married couple. One member of the couple could apply to adopt a child, but again the adoption agency may not regard such a placement as suitable. Some, albeit few, local authorities are prepared to consider individuals regardless of their sexual orientation, although many are likely to regard homosexuality as a bar in itself.

The difficulties relating to cohabitees adopting lead some couples to consider human assisted reproduction. Unlike adoption, such treatment is, at least in theory, available to any woman, whether married, single, heterosexual or homosexual. There is no bar on who can apply and there are certainly no rigorous investigation procedures to discover the suitability of the household for the child, although some counselling is usual. However, the availability of treatment varies from health authority to health authority. The legal status of the child born as a result of human assisted reproduction, or rather the status of the father, will vary depending on the nature of the treatment. In the case of AIH treatment, where the mother is artificially inseminated with her cohabitee's sperm, the child will be the genetic child of the parties, although as the parents are unmarried only the mother will have parental responsibility at birth. The father can, however, apply for a parental responsibility order or enter into a parental responsibility agreement in the same way as any unmarried father as described above.

If the AID method is used, whereby the mother is artificially inseminated by the sperm of an anonymous donor, the mother will have custody or parental responsibility from birth, and until recently her cohabitee was unable to apply for a parental rights or responsibility order as he is not the child's father. Although a child born by AID to a married couple is regarded as the child of the marriage where the husband consented to the artificial insemination (see s 27 FLRA 1987), there was no provision in FLRA 1987 extending parental rights to a cohabiting father in the same position. The CA 1989 does nothing to ameliorate the position, but the gap has been filled by s 28 Human Fertilisation and Embryology Act 1990 (HFEA 1990). Thus if cohabitees have a child as a result of artificial insemination, which treatment was provided by a licensed body for the man and woman together, then the man is treated as the father of the child. He can then obtain parental responsibility by virtue of a s 4 agreement or order in the same way as any other unmarried father.

Where a cohabiting couple has a child by virtue of the *in vitro* fertilisation method (IVF) and the egg is donated anonymously and fertilised by the male cohabitee's sperm, then by virtue of s 27(1) HFEA 1990, the mother in whom the egg is placed is regarded as the child's mother and if she is unmarried then she alone will have parental responsibility of the child at birth. However, her cohabitee can obtain parental responsibility by virtue of a s 4 agreement or order as if the child were conceived naturally as set out above. If the mother is married, s 28 provides that the child will be treated as a child of the marriage unless the husband is shown not to have consented. If both the egg and the sperm are donated, then the mother in whom the embryo is placed is treated as the mother of the child. Her cohabitee is in exactly the position described above in relation to AID. Providing the treatment was provided by a licensed body for the man and woman together, s 28 states that he is to be treated as the father of the child. He can therefore obtain parental responsibility in accordance with s 4 CA 1989.

Gay women can also undergo infertility treatment, although for gay men surrogacy is probably the only course and is fraught with legal and probably practical difficulties. An attempt has been made to curb commercial surrogacy, yet recognise that it happens. The Surrogacy Arrangements Act 1985 governs surrogacy agreements and, interestingly, s 30 HFEA 1990 now enables the court to make an order that the commissioning married couple should be treated in law as the child's parents, providing the surrogate mother and father consent. However, this provision does not apply to unmarried couples or, it seems, single commissioning parents, who would have to rely on wardship or apply for a residence order to obtain legal parental status. The child is deemed to be that of the surrogate mother even if both the egg and sperm were donated (s 27(1) HFEA 1990). This remains an area where cohabitees, compared with married couples, are disadvantaged.

Chapter 3

Housing

1. Introduction

At some point in their relationship, cohabitees have taken a conscious decision to share accommodation with one another. This could have involved one of them moving into their partner's accommodation and giving up their own; or they may have decided to rent accommodation jointly, or buy a property together.

Legal consequences flow from each of these possibilities, yet few couples seek, or even think of seeking, legal advice before they take the critical step, unless they happen to be in contact with an advisor about another matter. Some cohabitees may feel that the arrangement is, at first, very much on trial and is not something on which legal advice need be sought. More commonly, in the early stages, each cohabitee trusts the other and does not want to be seen questioning their faith in the relationship. There may be a rather vague intention to look into the position later. Yet all too often, it is only on breakdown of the relationship, or in the context of another crisis, such as threatened possession proceedings by a landlord or mortgagee, that the legal implications of a decision to rent or buy accommodation together will become apparent. The housing shortage in many parts of Britain makes it vital for cohabitees to know at the outset how a decision to share accommodation will affect each party's housing and property rights if the relationship comes to an end. Anything legal advisors can do to inform cohabitees of their respective positions before they commence living together may enable each of them to safeguard his or her interests as far as possible in advance of any crisis. It may of course not be possible or appropriate for a solicitor, who should generally take instructions rather than seek out problems, to take the initiative. Yet there are situations where an indication of the effects of cohabitation on housing rights may be welcomed and may elicit a request for more comprehensive advice.

Some of the more common problems can be illustrated. For example, where cohabitees purchase a property they will make the purchase either in their joint names or in the name of just one of them; this will have important ramifications if it becomes necessary to define their respective interests, either on breakdown of the relationship or on death. A non-owner cohabitee who has given up other accommodation may have little or no beneficial interest in the accommodation which he or she regards as home. Thus there may be no legal right to live there once the owner withdraws consent. Such cohabitees often believe that the act of cohabitation over a period of time will protect them from being "turned out of their homes", but this is not of course the case. Where cohabitees live in rented accommodation, their positions will depend on the name or names in which the tenancy is vested; and on whether the accommodation is rented in the private, public or newly named independent sector (which mainly comprises housing associations). This is so not only on breakdown of the relationship but also on the death of the partner or the granting of a possession order. Even where a property is jointly purchased, the death of one cohabitee may jeopardise the home of the other. Cohabitees may also find themselves homeless. In some situations, they may be eligible for rehousing by the local housing authority under their duties to the homeless as set out in the Housing Act 1985 Part III.

This chapter will consider the implications for cohabitees of the various forms of tenure in all contexts other than breakdown, and con-

sider the situations in which cohabitees may be assisted by the provisions of the homelessness legislation.

2. Rented accommodation

(a) Private rented accommodation

This area of law is highly complex and it is not proposed to attempt to
give anything other than a broad outline of the position as it affects
cohabitees, and to detail specific problems that cohabitees are most
likely to encounter. At present there are two statutory schemes which
govern private sector tenancies. If a tenancy was granted before 15
January 1989, it will be governed by the provisions of the Rent Act
1977. It is likely to be a protected tenancy (contractual or statutory)
or, possibly, a protected shorthold tenancy which affords less security
and must comply with the requirements of s 52 Housing Act 1980.
After 15 January 1989 all residential tenancies granted (with limited
exceptions where the tenant was previously a Rent Act protected tenant of the landlord) fall within the provisions of the Housing Act
1988. They will be either assured or assured shorthold tenancies
where the landlord may charge a market rent and, in the latter case,
there is only very limited security of tenure. A cohabitee's housing
rights thus depend on when the tenancy was entered into, and the type
of tenancy granted under the relevant statutory provisions.

As with any rented accommodation, another important factor
which will determine a cohabitee's position is whether the tenancy is
in joint names, or vested in the sole name of one of them. The importance of this distinction is discussed in (d) below. A joint tenancy is
more likely to have been granted if the cohabitees jointly looked for
and found the accommodation. However, even where this has happened, many private landlords insist on putting the tenancy in the sole
name of one of them, probably because this may prove advantageous
if possession is ever sought. Where the tenancy is in writing it is easy
to establish whether or not there is a joint tenancy by looking at the
tenancy agreement itself. In some cases the tenancy may have been
granted orally, and whether it is a joint tenancy or not is something
that will only ever be specifically determined if it becomes necessary

at a later stage. The matter will be decided by the court with reference to the parties' intentions at the time they reached agreement, and any other evidence (such as correspondence, the name or names on the rent book or which person paid the rent) available.

(b) Public sector secure tenancies

Cohabitees living in local authority accommodation are secure tenants, and their tenancies are governed by the Housing Act 1985. This is also the case with housing association tenancies granted before 15 January 1989. The advantages and disadvantages of a joint tenancy are discussed below. Public sector landlords are generally fairly willing to grant or transfer tenancies into the joint names of cohabitees.

An assignment of a secure tenancy generally results in the tenancy ceasing to be a secure tenancy, but not if the assignment is to someone who is entitled to be a successor to the tenancy, and, as set out below, a cohabitee may come within this definition providing he or she has lived in the accommodation for twelve months. Thus where these conditions are fulfilled the tenant cohabitee may assign the secure tenancy into joint names by deed.

Local authority secure tenants have a right to buy their accommodation at a discount providing they fulfil certain conditions (see Housing Act 1985 part V), and although a non-tenant cohabitee has no right to require to be a joint proprietor, a tenant has the right to require that up to three members of his family who are not joint tenants, but who occupy the accommodation as their principal home, purchase the property jointly with the tenant. Thus at the request of the tenant cohabitee, providing the non-tenant partner has resided in the property for the past twelve months, or providing the landlord consents, cohabitees can jointly purchase accommodation under the right to buy provisions, even if only one of them was the secure tenant. Conversely, a joint tenant has the right to buy the premises but could not do so without at least the consent of the other joint tenant. Cohabitees purchasing accommodation under the "right to buy" scheme must of course be advised of the implications of purchasing the property and the relevant considerations are set later in this chapter.

(c) Independent sector tenancies

Following the introduction of the assured tenancy by the Housing Act 1988, housing associations are no longer able to grant public sector secure tenancies, but must instead grant assured tenancies governed by Part I of the Act. Where a tenancy was granted by a housing association before 15 January 1989, it is likely to be a secure tenancy and the considerations set out above apply. Any tenancy granted after this time by a housing association (with limited exceptions where the tenant was previously a secure tenant of the association) will be an assured tenancy. Housing associations are not prevented by statute from granting assured shorthold tenancies for fixed term periods with little security of tenure, as is common in the private sector. They are at first sight entitled to charge a market rent. However, as a matter of policy, housing associations have been given a new role in the housing market and are seen as the new providers of "social housing". Despite a statutory right for landlords granting assured tenancies to charge a market rent, the Housing Corporation's Code of Guidance, which applies to all housing associations registered with it provides that rent levels should be kept within the reach of those in low-paid employment and assured shorthold tenancies should be granted only where, exceptionally, this is the only means of fulfilling the Association's housing objectives (see Guidance, para D2 & C3 respectively). None the less, new housing association tenants now come within the statutory provisions of the Housing Act 1988 and will grant assured tenancies. Thus there are different rules relating to assignment and succession for new tenants of housing associations, as opposed to local authorities; this is discussed below (see pages 52 and 55).

(d) General implications of joint tenancies for cohabitees

If cohabitees enter into a joint tenancy of private rented accommodation, or indeed any residential accommodation, then they both acquire under the terms of the tenancy agreement the right to occupy the accommodation specified in that agreement. Neither is at liberty to exclude the other from the accommodation save by court order obtained under, for example, the Domestic Violence and Matrimonial Proceedings Act 1976 (see page 115). Both are jointly and severally liable to perform the obligations under the tenancy agreement. Thus if one joint tenant who normally pays the rent fails to do so, the landlord can look to the other joint tenant to pay the whole of the rent, regardless of any arrangement made between the tenants. Failure to meet the rent demands will ultimately lead to possession proceedings which in the case of joint tenants must be taken against each of them.

Whatever the nature of the tenancy in other respects, where a joint tenancy has been granted and one of the joint tenants dies, the other will automatically become the sole tenant by survivorship. However, if one joint tenant leaves the accommodation permanently, then the remaining joint tenant, whilst continuing to have the right to occupy the accommodation, cannot usually become the sole tenant without the consent of the landlord or in limited circumstances where there are children by virtue of a court order under para 1(2)(e) Sch 1 CA 1989.

Generally, a joint tenancy gives each cohabitee security. Both have equal rights to occupy the accommodation and should therefore each be notified of alleged breaches of the terms of the tenancy agreement, or other statutory grounds for possession. There can be no challenge to the right of the survivor of joint tenants to continue to occupy the accommodation on the death of the partner, as, by operation of law, the survivor becomes the sole tenant. In addition, although not of personal concern to joint tenant cohabitees themselves, a joint tenancy which is protected by the Rent Act (in contrast to an assured joint tenancy under the 1988 Act), has the effect of enhancing statutory succession rights by permitting two further successions to resident members of the tenants' family following the death of the second joint tenant (see page 53). A joint tenancy is particularly advantageous for non-heterosexual cohabitees in relation to succession. As will be shown (see page 52 *et seq*), whilst heterosexual cohabitees do now have the statutory right to succeed to the tenancy of their deceased sole tenant partners, this is not the case for homosexual cohabitees, or indeed any people living together other than as husband and wife, unless they come within the definition of "a member of the tenant's family". This has been narrowly construed (see below) and in order to succeed to the tenancy, they must also fulfil the condition of having resided with the tenant for a period of one or two years (depending on the type of tenancy concerned) immediately before the death.

Conversely, as will be seen in the context of breakdown, there are situations where a joint tenancy may work to the disadvantage of a cohabitee. Both remain jointly and severally liable to pay the rent regardless of who remains in occupation, and as will be seen in Chapter 9, notice to quit the accommodation by one joint tenant may be sufficient to determine the whole tenancy even if the other cohabitee wishes to remain in occupation (see *London Borough of Greenwich* v *McGrady* (1982) 81 LGR 288). It is also possible that, if rendered homeless where previous accommodation vested in joint names has been given up, both cohabitees may be more readily found intentionally homeless if fault can be attached to the loss of the previous accommodation (see page 70 *et seq*).

Whether a joint tenancy will prove more or less advantageous to a cohabitee than a sole tenancy on breakdown of the relationship depends on which of them ultimately seeks to remain in the accommodation and whether or not that person is the tenant. At the outset it is not usually possible to foresee the circumstances which may arise, and of course the scenario which benefits one cohabitee is likely to disadvantage the other. None the less, it seems that overall the advantages of a joint tenancy outweigh the disadvantages for cohabitees in terms of achieving security. Such disadvantages as there are usually occur on breakdown of the relationship. Many of the disadvantages can be overcome, but security for a non-tenant cohabitee in accommodation which he or she regards as home, particularly if deserted by the tenant partner, or sometimes on death, may be more difficult, if not impossible, to achieve. All legal advisors can do is outline the implications of the options. Where appropriate, a written agreement or a Will drawn up in advance of any difficulties, can be suggested.

(e) Cohabitees and sole tenancies – the general position
Where cohabitees occupy accommodation the tenancy of which is vested in the sole name of only one of them, the non-tenant cohabitee is vulnerable. In the case of a married couple, a non-tenant spouse has the right to occupy the matrimonial home of which the other spouse is the sole tenant, by virtue of s 1 Matrimonial Homes Act 1983. A non-tenant cohabitee, on the other hand, is usually no more than his or her partner's licensee in law, and has no right at all to occupy the accom-

modation, no matter how long he or she may have lived there, once the partner revokes the licence to occupy or leaves the accommodation without an intention to return or even, in some situations, dies.

It may be possible to ameliorate this position by creating a joint tenancy, either by a grant of a new joint tenancy by the landlord, or in some cases by way of assignment by the sole tenant to the cohabitees as joint tenants. Much will depend on the nature of the tenancy. A non-tenant cohabitee does not have any right to insist that the tenancy be transferred into joint names, so the consent of the partner and, where appropriate, the landlord, will be needed. Advisers should be alert to the possibility of conflict of interest between the partners.

Broadly, statutory tenancies governed by the Rent Act 1977 and periodic assured tenancies arising under the Housing Act 1988 cannot be assigned without the landlord's express written consent (see Chapter 9). Contractual Rent Act tenancies and fixed term assured tenancies can be assigned during the fixed term period providing the terms of the tenancy permit assignment. Secure public sector tenancies can be assigned to a person entitled to be the statutory successor to the tenancy. Thus a tenancy can be assigned as between cohabitees providing the non-tenant cohabitee has been living with the tenant at the accommodation for the previous twelve months. In the case of local authority or housing association tenancies, it is usually possible to obtain the landlord's agreement to an assignment, or to a grant of a new tenancy in joint names. In the private sector, particularly where a Rent Act tenancy is concerned, a landlord's consent to an assignment or new tenancy which would retain Rent Act protection (see s 34 Housing Act 1988) is unlikely to be forthcoming and the parties may have little choice but to retain such security as is available to the sole tenant.

(f) Succession to tenancies on death
Where cohabitees are joint tenants, the survivor of them will automatically succeed to the tenancy on the death of his or her partner. Where cohabitees have lived together for a period of time in a private sector tenancy in the sole name of one of them, it may be possible for the surviving cohabitee to succeed to the tenancy. Succession to tenancies on death is now governed by statute and the position of non-tenant

cohabitees again varies according to the nature of the tenancy. The position is also very different for heterosexual and homosexual cohabitees.

(i) Rent Act tenancies: The Housing Act 1988 has made some significant changes to the law relating to succession of Rent Act tenancies. Before the 1988 Act, the Rent Act permitted a maximum of two successors to the tenancy after the original tenant's death. A spouse would automatically succeed to the tenancy provided he or she was living with the tenant immediately before the tenant spouse's death; in the absence of a resident spouse, any member of the tenant's family could succeed to the tenancy if he or she had lived with the deceased for at least six months before the death. The same rules applied again on the death of the first successor. Both the first and second successors became statutory tenant of the premises. However, cohabitees were not included in the definition of the word "spouse", although, finally, in the case of *Dyson Holdings* v *Fox* [1975] 3 All ER 1031 it was held that a woman who had lived with a man as his wife for forty years came within the definition of a member of the tenant's family and was thus entitled to succeed to the tenancy. However, in the later case of *Helby* v *Rafferty* [1978] 3 All ER 1022, cohabitees had lived together for some five years before the death of Ms Helby the tenant. The couple had retained their own names and did not hold themselves out to be married. There were no children. Mr Rafferty had nursed her when she was ill, and they had previously shared "bed and board". Nonetheless, he was held not to be a member of the tenant's family for Rent Act succession purposes. The law was therefore uncertain, and each case was very much judged on its own facts. Fortunately, the Housing Act 1988 has clarified the position to the extent that the definition of a spouse now includes a person living with the tenant "as his or her wife or husband" – further statutory recognition of the status of heterosexual cohabitees. It remains to be seen exactly how this will be interpreted by the courts.

Part I Sch 4 Housing Act 1988 amends Sch 1 Rent Act 1977 and the succession provisions for Rent Act tenancies are now as follows. The surviving spouse of an original tenant (which includes a person living with the tenant as the tenant's husband or wife), automatically succeeds and becomes the statutory tenant of the accommodation on the tenant's death, providing he or she was residing with the tenant in the accommodation at the time of the tenant's death. Providing it is the first succession, the statutory tenant will remain protected by the Rent Act 1977 as long as they continue to occupy the accommodation as a residence. There is now no qualifying period.

Homosexual cohabitees, however, have to prove that they come within the definition of a member of the original tenant's family. Even if able to do this, they must in addition show that they resided with the tenant in the accommodation for a period of two years before death. Such authority as there is indicates that they are highly unlikely to succeed. In the case of *Harrogate BC* v *Simpson* [1986] 16 Fam Law 359, which related to a public sector tenancy, it was held that a couple of the same sex cannot come within the definition of husband and wife. A subsequent complaint to the European Commission on Human Rights on the facts of this case was also rejected (see Application No. 11716/85 v UK). However, succession rules for public sector tenancies specify family members who are entitled to succeed, whereas the Rent Act definition is framed more broadly. It requires a successor to be "a member of the tenant's family" who has resided with the tenant in the accommodation for the two years prior to the tenant's death (see Sch 1 Rent Act 1977 as amended). Accordingly, it is still arguable, although without much hope of success, that a cohabiting couple of the same sex come within the definition of a member of the other's family and that therefore, provided there has been sufficient residence prior to their tenant partner's death, the survivor should be entitled to succeed to the tenancy.

The phrase "member of the tenant's family" does not completely exclude non-blood relatives. It has been held to include a woman who had been brought up by the tenant but never formally adopted (*Brock* v *Wollams* [1949] 1 All ER 715), but a *quasi* aunt and nephew relationship was not considered sufficient even though they had shared accommodation for eighteen years and the "nephew" had looked after the "aunt" during her failing health (see *Joram Developments* v *Sharratt* [1979] 2 All ER 1084.) Before the 1988 Act amendment, which brought couples living as husband and wife within the definition of spouse, it had been successfully argued that such couples were members of each other's families, although the authorities were not entirely consistent. It is thought unlikely even now that such an argument would succeed on behalf of homosexual cohabitees.

As noted above, in the absence of a spouse or cohabitee, a member of the tenant's family may succeed on the death of the original tenant providing the family member was living with the tenant in the accommodation for two years immediately before the tenant's death. However, this person succeeds to an assured tenancy at a market rent and does not now become a statutory tenant protected by the Rent Act 1977. Were a cohabitee of the same sex as the tenant partner to be successful in a bid to succeed to the tenancy, he or she would therefore become an assured tenant and be liable to pay a market rent for the premises. Where there has already been one succession under these provisions by the original tenant's spouse or cohabitee, that successor's spouse or cohabitee can succeed to an assured tenancy, as can someone who is a member of both the original tenant's and the first successor's family, providing that person lived in the accommodation with the first successor for two years immediately before the first successor's death. Again, the succession is to an assured tenancy.

(ii) Succession of assured tenancies: An assured tenancy held in a sole name remains an interest in property even on the tenant's death and thus, subject to the statutory provisions governing succession, will devolve according to the terms of any Will, or, in the absence of a Will, according to the intestacy rules. At first sight this appears to have a significant adverse effect upon cohabitees who are not joint tenants as the survivor of joint tenants succeeds to the tenancy by operation of law. Indeed, where a fixed term tenancy, as opposed to a periodic tenancy, is still in existence on the death of the tenant, the tenancy will indeed devolve in accordance with any Will or the rules of intestacy and will vest in the tenant's personal representatives under the Administration of Estates Act 1925. They should then vest the tenancy by a simple assent in the beneficiaries, who may or may not include a cohabitee. Where there is no Will, a cohabitee will not be a beneficiary and a claim under the Inheritance (Provision for Family and Dependants) Act 1975 may be the only means of attempting to vest the tenancy in the surviving cohabitee, notwithstanding

that the accommodation is that person's home. Even then, an application is fraught with difficulties. As shall be seen in Chapter 5, the court can look only to whether "reasonable financial provision" has been made. This phrase has been narrowly interpreted in the case of claims by non-spouse dependants; arguably it may not extend to tenancies which have no intrinsic financial value.

The situation for a surviving cohabitee is much better where there is a periodic assured tenancy, be it a statutory periodic tenancy arising on the expiry of a fixed term or a periodic tenancy from the outset. Section 17 Housing Act 1988 provides that the spouse, including a cohabitee living with the tenant as spouse, of a sole assured periodic tenant who was not himself or herself a successor to the tenancy, is entitled to succeed to the tenancy providing he or she occupied the accommodation as their only or principal home immediately before the tenant's death, notwithstanding the terms of any Will. The definition of "successor" includes a tenant who became a sole tenant by virtue of the Will or intestacy of the previous tenant or by the right of survivorship under a joint tenancy. This contrasts with the Rent Act position where a joint tenancy prolongs the potential succession rights. No other member of the tenant's family is entitled to succeed to a periodic tenancy, although where the tenant does not have a spouse or cohabitee, a tenancy which was periodic from the outset can be left by Will. However, unless the implied absolute covenant against assignment has been specifically overridden by the terms of the agreement, the personal representatives will, it seems, be unable lawfully to assign the tenancy to the beneficiary and the new tenant would not obtain security of tenure.

Another problem which may arise for cohabitees is that, in order to succeed by statute to an assured periodic tenancy, the requirement is for residence in the accommodation *by the tenant's spouse*, not residence *with the tenant*. To come within the definition of spouse, the cohabitee must show that he or she was living with the tenant as his or her wife or husband. Exactly how this will be interpreted remains to be seen. Where, for example, a tenant has been in hospital for a long time, leaving the partner in occupation of the accommodation, a landlord could argue that they do not fulfil the spouse condition as they are no longer living together as husband and wife. There is no requirement that the cohabitation should immediately precede the death, and it is hoped that the courts will not interpret the criterion too narrowly, but look to whether the nature of the relationship was akin to that of a husband and wife without also requiring the partners to have lived together in the accommodation immediately before the tenant's death where circumstances other than breakdown of the relationship prevented this.

(iii) Succession to public sector secure tenancies: A housing association tenant will now normally be granted an assured periodic tenancy. Accordingly, succession rights for such non-tenant cohabitees are as set out above in relation to private sector assured tenancies, and are significantly less favourable than those which apply to both protected and secure tenants. Where cohabitees are living in local authority accommodation they will be secure tenants and there tenancies are governed by Housing Act 1985. This is also the case with housing association tenancies granted before 15 January 1989.

There can be only one succession to a secure tenancy under the terms of the s 87 Housing Act 1985 and this can be to either the tenant's surviving spouse or a member of the tenant's family. Where there was originally a joint tenancy, on the death or surrender of the last surviving joint tenant, there can be no statutory succession. In order to succeed to the tenancy, the successor must have been living in the accommodation as his or her only or principal home. In the case of a spouse, there is no prior period of qualification but the spouse must have been living with the deceased tenant at the time of death. A spouse does *not* include a cohabitee under the 1985 Act, but a cohabitee can succeed as a member of the deceased tenant's family providing he or she resided in the accommodation with the deceased tenant partner as their husband or wife for at least twelve months before the death.

Cohabitees of the same sex do not come within the definition of "living together as husband and wife", as decided by *Harrogate BC* v *Simpson,* above. "Other members of a tenant's family" are defined in s 113 Housing Act 1985, and include children, parents, grandparents, siblings, aunts, uncles, nephews, nieces, step-and half relations.

Accordingly, succession and, to some extent, assignment, possibilities for cohabitees depend on the nature of the tenancy granted and the law of landlord and tenant, which, across different types of tenancy, is far from consistent in its treatment of cohabitees. Advisors need therefore to establish the nature of the tenancy before attempting to advise on cohabitees' housing rights.

3. Owner occupied property

Of the various courses open to cohabitees, purchasing a property together is the most likely to lead them carefully to consider their respective positions and to seek legal advice. They will usually instruct a solicitor, who should advise both on the implications of buying a property in their joint names. If the property is being purchased in the name of one of them alone, then the partner may not have access to advice, even if contributing to the purchase price. In this situation an advisor may still be required to take instructions from both cohabitees. Most building societies and banks who lend money secured by mortgage on residential property require, from all occupiers over the age of eighteen, signed consents agreeing to postpone any interest in the property they may have or acquire, to that of the mortgagee. This is so any person in occupation cannot prevent the mortgagee from realising its interest should the mortgagor default (see *Williams & Glyn's Bank* v *Boland* [1980] 2 All ER 408). An advisor who discovers that the purchaser's cohabitee will be living in the property must explain why the consent is required by the mortgagee. This provides an opportunity to indicate the legal implications of the whole transaction to both cohabitees, even though the property is to be in the sole name of one of them. Only one of the cohabitees would in fact be the advisor's client, but a duty is owed to the mortgagee to obtain consent for its charge to have priority over any interest of the other cohabitee. A letter to the non-client cohabitee should be written, outlining the consequences of the required consent and suggesting separate legal advice should they be concerned about the position. A legal advisor is clearly in a difficult professional position here, but it may be appropriate for a declaration of trust (see page 63) to be suggested.

(a) Purchase in joint names

As with rented accommodation, if a property is purchased in the joint names of cohabitees each has the right to occupy it. Neither can lawfully exclude the other without having first obtained a court order to do so. In addition, as both names are on the title deeds, one joint owner cannot sell, mortgage or charge the property without the consent of the other, whose signature will be required to effect the sale or create the legal charge. This also means that if one co-owner wishes to sell and the other refuses, an application has to be made to the court for an order for sale pursuant to s 30 Law of Property Act 1925. The court will either order the sale or agree to a postponement of the sale in certain circumstances. This situation usually arises on breakdown of the relationship between cohabitees and is explored in more detail in Chapter 10.

All joint purchasers hold the legal estate of their property as joint tenants in law. By virtue of ss 34 and 36 Law of Property Act 1925, where there is joint ownership, a statutory trust for sale of the land is implied. Co-owners are therefore trustees, and hold on trust for themselves as either joint tenants or tenants in common in equity and by virtue of the same provisions their interests are deemed to be in the proceeds of sale not in the land itself. As the law allows joint owners to hold their beneficial interest in the property either as joint tenants or as tenants in common, all co-owners should be advised at the time of purchase on the broad implications of both options, so they can make an informed decision as to which properly reflects their intentions. This decision is of tremendous importance to all co-owners, and particularly to cohabitees. Failure to explain and keep a record of the legal advice given at the time of purchase is likely to amount to negligence on the part of a solicitor (see *Walker* v *Hall* [1984] FLR 126, (CA)).

When purchasing a property, cohabitees may make different contributions to the purchase price. They may agree to make unequal contributions to the mortgage repayments or other outgoings. They may decide to apply one partner's income towards the mortgage repayments and the other income towards all the other outgoings. Very often, however, the agreement reached is not set out in any legal document. Many do not appreciate that these agreements may affect their beneficial interests in the property, and that these arrangements can prove critical. Solicitors are often criticised for failing to explain clearly to joint proprietors, at the time of purchase, the options and their implications. Where the advisor is on notice that the joint purchasers are cohabitees, the implications of purchasing in joint or sole names, and of purchasing as beneficial joint tenants or tenants in common, must be explained to both parties so that an informed and joint decision is taken. The legal documentation should be drawn up truly to reflect and record the intentions of the co-owners at the date of the purchase, and to provide an accurate starting point to determine any future dispute. It may also be appropriate to ask the cohabitees to consider whether they wish to reflect arrangements relating to other property in a written agreement, or to consider a cohabitation agreement.

(b) Joint tenancy or tenancy in common?

Regardless of their actual contributions to the purchase price, joint proprietors, whilst being obliged to hold as joint tenants in law under a statutory trust for sale, have the option of declaring that they hold their beneficial interests either as joint tenants or as tenants in common. One of the most important effects of this decision is seen on the death of one of the joint tenants. If the couple are beneficial joint tenants and neither has severed the joint tenancy thereby creating a beneficial tenancy in common, the survivor of them will succeed to the deceased joint tenant's legal and equitable interests by operation of law, and become the sole owner of the property, notwithstanding the terms of the deceased joint tenant's Will. However, where there is a beneficial tenancy in common, then the deceased co-owner's share will form part of that person's estate on death and devolve according to the Will, or the rules on intestacy in the absence of a Will.If there is no Will, the intestacy rules provide that the deceased cohabitee's share of the property will be inherited by his or her next of kin, and not by the partner. The surviving partner will have to rely either on the proceeds of any life policy to purchase the other share of the property from the partner's beneficiary; or apply for provision under the Inheritance (Provision for Family and Dependants) Act 1975, which would not necessarily enable the applicant to remain in the home (see Chapter 5 below).

What therefore should determine whether cohabitees should be joint tenants or tenants in common in equity, and how should this be reflected in the purchase documentation? Where the contributions made by each of the cohabitees are broadly equal, and it is intended that they should contribute to the mortgage in roughly equal shares, and they agree that their interests in the property are equal, the crucial issue is whether they wish the right of survivorship to apply. If they decide that they wish the other to inherit their share of the property without having to make a Will to that effect, then a beneficial joint tenancy should be created. In unregistered land, the conveyance should as a matter of course always contain an express declaration as to whether the purchasers hold beneficially as joint tenants or tenants in common. This, in the absence of any later evidence of a different joint intention or of fraud or mistake, will be conclusive. Where the purchase involves registered land, an express declaration can, and arguably should, be included in the transfer document, although probably the majority of solicitors do no more than complete the declaration on the standard form of transfer stating that the survivor can give a valid receipt for capital monies arising on disposition of the land. Whether or not this declaration is sufficient to create an express beneficial joint tenancy has not yet been specifically been decided. In *Bernard* v *Josephs* [1982] 3 All ER 162, the Court of Appeal held that where property had been transferred to two cohabitees jointly, without any express declaration as to the nature of the beneficial ownership, there was no presumption that the parties held the property in equal shares. Instead a court should look at all the evidence, such as respective contributions, and see whether it indicates any intention to hold the property other than in equal shares. In that case, it was decided that the parties did have equal interests in the property, but much time and expense would have been saved if the transfer had indicated the parties' intentions at the time of purchase. Where the conveyance or transfer does not include a declaration of the beneficial interests, a separate declaration of trust document, executed by both parties, should be drawn and placed with the title deeds. Once there is an express beneficial joint tenancy, then each party will be deemed to have an equal interest in the proceeds of sale even if the joint tenancy is subsequently severed (see *Goodman* v *Gallant* [1986] 1 All ER

311). Where there is an initial joint tenancy, it can later be severed by either of the joint tenants, by service of a notice of severance on the other party or by course of dealing. As soon as a joint tenancy is severed, a tenancy in common arises and the right of survivorship no longer applies. Each co-owner's share will then devolve separately with his or her estate. If instructed to sever a joint tenancy, the client should be advised to make a new Will.

Even if the parties have contributed in unequal shares to the purchase price of the property, they may still if they wish purchase as beneficial joint tenants. However, as has been seen *(Goodman* v *Gallant* above), even after the tenancy has been severed, they will still hold the property in equal shares, although where separation takes place some adjustment may be made to reflect varying contributions made after the separation.

Where there are unequal contributions to the purchase price and the parties wish this to be reflected in their respective interests in the property, then a beneficial tenancy in common is needed. To create a beneficial tenancy in common an express declaration should be made in the conveyance or transfer, or in a separate declaration of trust document, clearly stating the proportions in which the property is held by the co-owners. Express declarations of trust can be simple documents and must be in writing following the requirements of s 53(1) Law of Property Act 1925.

Where advisors are acting for joint purchasers, it should be standard practice to ask whether they wish to hold the property as joint tenants or tenants in common. Whatever the answer, an express declaration should be made at the time as it can avoid future disputes. It may well be appropriate to set out in a separate trust, not only the capital contributions to the deposit, but also any credit to be given for a "right to buy" discount; the parties' proposed present and future contributions to the mortgage and other outgoings; and the planned use of the property as a family home. In effect, a small scale cohabitation agreement dealing specifically with the parties' intentions in relation to the home could be drawn up.

To summarise, any advisor instructed to create a tenancy in common should immediately advise on the position of each cohabitee on death. Without a Will leaving their interest in the property to the other, a partner's share will devolve according to the intestacy rules on their next of kin, which may not reflect his or her true wishes. In the case of registered land, an advisor must also indicate on the transfer, and the Land Registry application form, whether or not the survivor can give a valid receipt on the subsequent sale of the property. As discussed above, this on its own is not sufficient to determine the interests in the property, and a declaration of the beneficial joint tenancy or tenancy in common, and the relative shares of tenants in common, must in any event be recorded on the transfer or in a separate declaration of trust.

(c) Purchase in sole name
If for tax or other *bona fide* reasons, cohabitees who are both contributing to the purchase of a property wish it to be purchased in the sole name of one party, it is still possible to have a declaration of trust as to how the equity is held. Although this would give only an equitable, rather than a legal, interest in the property to the non-purchaser cohabitee, it would still be clear evidence of the parties' respective interests in any subsequent dispute between them. A non-owner partner who has contributed in money or money's worth is likely in any event to be able to prove a beneficial interest in the proceeds of sale and can make an application under s 30 Law of Property Act 1925; see Chapter 10. Accordingly, although such situations are likely to be rare, where a beneficial interest is acknowledged or apparent from the outset, a declaration of trust should be drawn up, setting out the respective interests under the resulting trust and reciting the contributions made by each party.

The need for a declaration of trust may arise where parties agree to cohabit in a property already owned by one of them, and the in-coming partner pays for improvements to the property or contributes to the mortgage repayments. It is open to them to transfer the property into joint names, but this may involve obtaining a mortgagee's consent, and possibly paying stamp duty, land registration fees, legal costs and disbursements as on a new purchase. Some cohabitees may prefer to make a declaration of trust, although from the non-owner cohabitee's point of view, this would confer only an equitable rather than a legal interest and would be enforceable against the cohabitee only. The need for Wills to be drawn up should be considered, as, if they hold the property as tenants in common, their shares will devolve with their respective estates. A later purchaser for value of the property would normally raise enquiries about the interests of any other adult occupier of the property, and where the cohabitee is in actual occupation of the property, the owner cohabitee will not be able to give vacant possession without the partner's co-operation, and a purchaser is likely to be put on notice. The partner would in any event have an overriding interest where the title is registered (s 70(1)(g) Land Registration Act 1925). At the very least, a declaration of trust gives the non-owner cohabitee documentary evidence of his or her interest in the property which will prove helpful on relationship breakdown.

Unfortunately, express declarations of trust in these circumstances are rare. Where there is no declaration of trust, and a dispute arises on the breakdown of the relationship, the onus is on the non-owner cohabitee to prove that he or she has a beneficial interest in the property. The courts have in some cases been prepared to find implied, constructive or resulting trusts in a property of which only one cohabitee is the legal owner, deeming the owner to be holding the property in trust for both cohabitees. Another possibility where only one cohabitee is the owner is to find that a licence for life has been granted to the non-owner. This is only likely to arise in special circumstances and will never be easy to prove. These issues, which usually arise in the context of breakdown of the relationship, or, possibly, on death, are dealt with in detail in Chapter 10.

It should also be borne in mind that a non-owner cohabitee, or indeed in some situations a joint owner cohabitee, may wish to assert rights of beneficial ownership or occupation as against a mortgagee. The home may be mortgaged by one partner without the other's knowledge or consent; usually the mortgagee's rights will prevail, unless, in the case of registered land, there was actual occupation of the land before the creation of the charge (*Williams & Glyn's Bank* v *Boland,* above). Where the land is unregistered, the mortgagee's claim will only be defeated in this way if the mortgagee is on notice of the actual occupation. A detailed discussion of the issues is outside the scope of this book, but for a concise and most helpful account of the position, see Michael Daniel's article *Spouses, Cohabitees, Their Home and their Lenders* (Family Law, 1990, page 445).

4. Homelessness

Regardless of the tenure of their previous accommodation, cohabitees may find themselves, either as a family unit or following breakdown of their relationship, without any accommodation at all. The Housing Act 1985 Part III (formerly the Housing (Homeless Persons) Act 1977) gives local housing authorities specific duties to house certain categories of homeless people. In many instances cohabitees, particularly where they have children living with them, will fall within those categories. Homelessness arises in different ways, and how that situation arose may often determine whether or not a local authority has a duty to rehouse. Unfortunately, as will be seen, rooflessness of itself does not necessarily guarantee that a person is entitled to be found accommodation, even where there are dependent children. Homelessness has developed into a complex area of law. Although the statutory provisions are relatively concise, a plethora of case law now interprets the Act and only an outline of the main provisions and cases relevant to the unmarried family is attempted here. Further details of provisions relevant to homelessness caused by domestic violence are given in Chapter 6. Some general points are worthy of note.

Any challenge to a local authority's decision not to provide accommodation under the Act should normally be made by way of judicial review (see *Cocks* v *Thanet DC* [1982] 3 All ER 1135) rather than, as was originally thought possible, by an action for breach of statutory duty in the county court. It is still not clear whether it is possible to use the simple action for breach of statutory duty even to challenge the appropriateness of the manner in which the duty is being discharged, for example where the suitability of accommodation offered to an applicant to whom it is accepted that a duty is owed, is in question. This was left open in *R* v *City of Westminster ex parte Tansey* [1988] 21 HLR 57, although at least one county court has accepted that suitability can be challenged in this way (see *Guest* v *Manchester CC*, *Legal Action*, September 1990, page 7.)

An application for judicial review can be brought only in the Queen's Bench Division, Divisional Court; an applicant must obtain leave to apply and must fulfil the conditions of Order 53 of the Rules of the Supreme Court. The application for leave must normally be brought within three months of the decision, and, if the applicant is successful, the court usually makes an order for *certiorari* quashing the authority's decision but remitting it for them to make another decision in the light of the court's reasoning. Where leave is obtained to make an application for judicial review, it is always worthwhile pressing a local authority to reconsider its decision at that stage in the light of any further evidence available; this may bring about a different decision. Leave for judicial review following *dicta* in the House of Lords decision in *R* v *Hillingdon London Borough ex parte Puhlhofer* [1986] 1 All ER 467 should be granted only sparingly. Lord Brightman stated (474f): "Although action or inaction of a local authority is clearly susceptible to judicial review, where they have misconstrued the Act or abused their powers, or otherwise acted perversely, I think great restraint should be exercised in giving leave to proceed by way of judicial review." Nonetheless, it is often possible to persuade a local authority to reconsider a case using the threat of judicial review, and thus it is helpful to be able to use the case law to reveal the weaknesses in a decision which make it susceptible to challenge.

(a) Procedure

To be eligible to be housed as a homeless family, the Act provides that the applicant must:
  (i) be homeless or threatened with homelessness;
  (ii) have a priority need;
  (iii) not be intentionally homeless.

As we have seen, if a local authority has reason to believe an applicant is homeless and is in priority need, it must provide temporary accommodation pending a final decision (s 63). Many families, particularly in urban areas, are placed in bed and breakfast accommodation at this stage, and may stay there for several months whilst the authority completes its enquiries and decides whether all three conditions have been met.

Where cohabitees find themselves homeless or threatened with homelessness, they should be advised to apply to their local housing authority for accommodation pursuant to the Housing Act 1985 Part III. Where the authority has reason to believe that the applicant is homeless or threatened with homelessness, it has a duty to make enquiries (s 62(1)) and consider whether it owes a duty to secure them accommodation. If they also appear to be in priority need within the meaning of the Act (see below), for example if they have dependent children who reside with them, the authority also has a duty to provide temporary accommodation pending completion of its enquiries (s 63). Thus, making an application can of itself provide a family with immediate help. There is no particular application form but most authorities normally require an applicant to attend their offices for an interview. However, their duties take immediate effect and cannot be avoided by closing the offices; and in the cities at least, they are expected to provide a 24 hour service (*R* v *LB Camden ex parte Gillan* [1988] 21 HLR 114). The Act sets out various steps to be followed by the local authority, and hurdles which the applicant must clear before proving entitlement to accommodation. In addition the authority must also have regard to the Code of Guidance issued by the department of Environment and the Welsh Office (s 71(1)), which sets out matters to be taken into account. However, providing they have had regard to it, failure to comply with it will not of itself provide a base for a valid challenge to an authority's decision. A new code was published in August 1991 to replace the old 1983 code. The new code recommends that local authorities should set up internal procedures to review decisions on homelessness and provide an appeal panel. This would revolutionise present arrangements if adopted, and have serious implications in that legal aid would not be available to applicants at such a hearing, leaving Green Form advice the only possibility for a client who cannot afford representation.

(b) Homeless or threatened with homelessness
Persons are regarded as "homeless" if they have no accommodation in England and Wales which they, together with any person who normally resides with them as a member of their family or such other person for whom it is reasonable to reside with them, are entitled to occupy

(s 58(2)).

The applicant's entitlement to occupy accommodation may take the following forms:

(i) an entitlement to occupy by virtue of an interest in it or of an order of the court;

(ii) an express or implied licence to occupy;

(iii) occupation as a residence by virtue of any enactment or rule of law giving him the right to remain in occupation or restricting the right of another to recover possession.

Section 58(2A) provides that the accommodation must be such as is reasonable for the applicant to occupy and in determining this the local authority may have regard to the prevailing housing conditions in the local area. This is considered further in relation to the test for intentional homelessness (see page 72).

Accommodation will not constitute "available accommodation" if it is available to the applicant only and not to other members of the family or other persons normally and reasonably residing with him (s 75). It has always been thought that heterosexual cohabitees should come within the definition of a member of the other's family, and this is now specifically stated in the new Code of Guidance. However, each case will be considered by the authority on its individual facts. Certainly where there are children belonging to both the applicant and the cohabitee, and there is no care or custody, or residence, order removing or restricting either of the parent's parental rights, the applicant's cohabitee must be regarded as coming within the definition. It is submitted that if it were necessary to challenge an adverse decision by a housing authority on this point, the old Rent Act 1977 authorities cited above (see pages 54 to 55) in relation to successors to a tenancy could be used in support of a contention that a cohabitee should be regarded as a member of the applicant's family. This would not of course assist homosexual cohabitees who, as we have seen, are not regarded as family members in relation to public sector secure tenancies. However, it could be argued that where there has been cohabitation over a long period of time, it is reasonable for an applicant's partner to reside with him or her and that their needs as a unit should be taken into account in determining whether accommodation is available for occupation. Similarly, where a finding is made to rehouse an applicant, the suitability of the accommodation should be assessed according to their joint needs. Much of course will depend on the attitude of the authority concerned and the accommodation available in the area. It may be fruitful to ensure that the authority does categorise a partner as someone reasonably residing with the applicant, as this may assist in persuading them to place the tenancy in joint names. In practice an authority could not prevent a cohabitee applicant who has a priority need due to age or vulnerability (see below) from allowing his or her partner of the same sex to live with them in permanent accommodation; but, unless there is a joint tenancy, the partner would have no right to succeed to the tenancy if it were secure, and probably not even if it were an assured tenancy granted by a housing association. It has been held that occupation by way of licence of a battered wives refuge and a night shelter, which could refuse admission if the shelter were full did not amount to accommodation (see *R* v *LB Ealing ex p Sidhu* (1983) HLR 41, and *R* v *Waveney DC ex parte Bowers* [1983] QB 238) An applicant will also be homeless if unable to secure entry to the accommodation or at risk from domestic violence from a person residing there (s 58(3)).

A person is "threatened with homelessness" if they are liable to be made homeless within twenty-eight days (s 58(4)), and, for the purpose of the subsequent duties imposed on the authority, there is no distinction made between these two categories of people.

(c) Priority need
A duty to re-house will be owed only to an applicant who is in priority need (s 59). Applicants in priority need are:
  (i) a pregnant woman or a person with whom a pregnant woman resides or might be reasonably be expected to reside;
  (ii) a person with whom dependent children reside or might reasonably be expected to reside;
  (iii) a person who is vulnerable as a result of old age, mental illness or handicap or physical disability or other special reason or with whom such a person resides or might reasonably be expected to reside;
  (iv) a person who is homeless or threatened with homelessness as a result of an emergency such as a fire or flood:

(v) someone within a group of persons described as having priority need by the Secretary of State.

If homeless as a result of an emergency, cohabitees will automatically be considered to be in priority need. A homeless cohabiting couple has nothing to lose and a great deal to gain from applying to the housing authority to see whether they can be classified in any of these categories. It has been held that it is not lawful for an authority to have a policy of excluding childless couples from falling within priority need (see *AG, ex rel Tilley* v *LB Wandsworth* [1981] 1 All ER 1162).

"Dependent children" normally means children under sixteen or still in full time education. The test is a question of fact: are there dependent children who reside or ought reasonably to reside with the applicant? An authority cannot, where the parents are separated, insist that the applicant produces a custody order before accepting that a priority need exists (see *R* v *London Borough of Ealing ex parte Sidhu*, above).

To show vulnerability, an applicant must be of retirement age, or vulnerable in some other way. This has been defined as being less able to both find and keep accommodation (see *R* v *Lambeth LBC ex parte Carroll* (1988) 20 HLR 142). In the same case the court indicated that an authority must reach its own decision on vulnerability and not merely rubber stamp a medical opinion unless that is decisive on the only relevant issues. Accordingly advisors should in appropriate cases advise the applicant to submit independent medical evidence to the local authority. The local authority must provide accommodation temporarily where there is a *prima facie* priority need, but thereafter they further make enquiries to see if there is in fact such a need. Only if this is established will applicants proceed to the next hurdle.

(d) Intentional homelessness

It is this final hurdle which has spawned the most case law and undoubtedly causes hardship to people who fulfil the other criteria but are deemed to be the authors of their own misfortune. Where there is a finding of intentional homelessness, a local authority will not owe any duty to secure accommodation for the applicant, who may therefore literally be without a roof. A person is intentionally homeless if he or she does or fails to do anything which leads them to cease to occupy accommodation which is available and reasonable for them to occupy (s 60(1)). The definition of becoming intentionally "threatened with homelessness" is subject to a similar test. An act or omission in good faith by a person unaware of a relevant fact such as security of tenure, the availability of assistance with rent or mortgage payments, or the validity of a notice to quit, is not to be treated as deliberate (s 60(3)). A person is not intentionally homeless if they give up accommodation which is not available for both the applicant and any person with whom they might reasonably be expected to reside (s 75). Thus in *R* v *Peterborough CC ex p Carr* (1990) 22 HLR 206 (QBD), a pregnant woman who left her accommodation with her sister due to her sister's refusal to allow her prospective child's father to live with her was not intentionally homeless. Where one cohabitee has done an act, such as giving up a job, which has meant the loss of tied accommodation, then it may be possible for their spouse or cohabitee or another adult who usually and reasonably resides with them, to make the application under the Act in order to avoid a finding of intentionality (see *R* v *North Devon County Council, ex parte Lewis* [1981] 1 WLR 328 and *R* v *Swansea City Council* (1983) 9 HLR 64). Each case will depend on its own facts, but to be successful the applicant must not have acquiesced in the act which led to the loss of accommodation. Thus, in *Lewis* above, although it was accepted that a cohabitee was entitled to make an application following her partner's quitting his job and losing accommodation, she was equally found to be intentionally homeless because she had acquiesced in his decision to leave. It would have been otherwise if she had done all in her power to prevent him from resigning.

Cases of mortgage and rent arrears often lead to intentionality findings, as do possession orders granted on the basis that the applicant has caused nuisance and annoyance to other occupiers. The Code of Guidance suggests that a lenient view may be taken where these arise due to ignorance of the availability of welfare benefits. Where one party has spent the rent money on drink or caused nuisance and annoyance despite the attempts by the other to prevent it, the "innocent" cohabitee or spouse can argue that they are not intentionally homeless, particularly if financially dependent on their partner, or for other reasons were not in a position to prevent the situation. It is submitted that this should be the case regardless of whether the parties are joint tenants or the tenancy is vested in the other's name. It has been held that mere knowledge of rent or mortgage arrears by a partner is not necessarily enough to constitute intentionality as they may not have learned of the situation until it was too late to forestall. However, where there is a joint tenancy, lack of knowledge may be difficult to uphold as both parties should be communicated with and served with proceedings. Many couples in severe financial straits may decide that what money is available should be spent on food rather than housing costs. They may be helped to some extent by the case of *R* v *LB Hillingdon ex parte Tinn* (1988) 20 HLR 305 where it was held that it could not be reasonable to occupy accommodation where to meet the mortgage repayments the family had to go without food and the other necessities of life.

Whether or not it is reasonable for an applicant to continue to occupy accommodation involves many questions, but an authority must take into account the housing conditions in its area in reaching a decision on reasonableness, and the worse these conditions are, the more an applicant is expected to put up with before quitting accommodation. In *R* v *LB Tower Hamlets ex parte Monaf* (1988) 20 HLR 529, it was held that the authority must perform a balancing exercise between the reasons for departure and housing conditions in that area. However, the authority must compare the applicant's actual housing conditions with those in the *authority's* area and not with the conditions of residents in the area or country where the applicant had left the accommodation (see *R* v *Newham LBC ex p Tower Hamlets LBC* (1990) 22 HLR 298). Another important factor is that the authority can look beyond the immediate cause of homelessness to see if the real cause of the homelessness is intentional.

Unless settled accommodation has been lost unintentionally, a finding of intentional homelessness is valid. There is no definition of settled accommodation and it may now be that if Rent Act security is given up and better accommodation is taken under a new style assured shorthold tenancy with an initial period of only six months that this would lead to an intentionality finding. In *Dyson* v *Kerrier DC* [1980] 1 WLR 1205, a writer gave up a secure tenancy to take a winter let. When this expired she applied under the Act. However, it was held that the cause of her homelessness was the giving up of the secure tenancy which was a deliberate act, and as her subsequent accommodation could not be regarded as settled, as it was so short term, she was intentionally homeless. Indeed in *Din* v *LB Wandsworth* [1983] 1 AC 657, where a family ignored advice to remain in accommodation until the court order for possession expired, although it was accepted that by the time they applied to the authority they would in any event have been homeless unintentionally, the act of leaving available accommodation before being required to leave was sufficient to render them intentionally homeless in the view of the House of Lords; as none of the accommodation they had subsequently occupied had been settled, they were still intentionally homeless despite the fact that a considerable period of time had elapsed; a finding of intentional homelessness can only be redeemed after an applicant has lost subsequent settled accommodation *unintentionally*. Thus cohabitees should not surrender settled accommodation which it is at that time reasonable for them to continue to occupy; clearly this has been very strictly interpreted by the courts.

It may be possible for advisors to suggest that homeless clients apply to another authority after a finding of intentionality, as an authority's discretion is wide and another may justifiably come to a different conclusion on the same facts. If they have a local connection under s 67, they then may be referred back to the first authority and, surprisingly, there is nothing to prevent this "merry-go-round" effect (see *R* v *Slough BC ex parte Ealing LBC* [1981] 2 WLR 399). However, the referring authority should treat the application carefully and give the other authority the chance to discuss any discrepancies between the applicant's accounts to each of them (*R* v *LB Tower Hamlets ex parte LB Camden* (1988) The Times 12 December). If the referral is unsuccessful, the second authority must then house the applicant.

(e) Duties of local authorities; local connections
Once an authority has made its decision it must notify the applicant, giving reasons if it finds no duty to rehouse or that there is a local connection elsewhere (s 64). If the authority finds there is no priority

need, then advice and assistance, but nothing further, must be provided. If there is priority need but the applicants are judged intentionally homeless, then accommodation must be provided for such period as will allow them to find other accommodation (typically twenty-eight days) and advice and assistance should also be provided. At this point, a family is often left unable to afford, or even find, private sector accommodation, yet nothing further has to be done by the local authority. Although the Act aims to keep families together, once this point is reached, the only course is to ask Social Services to provide accommodation for the children pursuant to s 20 CA 1989, or to provide help to enable the family to stay together pursuant to s 19 CA 1989. It remains to be seen whether the new duties placed on local authorities by the Children Act 1989 will result in more practical help being available to families in these desperate circumstances. Housing associations or other charitable organisations such as SHELTER may sometimes be able to assist.

If an applicant has succeeded in overcoming the three hurdles above, then the authority has a duty to secure suitable accommodation. However, if there is no local connection with that authority but there is with another authority, then s 67 provides that the applicant can be referred back to the authority with whom he or she has a local connection, providing the applicant does not run the risk of domestic violence in that area. Section 61 defines "local connection" in terms of periods of residence (past or present), employment, family associations and special circumstances. Where an applicant does not have a local connection with any area but fulfils the other criteria, then the local authority to whom he or she has applied must secure suitable accommodation, although this may be done through another authority or housing body (see *R* v *LB Hillingdon, ex parte Streeting* [1980] 3 All ER 413).

Homelessness on family breakdown due to domestic violence is a problem often affecting cohabitees with children, and is dealt with in Chapter 6.

Chapter 4

Tax and social security

It is in the areas of tax and social security that some of the greatest anomalies in the legal treatment of cohabitees become apparent. Despite statements of intent by politicians at various times to integrate the welfare benefit and tax systems, it has yet to be achieved. But changes have been made, for public policy reasons, to both tax and social security legislation, to limit any advantages heterosexual cohabitees had had over married couples. It is not proposed here to look at the substantive law in any great detail, but to outline the general principles, and points of particular relevance to cohabitees.

1. Income tax

Both heterosexual and homosexual relationships are treated by the Inland Revenue as separate individuals for income tax purposes and the increased married couples allowance, which is awarded to married couples by virtue of the act of marriage, cannot be extended to cohabitees, regardless of whether one or both of them works or has an income. The relevant provisions are now to be found in the Income and Corporation Taxes Act 1988, which is principally a consolidating Act.

A recent attempt to extend the meaning of the word "wife" under the Income and Corporation Taxes Act 1970 to a woman cohabitee living with a man failed. A decision by the General Commissioners for New Forest (West) to allow a man, who had cohabited for eleven years with a woman, who had changed her surname to his and whom he had wholly maintained, to claim the then married man's allowance under s 8 was overturned by the Chancery Division. Ferris J in *Rignell (Inspector of Taxes)* v *Andrews* [1990] STC 410, stated:

"....the term 'wife' was used only to denote a woman who had entered into a marriage that was recognised by the civil law of England, with a particular man and that the term was not apt to cover a woman who had not entered into a marriage but was merely cohabiting, however close or permanent the relationship might be."

Where cohabitees have no children, they will each receive a single person's personal allowance which they can set off only against their own income in each tax year. The single allowance for the tax year 1991/92 is £3,295.

Where cohabitees have qualifying children living with them, they are entitled to an additional personal allowance, currently £1,720. The married couple's allowance is also £1,720, and is awarded to all married couples regardless of whether or not they have children. However, this is credited automatically to the husband first and can be transferred to the wife only if his income is insufficient to use the allowance.

Cohabitees with children can choose which of them claims the additional personal allowance. If only one partner is working, or only one of them earns sufficient to take full advantage of the additional allowance, then that partner should claim the allowance, or no benefit will be derived from it. Interestingly, where both partners have incomes, and there are at least two qualifying children residing with them, cohabitees may *each* claim an additional allowance, one for each child, and providing they each have sufficient income, will obtain greater relief than that available to married couples. Thus if cohabitees either have two children of their own or each has one or more children of former relationships, or a combination of children of former relationships as well as at least one of their own, they can take advantage of this situation. It is to be remembered, though, that only one additional allowance can be claimed by each partner, regardless of how many children are living with the couple.

Cohabitees who purchased a property jointly before 31 August 1988 were *each* entitled to mortgage interest relief on capital sums borrowed of up to £30,000 per person in relation to a property which was their only or principal residence, whereas married couples were limited to relief of a maximum of £30,000 per couple. Relief is now limited to a maximum of £30,000 *per property* and one of the reasons justifying the change was that the previous system unfairly favoured unmarried couples over married couples, although of course the changes affected not only cohabitees living together as husband and wife, but all unmarried joint purchasers.

It should be borne in mind that everyone, regardless of age, is entitled to a personal allowance. Allowances are increased for those over 65; and children, however young, are entitled to a single person's allowance. Thus it used to be the position that maintenance payments paid directly to the child were most tax efficient. Providing the child had no other income to absorb the personal allowance, this method saved the custodial parent, who may have had income of his or her own, having to pay income tax on the payments of maintenance for the child(ren). In addition, the non-custodial parent could, depending on the size of the payments, deduct or reclaim tax from the maintenance. However, since 1988, maintenance payments are no longer taxable in the hands of the recipient and thus do not constitute income for tax purposes (s 51A ICTA 1988). All payments must therefore be paid gross and there is no tax relief available in respect of maintenance payments to children.

2. Capital gains tax

The Capital Gains Tax Act 1979 provides that capital gains tax is payable on all chargeable gains made in respect of chargeable assets, after deduction of all allowable losses and subject to an annual exemption, currently £5,500. Cohabitees, unlike married couples, have always been entitled to an annual exemption each. However, with effect from 6 April 1990, married couples are similarly entitled to two exemptions and in addition, disposals between spouses are deemed to be neither at a loss or a gain. However, disposals between cohabitees do not attract any special treatment and are thus chargeable either as a gain or a loss as appropriate.

The main asset of most cohabitees is likely to be the home, although a sole or principal residence does not attract capital gains tax, and any profit made on a sale is not considered a gain (s 101 CGTA 1979). A married couple can have only one sole or principal residence, whereas cohabitees may have one each. Accordingly, providing one property is vested in each of their names, and they can each satisfy the residence condition, it is possible to avoid paying capital gains tax on either property no matter when they are sold.

3. Inheritance tax

While no inheritance tax is payable on transfers between spouses, there is, again, no like treatment of cohabitees, who are treated as strangers. Inheritance tax is payable on "transfers of value", that is those which reduce the value of the transferor's estate, made either *inter vivos* or on death. However there is a threshold of £140,000 below which no tax is payable in respect of transfers made after 5 April 1991. Although this may seem a fairly large sum of money, there is, unlike capital gains tax, no exception in respect of the transferor's residence, and thus the value of the deceased's share of his or her property will be taken into account in calculating when the threshold is reached. Where jointly owned property is held as tenants in common in equity, the deceased's share forms part of the estate and tax will be payable in accordance with the terms of the Will.

Where there is an equitable joint tenancy, the deceased's share in the property will pass to the co-owner in accordance with the right of survivorship. However, although this share of the property will not form part of the estate, the surviving co-owner will be liable for any inheritance tax due in respect of the share.

After the first £140,000, tax is payable, currently at 40%, either by the estate or by the beneficiary. Thus where a cohabitee is the only beneficiary, his/her inheritance will be subject to tax where the total value exceeds this threshold. Where gifts are made before death, and providing the transferor lives for seven years after the making of the gift, then no inheritance tax is payable on such a gift and its value will not form part of the transferor's estate on death. Even if the transferor dies within the seven year period, liability to tax will normally be reduced on a sliding scale, although if death occurs within three years of the gift, then tax is still payable at the full rate. If the donor survives three years but less than four, then 80% of the full rate of tax is payable; tax is payable at 60% of the full rate if the death occurs after four years but less than five; at 40% of the full rate after five years but less than six; and at 20% after six years but less than seven. In addition there is an annual exemption of £3,000 which reduces liability on *inter vivos* gifts.

Cohabitees making Wills, perhaps even more than other clients, need to be advised of the inheritance tax implications of their proposed gifts, and to consider the advantages of making use of the annual exemption and of effecting life assurance for the benefit of their partners, as discussed in Chapter 1.

4. The community charge

Although the community charge now seems unlikely to survive for much longer, it remains payable in 1992 at least.

This is the only tax in respect of which cohabitees can be made liable for their partners' unpaid charges in the same way as for married couples. The provisions relate only to couples of the opposite sex and thus homosexual couples are not rendered liable for their partners under these provisions, although if they are co-owners they may become so liable in respect of standard community charge. Everyone over the age of eighteen years is now liable to pay the personal community charge, unless they fall within one of the very restricted exempt categories. There are three types of community charge: personal, standard and collective. The amount payable is fixed each year by each local authority and varies from area to area. In an effort to reduce the unpopularity of the charge, all bills for the year commencing 1 April 1991 were reduced by an average of £140, paid out of central taxation funds.

(a) Personal community charge

A person is liable to pay the personal charge in the area in which his or her main or principal residence is situated; when a person moves, they cease to be liable in the area from which they have moved and become liable in the new area. Students in advanced education and persons claiming income support are normally liable to pay only 20% of the charge. Community charge benefit may be available for those on low incomes, although, unless a person falls within an exempt category, every one has to pay at least 20% of the charge from their own resources. This 20% rule applies even to people claiming income support, regardless of the level of charge in their area. Given the new government subsidy of £140, the liability of people on low incomes will be greatly reduced, however. Although each partner is individually billed for community charge, any claim for community charge benefit (see below) must be made jointly, and the means of both partners, if they are living together as husband and wife, will be aggregated. Benefit will, though, be paid to each of them individually.

As indicated above, cohabitees may have to pay one another's personal community charge regardless of whether they themselves are exempt or registered students. The rule applies only for any period during which the partners are members of the same household living together as husband and wife. Local authorities should not assume that two people of the opposite sex living at the same address fall into this category. The test to determine whether or not a couple live together as husband and wife is the same as that for applications for income support. The factors which will be taken into account are therefore as follows:

    (i)   whether the couple are members of the same household and the stability of relationship;

    (ii) whether there is financial support;

    (iii) whether there is a sexual relationship;

    (iv) whether the couple have children; and

(v) whether the couple are publicly acknowledged as living together as husband and wife.

This is not to say that unless all these factors apply, there will be no
joint and several liability. However, officers are not entitled to insist
upon this information until after an order for joint and several liability
has been made. It may be possible to appeal against a liability order
made against the partner of a defaulter if it can be shown that they
were not living as husband and wife, although if they are co-owners
then they may in any event be liable if standard community charge is
payable.

The joint and several liability rule cannot be invoked in respect of
any period after cohabitation has ceased, including the day of separation.

Liability arises only if the authority issues a bill to the partner, and
this can only be done when the charge payer has failed to pay the bill
himself or herself. The bill to the partner will request the whole outstanding amount be paid within a specified period of at least fourteen
days. The partner who pays on behalf of his or her cohabitee then has
the right to recover that money as a debt from the defaulting partner
where the default was the result of "wilful refusal or culpable
neglect", but will have to prove this on the balance of probabilities at
court if necessary. In all other cases, the couple are left to resolve the
matter themselves. If neither the defaulter nor the partner pays the
bill, and a reminder is sent to both of them, then the authority can
obtain a liability order against both the defaulter and the partner, but
not against the partner alone. However, the partner is then liable to
pay the whole amount and the authority can enforce the bill against
either of them in full.

On breakdown of the relationship, it is clearly important for the
partner remaining at the couple's joint address to check the community charge position and ensure that payment is made by the partner if at
all possible. In any event it would be prudent to inform the local
authority that a separation has taken place.

Local authorities should be pressed to try and recover the charge
from the defaulting partner before issuing a bill to a former cohabitee
and indeed the Practice Note no 16, para 3.3 strongly recommends
that joint and several liability should not be automatically invoked.

Indeed the same practice note goes on to state that in some circumstances it may not be appropriate to apply the joint and several liability rule at all, and cites the example of where one partner has fled the home due to domestic violence. In such cases the authority should be willing to wait until the violent partner can be forced to pay. However, the local authority is left with a broad discretion as to when to invoke the joint and several liability rule, and policy varies from area to area.

(b) Standard community charge

Standard community charge is payable by owners or, in certain cases, tenants, of empty properties, and where these are jointly owned or rented each co-owner or joint tenant is jointly and severally liable for the standard community charge. Accordingly, where cohabitees jointly own or rent a property which is not occupied by any person as their sole or main residence, the standard charge can be enforced *in toto* against either of them for the period of co-ownership or the joint tenancy as appropriate. Again, this has most significance on breakdown of the relationship. Community charge benefit is never payable in respect of liability to standard community charge.

(c) Collective community charge

Finally, the collective community charge is payable to the authority by landlords of properties where there is a high turnover of occupants from whom the authority considers it would be too difficult to collect the personal charge. The freeholder or leaseholder of the whole building is then liable to pay the charge, and it is that person's responsibility to collect community charge contributions from the residents. Where the property is jointly owned by a couple, then again they are jointly and severally liable for the period of co-ownership. On the other hand, a couple *resident* in such a property are not jointly and severally liable for each other's contributions to the collective community charge.

5. Welfare benefits

The law is by no means even handed in its treatment of heterosexual

cohabitees in the area of welfare benefits and once again it is not possible here to do more than give a summary of the main points relevant
to cohabitees. There is a tendency to treat cohabitees in the same way
as spouses where this is to the advantage of the State purse, but not
when this would involve extra cost. As in the taxation system, there is
no recognition of cohabitees of the same sex, who are therefore
always treated as separate individuals.

(a) Contributory benefits

Contributory benefits are those which are payable upon condition that
sufficient National Insurance contributions have been made; they are
not means-tested. In some circumstances contributions by a person's
spouse are taken into account in assessing entitlement to a contributory benefit, but this is never the case for cohabitees. Sometimes, however, a person is entitled to an increased payment for a cohabitee, as
shall be seen.

A person entitled to a contributory benefit may in addition need to
claim Income Support (see page 86) to supplement his or her income;
this is a non-contributory and means-tested benefit. It is most likely to
be appropriate where the claimant has dependants for whom the contributory benefit does not provide or where the claimant is liable for
mortgage repayments, which are only provided by income support. If
accommodation is rented, then a claim for Housing Benefit (see page
91) should be made to cover rent payments. Again this is non-contributory and means-tested, and is administered by the local authority
rather than the Department of Social Security.

(i) Unemployment and other contributory benefits and additions for cohabitees:

*(i) Unemployment and other contributory benefits and additions for
cohabitees:* Entitlement to unemployment benefit depends upon the
claimant's having paid sufficient class 1 National Insurance contributions, which are payable by those in employment only, and not by the
self-employed. There are now further stringent conditions specified in
ss 17 and 20 Social Security Act 1975 as amended, which also have to
be met in order for a claimant to be eligible. These include being
available for work, actively seeking employment and establishing that
the unemployment is not voluntary. Once entitlement has been established, the claimant is paid unemployment benefit for a period of up

to one year at a flat rate. This is currently (in the year 1991/92) £41.40 per week for those under pensionable age.

The legislation does not refer to, or require the couple to be, living as man and wife in order to claim adult dependant addition. It is not possible to claim this increased benefit unless the partner is dependent on the claimant (having earnings less than £37.35 per week) *and* is caring for a child for whom the claimant is entitled to claim child benefit. Thus a cohabitee with children and without a disqualifying income will be entitled to claim an additional £25.55 for his or her partner. £10.70 is payable for each child. It should be noted that if an increased payment is being made to a claimant for a spouse, the claimant is not eligible to claim a payment for a cohabitee in addition.

Other contributory benefits such as sickness benefit, retirement pension, invalidity pension, severe disablement allowance, and invalid care allowance are subject to the same limitation, and thus an additional payment is only made where the claimant's cohabitee is dependent and has child care responsibility. Sickness benefit has now been largely superseded by statutory sick pay which is payable to employees by their employers for the first twenty-eight weeks. It is paid at one of two rates depending on the claimant's income and there are no additional payments for spouses or dependants of any kind. This is also the case with statutory maternity pay. Those who are not eligible for this may qualify for maternity allowance, payable at a flat rate, without any adult dependant addition.

(ii) Widows' benefits: Widows' benefits comprise a widows' payment on death of a lump sum of £1,000; widowed mothers' allowance where there are minor children; and widows' pension. There is also a non-contributory widows' pension. No payments of any of the benefits to which widows are entitled can be made to cohabitees on the death of his or her partner, no matter how long they lived together. However, it is important to note that if a widow receiving widows' benefit cohabits with a man, then her widows' benefits will be suspended. If cohabitation ceases, then the entitlement to widows' benefits revives. If the widow was cohabiting with another man at the time of her husband's death, then she is not entitled to the lump sum widows' payment. The definition of cohabitation or "living together as

husband and wife" adopts the same criteria as for income support and community charge liability as outlined above (see pages 80 and 87). It is for the adjudication officer to show that there is cohabitation.

(b) Non-contributory benefits

(i) Child benefit is a universal benefit payable regardless of means in respect of all children under the age of sixteen and those under the age of nineteen undertaking non-advanced full-time education at a recognised establishment (ss 1 & 2 Child Benefit Act 1975 as amended. See also Child Benefit (General) Regulations 1976 as amended). The benefit is payable to the person who is responsible for the child and does not necessarily have to be a parent.

Responsibility comprises either having the child living with the claimant; or contributing to the expenses of the child at a rate no less than the weekly benefit payable (s 3). However, where one person contributes and another has the child living with him or her, the person with whom the child resides will be the person entitled to claim.

Cohabitees with children will normally be entitled to child benefit for each child living with them. The Regulations provide that where parents are married, the wife is the person entitled to make the claim. Similarly, where the child lives with cohabitees who are both parents, it is the mother who must claim. However, where one cohabitee is a parent and the other is not, it is the parent who is entitled to claim. If neither partner is a parent, then it is for the couple to decide between themselves. From 7 October 1991, £9.25 is payable weekly in respect of the eldest child, and £7.50 for other children. Where cohabitees each have children from previous relationships, it seems that there can be two eldest child payments.

A supplemental one-parent benefit, currently £5.60 per week, is payable to a person who has sole responsibility for bringing up a child. Cohabitees are not eligible for this when they are living together as husband and wife regardless of whether or not the claimant's partner is the child's other parent.

Following separation, however, entitlement to one-parent benefit revives automatically. This contrasts favourably with the position of spouses, who have to wait 91 days following separation before becoming eligible.

(ii) Income support: This is now the welfare benefit of last resort, the safety net for those with no other means of support. It can also be claimed as a supplement to a low income where less than twenty-four hours per week are worked, or to contributory benefits where these alone amount to less than a claimant's entitlement to income support.

Income support is a means-tested benefit and cohabitees who are living together as husband and wife are treated in exactly the same way as married couples. The rationale for this is that to do otherwise would be to discriminate against married couples. On the other hand, married couples have a mutual and legally enforceable duty to maintain each other, this is not the case as between cohabitees. Thus whilst only one partner can claim income support on behalf of a couple, if one cohabitee fails to support the other from the benefit received, the partner has no legal redress.

Similarly, if one partner is employed, earning more than the income support that would be paid if the family had no income, but fails to support the partner, the unsupported partner may not claim income support. Co-operation is presupposed between the partners as it is between spouses, but cohabitees cannot bring pressure to bear by applying for a maintenance order. In this situation where the couple has a joint claim for income support, the aggrieved partner can either apply for the benefit to be paid directly to him or her instead of to the partner on the grounds of failure to maintain; or commence living in a separate household to gain individual entitlement to benefit. For those whose partners are in employment, the latter is the only option.

The so-called "cohabitation rule" has been preserved in the Social Security Act 1986, which introduced the new benefits of income support and family credit, although the word "cohabitation" has been omitted from the statute, as it was thought to have pejorative overtones. Instead, references are made to unmarried couples living together in the same household as husband and wife (s 20 Social Security Act 1986), and such couples are to be treated in the same way as married couples for income support purposes. Where a couple admits living together as husband and wife, their benefit will be calculated in the light of their aggregated income and capital. The capital limit is currently £8,000, although capital in excess of £3,000 is deemed to provide income and is taken into account in assessing income eligibility. In general terms, income eligibility is assessed by deducting actual income from the total sum prescribed by the state as necessary to meet the needs of the particular family unit, and where there is a deficit the balance will be paid. Mortgage interest repayments will form part of a claimant's needs, although only one half of the interest is payable for the first sixteen weeks.

Where an unmarried couple does not admit to living together as husband and wife, it is for the DSS adjudication officer, if the benefit claim is to be rejected, to show that the couple cohabit in this sense. The factors to be taken into account have been developed through case law and DSS guidance pertaining to similar provisions in the legislation relating to supplementary benefit, the predecessor of income support. It seems that the criteria remain the same in relation to the new benefit. The factors to be shown are as follows:

• *The couple are members of the same household* – The concept of sharing a roof but maintaining separate households is found in matrimonial law where separation is recognised for the purposes of the Matrimonial Causes Act 1973 if spouses live in separate households but not necessarily at different addresses (see for example *Mouncer* v *Mouncer* [1972] 1 WLR 321). For the purposes of social security law, there is no statutory definition of a household but there is much case law on the subject. If one member of the couple usually lives at another address, the cohabitation rule should not be applied. Liability for separate housing costs was held to be enough to show two separate households, regardless of living arrangements, in *R(SB)* 13/82. It is not possible for a person to be a member of more than one household at the same time, but the mere fact of marriage to another person does not prevent a person being a member of a household with a cohabitee as was indicated in *R(SB)* 35/85. The question of whether a person can be a member of one household for part of the week and a member of another for the remainder has not yet been decided.

The couple's reason for, and manner of, living together will be significant and the DSS must not assume that people of different sexes living at the same address and in the same household are cohabiting as husband and wife.

In the cases of *Crake & Butterworth* v *SBC* [1982] 1 All ER 498, two cases which were reported at the same time, it was held that a person who moved in with a disabled friend to provide assistance and company did not become a member of the same household, living together as husband and wife. Neither was this the case where a woman and her children had moved in with a man for whom she acted as his housekeeper. However, in *R(SB)* 30/83, a couple were regarded as members of the same household notwithstanding that one of them lived away in order to attend a university course for thirty weeks of the year. It should be noted that the cases are not particularly consistent in applying this test.

• *The length and stability of the relationship* – This is another critical factor and each case will turn on its own facts. If the relationship is brief or temporary, it should not fall within the category of living together as husband or wife. However, cohabitation of a few weeks is likely to be sufficient evidence of a couple's having formed a relevant relationship.

•   *Financial dependence* – Where one partner is financially dependent on the other this is strong evidence of living together as husband and wife. Separate financial arrangements of themselves will not be conclusive as to the absence of cohabitation either, and evidence of how household expenses are shared will be taken into account.

• *Sexual relationship* – Although the DSS is not permitted to ask direct questions about whether or not there is a sexual relationship, its assessment of the position will in practice be important in deciding whether two people are living together as husband and wife, as this is usually a normal facet of marriage. It will not, though, be conclusive, and evidence disproving such a relationship, such as separate sleeping arrangements, should be volunteered to the DSS.

• *Children* – Where there are children of the relationship, or children of one of the parties who are cared for or have been maintained by the other, there is a strong presumption of living together as husband and wife.

• *Public acknowledgement* – Where two people held themselves out to be husband and wife, or where a woman has adopted a man's surname, this will be strong evidence that they are living as husband and wife. It is none the less also acknowledged that many couples who do not in any way pretend to be married, may be cohabiting.

If, having considered all the above factors, the DSS decides a couple is living together as husband and wife, then only one claim for income support can be made for the household, and any other benefit will be withdrawn. Either of the partners may make the joint claim.

Where a couple wishes to dispute the decision, they may appeal to the Social Security Appeal Tribunal within three months of the decision, and are entitled to request reasons for the adjudication officer's decision.

It is also possible to ask for the decision to be reviewed, and this will be particularly appropriate where the reasons for refusal show that an important fact has not been properly taken into account.

If partners separate, a new claim will have to be made. In practice, if they continue to live at the same address, it may be difficult to show that they are now living in separate households. In the case of married couples, the fact that a solicitor has been approached with a view too matrimonial proceedings will often back up the contention that a *de facto* separation has taken place. With cohabitees, this is, ironically, sometimes more difficult to prove, and separate arrangements for cooking, sleeping, shopping, washing and payment of bills may need to be shown to convince the DSS of a change in the arrangements.

Another factor relevant to claims for income support following breakdown of a relationship where there are children is the "liable relative" procedure. Sections 24(4) and 21(1) of the Social Security Act 1986 enable the DSS to claim payments by issuing proceedings in the magistrates' court against a person liable to maintain another person in respect of whom a claim for income support has been made. Thus they can claim against an unmarried father or mother of a child, payments up to the sum paid out in income support, although this will not increase the sum paid to the child in any way. Furthermore, the Social Security Act 1990 introduced a new s 24A into the 1986 Act, extending this power to apply for an order in respect of the unmarried residential parent as well as the child, where that parent is claiming income support for himself or herself and the child. This introduces a duty to maintain an unmarried partner where there are children of the relationship in respect of whom income support is being claimed, although again neither the parent nor child will derive any benefit from this as it will not increase the payments made to them. The purpose of this provision is to reduce the cost of such families to the state. Where there is a maintenance order in respect of the child paid by the other parent, this sum is deducted from the benefit entitlement of the residential parent and child.

These provisions are to be greatly strengthened by the much publicised Child Support Act 1991. Any single parent on income support or family credit must, by s 6(1), authorise the DSS to recover child maintenance unless this might reasonably cause harm or undue distress to the child or resident parent. The Act also introduces an arithmetical formula (found in Sch 1 to the Act) to calculate what every non-residential parent should pay in respect of their child, regardless of any court maintenance order in existence. Publication of all-important Regulations are awaited at the time of writing (January 1992), but it is anticipated that the statutory maintenance level will substantially exceed that which the courts have held reasonable, having regard to the payer's income. It is consequently feared that the new provisions, which will not come into force until 1993, and which are to be administered by a new body – the Child Support Agency – will cause financial hardship and provoke further bitterness between separated parents. Even where the non-residential parent is on income support it seems deduction from their benefit may be made in recognition of their duty to support their child if the non-residential parent has no new dependent children. Section 43 permits the Secretary of State to make regulations prescribing the amounts of maintenance which can be deducted. The 1991 Act will, in the vast majority of cases, take the assessment of maintenance orders away from the courts even where the residential parent is not in receipt of benefits.

(iii) Family credit: This benefit replaced family income supplement by virtue of the Social Security Act 1986, and is aimed at low income families with children who are not entitled to claim income support because one of them is in remunerative work. As with income support, regulations provide the detail of entitlement, and unmarried couples are treated in the same way as married couples. The criteria for identifying a couple living together as husband and wife are as described for income support above.

In order to be eligible, the claimant must be engaged in remunerative work for at least twenty-four hours per week; earnings must not exceed the prescribed limits, which are reviewed annually; and the claimant must not have capital over £8,000. Income and capital are once again aggregated with that of the partner. In addition, the claimant or the partner must be responsible for a qualifying child who is a member of the household. The definition of a qualifying child for the purposes of child benefit (see above) is also adopted here.

Family credit, like child benefit, is normally paid to the woman unless the Secretary of State is satisfied that it is reasonable for it to be paid to the man. In contrast to income support, once eligibility is accepted benefit will be paid for twenty-six weeks and any change of circumstance will be taken into account only upon renewal of the claim at the end of that period. As noted above, single parent recipients of family credit will be required to authorise the DSS to recover child maintenance once the Child Support Act 1991 comes into force.

(iv) Housing benefit: This is another means tested benefit available to help pay rent. It is administered by the local authority, although the DSS will automatically notify the authority of a claimant's eligibility for housing benefit. Those on low incomes, or claiming any benefit other than income support, must apply directly to the local authority for housing benefit. Once again, couples living together as husband and wife are entitled to make only one claim in respect of their household, and their capital and income will be aggregated. If the rent exceeds the prescribed maximum for that area, no benefit will be payable for the excess, regardless of the claimant's ability to pay from other sources.

Eligibility is assessed in accordance with a specified calculation but the capital cut-off limit is £16,000, although there is deemed income added to actual income in respect of capital in excess of £3,000.

Housing benefit is not payable in respect of mortgage repayments, although the interest element of such payments may be paid as part of a claim for income support. Recipients of Family Credit cannot claim any benefit to help with mortgage repayments.

(v) Community charge benefit: As mentioned above (see page 80), benefit is payable for those paying the personal or collective commu-

nity charge contribution, but not in respect of the standard community charge.

Like housing benefit, the claim must be made direct to the local authority, and can only be claimed in respect of 80% of the bill. In assessing eligibility for benefit, an unmarried couple's means will be aggregated and the capital limit is £16,000 and operates in the same way as that for housing benefit described above. The same test applies to determine whether a couple lives as husband and wife.

(vi) The social fund: By virtue of s 32 Social Security Act 1986, the social fund replaced the previous grant based system of single payments and urgent needs payments. It introduced a much narrower grant system for specific circumstances, and, more controversially, crisis and budgeting loans which are repayable to the DSS. For the purpose of determining eligibility, married and cohabiting couples are once again treated alike.

The fund is divided into two distinct parts. The first consists of non-discretionary payments in relation to maternity, funeral and cold weather expenses. For the purpose of the maternity expense payment, which is currently limited to £100, the claimant or their partner must be in receipt of income support or family credit. The claim must be made within three months of the birth and any capital over £500 will be deducted from the payment.

Funeral expense payments and cold weather payments are subject to a similar capital deduction rule. Cold weather payments are available only to households claiming income support, whereas funeral expense payments are payable to those in receipt of any of the means-tested welfare benefits referred to above who take responsibility for a funeral.

All other payments from the social fund are discretionary. In general terms, community care grants are payable to those coming out of institutional care, or where a payment will prevent institutional care being necessary. These are not repayable.

Budgeting loans are available only to those in receipt of income support, to meet large expenses. There are strict criteria, and any loan is repayable, although interest free. Crisis loans are available to all those who do not have sufficient savings to meet expenses incurred as a result of an emergency and have no other means of meeting the expense. Such a loan will not be made unless the claimant is able to repay it. Where a loan is made, it can be recovered both from the person to whom it was made, and from a person for whose benefit it was made. This may be of particular relevance to cohabitees.

Chapter 5

Inheritance and succession

The desirability of unmarried couples making Wills and taking out life assurance has been discussed in Chapter 1. Cohabitees, whether of the same or opposite sexes, are vulnerable on the death of their partners if no provision has been made by Will to cover such an eventuality. Where a cohabitee dies intestate, the distribution of the estate is governed by s 46 Administration of Estates Act 1925 ("AEA 1925"). Any children of the the deceased, including those of the relationship, will inherit from the estate under these provisions unless there is a surviving spouse and the value of the estate is less than £75,000, in which case the whole estate passes the the spouse. Although the Family Law Reform Acts 1969 and 1987 have effectively given children of unmarried parents the same succession rights as those of married parents, the deceased's partner will never be a beneficiary on intestacy under s 46.

The surviving cohabitee may, however, have a claim under the Inheritance (Provision for Family and Dependants) Act 1975 ("I(PFD)A 1975") for financial provision to be made out of the deceased's estate. Even where a Will has been made, benefiting a cohabitee and any children of the relationship, should the deceased also leave behind a spouse, or former spouse who was being maintained by the deceased, or any children by other relationships, they may all, by virtue of the same statute, have a claim against the deceased's estate. This could of course substantially reduce the provision the deceased believed would be available for his or her partner and their children. If the deceased had had the necessary means, life assurance could have ensured provision was made for all those to whom the deceased owed financial responsibility. Unfortunately, such foresight is rare. The first part of this chapter will therefore deal with the claims that can be made under I(PFD)A 1975, either by or against a deceased cohabitee's partner.

The cause of death may have a bearing on the financial provision available to those left behind. Where it can be shown that death resulted from the fault of a third party, then the partner may well, and any children of the relationship certainly will, have a claim for compensation against the third party under the Fatal Accidents Act 1976 (FAA 1976) as amended. As will be seen, this is true for heterosexual cohabitees only, and most unusually in English law, a minimum period of cohabitation of two years is required by the statute as a prerequisite for a claim. The second part of this chapter will therefore consider the law relating to Fatal Accident Act claims, as it affects cohabitees.

1. Inheritance Act claims

In broad terms, the I(PFD)A 1975 enables claims to be made by specified categories of person against a deceased's estate, where either the deceased's Will or the law on intestacy does not make satisfactory provision for them. The rules as to what sort of provision should be made varies according to the category of person. It should be remembered that on intestacy, although cohabitees never inherit from their partners (s 46 AEA 1925) and may therefore need to make a claim under the 1975 Act, any children of that relationship will usually inherit on a parent's intestacy regardless of the fact that their parents never married.

Where there is no surviving spouse, the deceased's estate will be divided equally between his or her children, regardless of whether those children were born inside or outside marriage. Thus account will be taken of all the deceased's children. If there is a surviving spouse, (and significantly this definition includes a spouse in the process of divorcing until the time a decree absolute is pronounced), then the first £75,000 will go to the spouse, who will also have a life interest in one half of the remainder of the estate (s 46(1) AEA 1925). The other half of the residuary estate is held upon the statutory trusts for the deceased's children in equal shares, and on the death of the spouse the children become entitled to the spouse's half share also. These rules apply regardless of the ages of the children. Only where the deceased's estate passes *bona vacantia* to the Crown because there are no beneficiaries at all on the deceased's intestacy, may a surviving cohabitee, at the discretion of the Crown (see Chapter 1), receive provision out of the deceased's estate without having to apply under the 1975 Act.

Should the deceased's children have been omitted from their parent's will as beneficiaries, if they are to receive provision out of the estate, they also must make a claim under the Act; in this situation whether or not they are minors is significant, as will be discussed below.

(a) Claims by cohabitees

(i) Eligible applicants: Providing a cohabitee can show he or she is an eligible applicant under the Act, the claim will proceed to be considered on the merits. Cohabitees in themselves are not a specified category of applicant eligible to make a claim under the 1975 Act. The Act does not refer to persons "living together as husband and wife" as is to be found in other statutes. However, s 1(1)(e) of the 1975 Act provides that an application for provision may be made by any person "... who immediately before the death of the deceased was being maintained either wholly or partly by the deceased."

Thus cohabitees can make a claim under the Act only if they can show that they were financially dependent upon the deceased, and such dependence must have existed immediately before the death. It was considered by Megarry V-C in *Re Beaumont* [1980] 1 All ER 266 (at page 272 b) that a temporary interruption of maintenance just before death would not necessarily defeat the claim, as what the court had to decide was whether there was in existence a settled arrangement between the deceased and the claimant at the time of death. This reasoning was considered fully and followed in *Kourkgy* v *Lusher* (1983) 4 FLR 65. A man who had left his cohabitee returned to live with his wife just nine days before he died. This alone was not fatal to the cohabitee's claim. However, as there was evidence which revealed that the deceased had slowly been divesting himself of responsibility towards the applicant over a much longer period, this defeated her claim to maintenance out of the estate. The Act provides further definition of the necessary degree of maintenance. Section 1(3) goes on to state:

"For the purposes of subsection (1)(e) above, a person shall be treated as being maintained by the deceased, either wholly or partly, as the case may be, if the deceased other than for full valuable consideration, was making a substantial contribution in money or money's worth towards the reasonable needs of that person."

Although it might seem that the Act creates two categories of claimant – those who were actually being wholly or partially maintained by the deceased, and those who could be construed as so being by virtue of the test in the later subsection – this was held in *Re Beaumont* (above) not to be the correct approach. In that case, the deceased was a woman with whom the applicant had lived for some twenty-six years. She died leaving him nothing in her Will. She had owned the bungalow in which they lived, paid all the outgoings and performed the domestic chores. He owned a car in which he used to drive the deceased around; paid for his accommodation; contributed to the shopping bill and did gardening and repair jobs around the home. Megarry V-C held that s 1(3) qualified s 1(1)(e), and was not an alternative. Accordingly, the applicant's claim failed as the maintenance of the claimant by the deceased was a substantial contribution to his needs for full valuable consideration.

Again in the leading case of *Jelley* v *Iliffe* [1981] Fam 128, the Court of Appeal held that rent-free accommodation provided for the applicant by the deceased was capable of being a substantial contribution to his needs. Whether or not this was for full valuable consideration depended on whether the applicant's contribution to household expenses equalled or outweighed the value of the deceased's contribution by virtue of the accommodation. Thus where cohabitees make equal contributions, or indeed where the surviving partner was maintaining the deceased, no claim is available under the Act. A degree of financial dependency must be established.

In the recent case of *Bishop* v *Plumley and Another* [1991] 1 All ER 236, 29 June 1990, the Court of Appeal held that in order to decide whether the deceased had been making a substantial contribution, the matter had to be looked at in the round, and a common sense approach applied, avoiding fine balancing computations involving the value of normal exchanges of support in the domestic sense. Interestingly, Lord Justice Butler-Sloss commented that it could not have been Parliament's intention to place an applicant who was less devoted and contributed less to the deceased partner's needs in a more advantageous position than a more caring applicant. Thus, although the wording of the Act appears to be capable of leading to an anomalous position, in this case, the applicant was allowed to proceed and have her application considered on the merits. She was herself in poor health and 64 years of age, and had lived in a property owned by the deceased with whom she had lived for ten years, performing the domestic chores and caring for him during years of bad health.

Homosexual cohabitees, providing they can show the necessary degree of dependency immediately before death, seem to fall within the category of eligible applicants, although this has not to date been tested in the courts.

(ii) Criteria relevant to the claim: The next hurdle an applicant must overcome is to show that the distribution of the deceased's estate, either in accordance with any Will or pursuant to the law on intestacy, "is not such as to make reasonable financial provision for the applicant" (s 2(1)). In the case of a cohabitee this has to be considered in the light of s 1(2)(b) which defines reasonable financial provision as "such financial provision as it would be reasonable in the circumstances of the case for the applicant to receive for his maintenance".

This is deliberately less generous than the test applicable to spouses, where provision is not limited to that needed for maintenance (see below). In addition, it will not be sufficient for a cohabitee to show that he or she needs maintenance, but also that it was objectively unreasonable in the circumstances of the case for the deceased to have failed to make provision. Thus in *Re Coventry* [1980] 1 Ch 461, the Court of Appeal held that an adult son who was undoubtedly in need of maintenance and whose father died intestate, resulting in a fairly small estate devolving to his wife, received an award of only £2,000. It was stressed that each case will depend on its own facts, but it is not for the court to decide how the deceased's assets should have been fairly divided, but rather whether it is unreasonable that the estate does not provide reasonable maintenance for the applicant.

Section 3(2) sets out the principal factors to be taken into account by the court deciding whether the estate has provided "reasonable financial provision". These can be summarised as follows:

- the financial resources and needs the applicant, any other applicant and any beneficiary of the deceased's estate have or are likely to have in the forseeable future;
- any obligation and responsibilities the deceased had towards any applicant or beneficiary of the estate;
- the size and nature of the net estate;
- any physical or mental disability of any applicant or beneficiary of the estate;
- any other matter including the conduct of the applicant or any other person, which in the circumstances of the case the court may consider relevant.

These factors echo those to be taken into account by a court when making an order for financial relief on divorce as set out in s 25(2) Matrimonial Causes Act 1973. However, whereas the provision relating to conduct has been amended in the matrimonial situation to limit its scope to conduct which it would be inequitable to disregard, the 1975 Act has not. "Relevant conduct" had been narrowly interpreted by the courts and it is submitted that this interpretation of relevant conduct may well be imputed into the workings of the 1975 Act in the future. Generally, it can be seen that the relative needs and resources of all the potential beneficiaries have to be weighed against each other and the existence of life assurance benefiting one or more of them will be of great relevance. In addition the size of the net estate will be critical to the approach and outcome of any claim.

Where an application is being made under s1(1)(e), which is the only possibility open to cohabitees, s 3(4) provides that the court also has to take into consideration "the extent to which and the basis upon which the deceased assumed responsibility for the maintenance of the applicant and ... the length of time for which the deceased discharged that responsibility." In *Jelley* v *Iliffe* (above), it was held that the provision of rent free accommodation over a period of time did reveal an assumption of responsibility.

The relevant date for assessing the factors is the date of the hearing not the date of death. The right to bring a claim under the Act is a personal one and it cannot therefore be continued by the applicant's personal representatives should the applicant die before the court has determined the application.

(b) Claims by children

Unlike cohabitees, children of the deceased are eligible as of right to bring an action against the deceased's estate, claiming that the reasonable financial provision has not been made for them out of the deceased's estate (s 1(1)(c)). The relevant criteria for assessing whether or not reasonable financial provision has been made are as set out above, but with some important distinctions. In particular, s 3(4) does not apply to children and thus no assumption of responsibility needs to be shown. Provision is not limited to maintenance and so more generous orders may be made. However, minor children (as opposed to adult children) are likely to be treated far more generously as there is no duty to maintain an adult child.

(c) Orders available to the court

The court, by virtue of s 5, has power to make interim orders in favour of an applicant who is "in immediate need of financial assistance". This is likely to take the form of periodical payments, but a lump sum may be made if the circumstances merit it.

The final orders available to the court, which are set out in s 2, once again resemble those which can be made on divorce and are:

- periodical payments;
- lump sum;
- transfer of property;
- settlement of property;
- acquisition of property not comprised in the estate out of property which is so comprised for transfer or settlement to or settlement on the applicant

Notwithstanding that an order in favour of a cohabitee can extend to reasonable provision for his or her maintenance only, this can still take the form of any of the orders listed above. Unlike the provisions on divorce contained in the Matrimonial Causes Act 1973, the court can actually order that specific property be acquired for the benefit of a claimant. For example, a smaller home may be ordered to be purchased rather than transferring the existing home to the applicant.

In addition, under s 9, the court has a discretion to order that the deceased's severable share of a beneficial joint tenancy be treated as part of the net estate, but the court must rule on this when it is deciding the preliminary issue of whether or not reasonable financial provision had been made and not when it is making the final orders. Further this can be done only where the application is brought within the initial six month time limit for bringing an action as discussed below. The effect of this rule is that where the deceased was a co-owner of a property his share in which would normally pass to the other co-owner by virtue of the rule of survivorship, the court can rule that the deceased's share of the property should, for the purposes of the Act, be deemed to form part of his net estate. Severance of a joint tenancy will be ordered only where it is "just in all the circumstances of the case" and only in so far as is necessary. Thus if some but not all of the value of that share is needed, the balance will still pass to the co-owner by right of survivorship.

Where a successful claimant is legally aided, the legal aid statutory charge will apply to any property exceeding £2,500 in value recovered or preserved as a result of work carried out under the legal aid certificate (reg 94(d)(ii), Civil Legal Aid (General) Regulations 1989). Usually, but not necessarily, an order for costs will be made against the estate where a claimant is successful. However, this will affect the size of the estate available to be distributed and thus may be taken into account in evaluating the appropriate sum to be awarded. Any costs not recovered by a legally aided claimant from the estate but incurred under the certificate will have to be paid to the Board by the claimant; again this will affect the amount ultimately in the hands of the claimant. Where property which the court has ordered is to be used as a home for the claimant or their dependants is transferred, reg 97(1) provides that the Legal Aid Board may, if satisfied that the property will provide adequate security for the sum which is the subject of the charge, agree to defer the enforcement. The Board will take a legal charge over the property, and simple interest will accrue to the initial sum charged at a rate of 12% per annum. In addition if a sum is recovered by a legally aided claimant under the 1975 Act which the court orders is to be used to purchase a home for the claimant or their dependants, the Board may again, on the same conditions, agree to postpone enforcement by taking a legal charge over the property purchased. Where the Board does agree to postponement and the claimant subsequently wishes to move to a new home, reg 98 gives the Board discretion to accept a substitute charge on the new property.

The form of the court order is critical to the Board's agreement to deferment of the statutory charge, and practitioners must ensure that it clearly states that the property transferred or to be purchased is to be used as a home by the legally aided party or his/her dependant(s). The Board will require the assisted person to agree in writing to the conditions of deferment of enforcement. No interest will actually have to be paid until the legal charge in favour of the Board is redeemed, although the Board will of course accept any repayment which the assisted person wishes to make and will deduct this from the total sum repayable. Statements of interest accrued are issued each year by the Board.

(d) Defending a claim

Defending a claim will arise only where the deceased's Will benefits his or her cohabitee but fails to provide reasonable financial provision for other eligible applicants – principally a spouse, a former spouse who has not remarried, children of the deceased and any other adult dependants falling within s 1(1)(e), discussed above.

The terms of the Act are to the effect that a spouse (who remains such until the day any decree absolute of divorce is pronounced) is able to receive more generous provision than any other type of applicant. The test is whether reasonable provision, and not reasonable provision *for his or her maintenance,* has been made by the estate. However, all the circumstances of the case, including, it seems, the existence of any divorce proceedings, will be taken into account, as well as the general factors set out above and contained in s 3. A spouse is likely to receive provision similar to that which he or she would have received on divorce. Any other person who is supporting the spouse will of course be relevant, as will any provision which has been made by way of life assurance, and the size of the estate.

A former spouse is in a much weaker position, as the question of financial provision between the spouses will have been decided by the court. Indeed many orders made on divorce specifically preclude an application under the 1975 Act.

Any children of the deceased may likewise make a claim against the estate.

Where a cohabitee beneficiary is faced with a claim, it is clearly preferable to reach agreement by negotiation. Litigation is costly and will quickly deplete the estate available for distribution. Although costs will normally be awarded to the successful party against the loser(s), where a claimant is legally aided, any order for costs is likely to be unenforceable in any event.

(e) Procedure

An important requirement in relation to inheritance claims is that they comply with a strict time limit. Section 4 stipulates that applications must be made within six months of the date on which representation (a grant of probate or letters of administration as appropriate) with respect to the estate of the deceased was taken out, unless the court grants permission for a late application. Good reason will be needed for a late application, as explained in the Practice Direction [1976] 1 WLR 418, and an application for leave must set out the grounds for the request.

From 1 July 1991, an application under the Act should be made to the county court by way of originating application, supported by affidavit. Previously, the county court had jurisdiction only where the deceased's net estate was worth less than £30,000. Property jointly owned by the deceased and subject to the right of survivorship will not form part of the value of the deceased's net estate.

2. Fatal accident claims

Following amendments introduced by the Administration of Justice Act 1982, a cohabitee who can show dependence on the deceased may well be able to bring a claim under the Fatal Accidents Act 1976 ("FAA 1976") against a third party who was responsible, due to a wrongful act, for the death of the partner. The act needs to be such as would have entitled the deceased to bring an action and recovered damages if death had not ensued. Thus where a cohabitee dies due to a road accident or an accident at work caused by another party's negligence, a claim will lie. A child of the deceased who was dependent on him or her at the date of the death also has a right of action under the Act.

A quite separate action brought by the personal representatives of the deceased in his or her name under the Law Reform (Miscellaneous Provisions) Act 1934 for compensation for loss incurred up to the date of death, may also benefit a cohabitee and any children who are beneficiaries under the deceased's Will. However, any damages payable are assessed quite independently of any claim under the 1976 Act, and will not be taken into account in assessing quantum in a successful Fatal Accidents Act claim.

Section 1(3) of the FAA 1976, as amended, provides that an application may be made by any person who:
  (i)   was living with the deceased in the same household immediately before the date of death; and
  (ii) had been living with the deceased in that household for at least two years before that date; and
  (iii) was living during the whole of that period as the husband or wife of the deceased.

The definition resembles those appearing in both the Domestic Violence and Matrimonial Proceedings Act 1976 and in the social security legislation discussed in Chapter 4, save that the two year qualification period appears to be unique in English law and is not yet to be found in any other statutory provision.

Section 3(4) of the Act goes on to provide that the fact that such an applicant has no enforceable right to financial support by the deceased as a result of their living together must be a consideration. Thus in determining the appropriate multiplier to be applied in assessing damages, the fact that either party could have determined the relationship at will, without any right to maintenance ensuing, will be taken into account and is likely to reduce awards made to cohabitees as opposed to spouses. It is thought that the greater the degree of stability of the relationship shown, the greater the award. Any cohabitation agreement could be of great significance in such a situation. Apart from this additional consideration, damages will be assessed in accordance with the normal principles of tort.

Cohabitees are not entitled to statutory bereavement damages (currently £7,500) for deaths occurring after 1 April 1991, which are automatically awarded to a spouse where liability is proved under the 1976 Act.

Even before the 1982 amendments to the Act, the courts, in *K* v *JMP Co Ltd* [1975] 1 All ER 1030, had sought to assist a cohabitee who was the mother of the three children of the relationship and where the couple and their children had lived together as a family unit before the death of the children's father. Only the children could at that time being a claim. However, in assessing the multiplicand, the Court of Appeal deducted a sum in respect of the deceased's expenses, but decided not to deduct a sum in respect of the applicant's expenses previously paid by the deceased, resulting in a larger sum to be paid to each of the children. Although the award went to the children, it was recognised that the children could not without their mother do certain things, such as visiting their relatives in Ireland, and provision was made for her expenses in this regard. The court was clearly keen that she should have this assistance.

This decision is not entirely redundant. There will be cases where a cohabitee has the responsibility of bringing up the child of the deceased, but cannot make a claim under the Act because they had not lived together for two years. In such a situation, it might be felt appropriate to increase provision for the children in accordance with the reasoning in *K* v *JMP Co Ltd* (above).

Dependency is also a prerequisite of a successful claim under the Act for all categories of applicant. Any dependent child of the deceased will also have a claim under the FAA 1976, but any child who cannot prove dependency will not be eligible.

Unlike the I(PFD)A 1975, cohabitees of the same sex are specifically excluded by the prerequisite in the FAA 1976 that the claimant and the deceased were "living together as husband and wife". As was seen in Chapter 3, this has been held to exclude couples of the same sex in the context of succeeding to a secure tenancy (see *Harrogate BC* v *Simpson,* above). Thus, notwithstanding dependency, only a heterosexual cohabitee who fulfils all the conditions can make a claim under the 1976 Act.

3. Criminal Injuries Compensation Board scheme

Cohabitees used to be specifically excluded from recovering compensation where a partner dies as a result of a violent crime. However, the new statutory scheme introduced by s 111 Criminal Justice Act 1988 enables dependants to make a claim under the CICB scheme and "dependant" is defined with reference to s 1(3) FAA 1976, set out above. Thus, only cohabitees who come within the definition of "dependant" in the 1976 Act can apply. In fact, these statutory provisions have not yet been brought into force, but the revised 1990 guidelines have incorporated this, and many of the other changes envisaged in the statutory provisions, into the current scheme. Thus cohabitees who come within the 1976 Act definition are eligible to apply, as are dependent children. A claim must be made within three years of the death and compensation is awarded on the basis of common law damages. It will normally be in the form of a lump sum. Funeral costs can be recovered under the scheme by any person who is responsible for payment and there is no dependency requirement here. For details, write to the CICB, Blythswood House, 200 West Regent Street, Glasgow G2 4SW, from whom the appropriate application form is also available.

The scheme only requires an application to be completed and sent to the CICB for consideration. There will not normally be a hearing and the assessment of the compensation will be determined by the Board and notified through the post to the applicant. However, it should be noted that there are presently long delays in processing compensation claims.

PART II
RELATIONSHIP BREAKDOWN

It is on relationship breakdown that legal advice is most often sought by cohabitees. As has been noted in Chapters 1 to 5, the legal position of cohabitees on breakdown of the relationship depends to a large degree on any legally binding arrangements that have been made between them. At the present time there is no "divorce law equivalent" for those who have not made pre-emptive arrangements by entering into full or partial cohabitation agreements as discussed in Chapter 1 or who cannot otherwise reach agreement on breakdown. The fallback position is the general law applicable to the area or areas of dispute. As a rule, the more comprehensive the arrangements which have been made between cohabitees, the less scope there should be for lengthy and bitter litigation. However, most cohabitees fail to make any arrangements at all. Faced with this situation, as in divorce, the aim should be for the parties to reach agreement without having to resort to the courts, particularly in relation to the arrangements for any children.

Legal advice on the appropriateness of tentative agreements reached between the parties is often sought. This can place the advisor in the position of having to indicate that the agreement is not in the client's best interests. Whilst there is a duty to explain why this view has been formed, it is also important for practitioners to explain that, despite this, bitter litigation rarely allows amicable relations between the parties in the long term. None the less instructions must be followed, yet no client should be allowed to agree to an arrangement which would severely prejudice his or her long term future unless all the other options have been explained, explored and rejected. Solicitors are often criticised for tending to exacerbate the tension between parting couples. The possibility of counselling, conciliation or mediation for cohabitees on relationship breakdown may be overlooked. The availability of such services will depend on the area in which the couple live, but, particularly in relation to disputes about children, this is an avenue of help of which the client should at least be aware. Amicable settlement is not, however, always possible. The prime example is a case of domestic violence. Here the only remedy available may be prompt court action. This is addressed next, in Part II of this book. Disputes about the children will be considered in the following chapter, and the law relating to financial provision for children, and housing and property rights between cohabitees will be considered in later chapters. Finally, a conclusion will attempt to identify and draw together the most unsatisfactory aspects of the law relating to cohabitation, and suggest possibilities for reform.

Chapter 6

Domestic violence

The home is at times violent for some families, married or unmarried. Although less publicised and researched, violence can also be found in relationships between couples of the same sex. Even after couples separate, violence may still occur. Depending on the effects of an assault, criminal and/or civil remedies may be available to a cohabitee victim, although the often half-hearted police response to "domestic" crime is well documented. Unmarried victims have been shown in practice to experience a more positive police response to domestic violence than married victims, as the public policy factor of recognising the unity of those bound in marriage does not apply (see J. Pahl, *Police Response to Battered Women* [1982] Journal of Social Welfare Law 337). Nevertheless, other factors, which have traditionally been cited by the police as justification for declining to bring charges against violent spouses, have undoubtedly also deterred the bringing of charges against violent cohabitees. Examples are an alleged propensity for victims to change their minds about pressing charges, and reluctance to testify against their partners, although these have never been insuperable hurdles in the cases of cohabitees who have always been compellable witnesses.

Whilst the police response still varies tremendously from area to area, it is encouraging that some steps to change police policy have been taken. In the Metropolitan Police area, following the report of a multi-agency working party in 1986, new guidelines were issued and implemented in June 1987. These aim to lower the threshold at which police intervention in domestic disputes occurs, and to enhance support for victims. A change in attitude is reflected in their leaflet published in 1988 which reads "Domestic Violence ... not just a family affair – It's a crime". In many areas specialist domestic violence units, which have significant numbers of women police officers and aim to provide support for women victims, have been set up. A similar development is being made in relation to child abuse, although this subject is outside the scope of this book.

1. Criminal proceedings

(a) Prosecution

Although rarely appropriate, there may be circumstances in which both victim and perpetrator may benefit from the knowledge that domestic violence is increasingly viewed by the police as a serious criminal offence warranting prosecution.

The proceedings which may be brought, whether victim and aggressor are of the same or the opposite sex, are identical, but how effective they are usually depends on the police response, and the seriousness of the assault. The most serious incidents of domestic violence involve charges of murder or manslaughter. The Offences Against the Persons Act 1861 enables prosecution for assaults occasioning actual bodily harm (at least bruising usually – s 47); grevious bodily harm (very serious harm – s 18); or wounding (some puncturing of the skin – s 20). Section 39 Criminal Justice Act 1988 also provides a statutory offence of common assault for which the police themselves will now often prosecute, rather than, as was their previous policy, suggesting that the victim take out a magistrates' court summons for common assault. Although the latter is still an option, it is rarely appropriate as legal aid is not available, leaving the victim to bring his or her own case.

The recent change in police policy towards domestic disputes has meant an increase in the number of prosecutions brought in domestic disputes to the point that some victims then find that they cannot withdraw the charges should they wish to effect a reconciliation. Yet there are many reasons why a cohabitee may not want his or her partner prosecuted, as where the victim is financially dependent upon their assailant, particularly if there are children. Pressure is often brought to bear on victims in these situations to withdraw the charge, although the victim, having made a statement and been summoned to give evidence, can be jailed for contempt, however frightened about his or her personal safety, if he or she does not attend court.

One advantage of calling the police and allowing the perpetrator to be charged is that it will almost certainly result in the court's imposing a bail condition that the defendant must not contact the victim pending trial. This is often an effective way of keeping the violent partner at bay, allowing time to dwell on the seriousness of the situation. On the other hand, prosecution can result in a guilty plea and the matter being dealt with by the magistrates' court on the day after the incident, with nothing more than a fine being imposed, particularly if it is a first offence. This may leave the perpetrator at large, angry and vengeful, placing the partner in a vulnerable position and in need of the additional protection of the civil law. Any decision made by a victim of domestic violence in relation to pressing charges must be an individual one, but where possible it should be one made in the fullest possible knowledge of the benefits and disadvantages at that time and in the future.

(b) Compensation for criminal injury

A criminal court, on conviction, has power to make a compensation order pursuant to s 35 Powers of Criminal Courts Act 1973 in a domestic violence case where the victim has been injured. However, the defendant's means are taken into account and where the assailant is on a low income an order is unlikely to prove very satisfactory from the victim's point of view. Such orders are usually payable by instalments and their effectiveness is subject to the defendant's regularity of payment.

(c) The Criminal Injuries Compensation Board

One advantage of using the criminal law against a violent partner is the possibility of obtaining compensation for injuries under the Criminal Injuries Compensation Board Scheme. Although ss 108-117 Criminal Justice Act 1988 were enacted to put the scheme on a statutory footing, the implementation of the statutory scheme has been postponed. Instead a new scheme incorporating some of the features provided for by statute was introduced on 1 February 1990. The scheme does now allow a claim for compensation where the victim and the person responsible for the injuries were, at the time of the injuries, living in the same household as members of the same family. This definition includes a man and woman who are living together as husband and wife.

However, for the victim to qualify for compensation, the assailant should normally have been prosecuted, unless the Board considers there are good reasons why this has not happened. In addition, where the incident involves violence between adults in the family, they must have ceased living together before the application was made and seem unlikely to resume cohabitation again. Where a child is the victim, the award of compensation must not be against the minor's interests.

Where a criminal compensation order or a civil award of damages has been made, then any compensation awarded under the scheme will be reduced by the sum received from that other source. If such sums are awarded after compensation has been paid under the scheme, they must be paid over to the Board.

Applications for compensation must be made within three years of the incident giving rise to the injuries, and compensation is awarded on the basis of the common law rules for assessment of general damages in tort actions. The only special damages payable relate to loss of earnings and certain restricted out of pocket expenses.

Claims are limited now to those meriting a minimum award of £750. Thus, if a victim has suffered minor bruising and no loss of earnings, he or she may not receive any compensation, as their entitlement is to less than the minimum, after the deduction of any social security payments paid as a direct result of the injuries.

Nonetheless, advisors should be aware of the existence of the scheme and despite the minimum level rule, and the fact that applications are taking more than twelve months to process, there is usually nothing to be lost from making an application even in marginal cases. Legal costs are not recoverable and where advice is given under the green form legal advice scheme, the statutory charge applies and costs are deductible from compensation obtained. Application forms are obtainable from the CICB, Blythswood House, 200 West Regent Street, Glasgow G2 4SW; tel: 041-221-0945.

Criminal prosecution may serve only to exacerbate a victim's vulnerability when the partner is once again outside the confines of the criminal justice system, and compensation under the CICB scheme will not of itself remove the threat of violence. Thus additional remedies may be required. Even where the victim wishes the criminal law to be used, civil proceedings may also be appropriate. The housing situation may also need urgent consideration by the victim's legal advisor.

2. Civil remedies

Cohabitees, particularly those of the same sex, are offered fewer remedies in respect of domestic violence through civil law channels, than are spouses. There is only one court to which cohabitees can apply for a specific remedy, and that is the county court, under the Domestic Violence and Matrimonial Proceedings Act 1976 ("DVMPA 1976"). Even this is available only to couples living together in the same household as husband and wife. Before the Children Act 1989 ("CA 1989"), where there was a child living with the party seeking the court's protection from the child's other parent, but the parents did not live together as husband and wife in the same household, a non-molestation injunction could be obtained, protecting both the child and the custodial parent, ancillary to a claim for custody in the county court or High Court, under the Guardianship of Minors Act 1971. It was uncertain whether a court had jurisdiction to order an ouster injunction ancillary to such applications. Now, there seems to be no reason why a non-molestation order could not be made ancillary to an application for a residence order under s 8 CA 1989 upon the same basis. Whereas spouses can apply to the magistrates' court under s 16 Domestic Proceedings and Magistrates' Courts Act 1978 ("DPMCA 1978") for personal protection and exclusion orders, cohabitees cannot, despite the fact that this is often the most accessible court.

The Children Act 1989 does not directly ameliorate this situation. As will be seen in the next chapter, although it allows orders under s 8 of the Act, including residence and contact orders, to be made in proceedings under the DVMPA 1976, such proceedings themselves remain limited to the county court. However, s 11(7) CA 1989 provides that any court, including the magistrates' court, may, when making a s 8 order, impose conditions on any person, including the parent of the child, or a person with whom the child is living; and may make such incidental, supplemental or consequential provision as the court thinks fit. How this will be used by the courts remains to be seen. Nonetheless, it is and will continue to be the county court which provides the most comprehensive civil remedy for violence against cohabitees, although such relief as can be afforded is usually of a temporary nature only, as shall be seen.

(a) Domestic Violence and Matrimonial Proceedings Act 1976
Section 1 of the DVMPA 1976 provides:
"1(1) Without prejudice to the jurisdiction of the High Court, on an application by a party to a marriage a county court shall have jurisdiction to grant an injunction containing one or more of the following provisions, namely–
   (a) a provision restraining the other party to the marriage from molesting the applicant;
   (b) a provision restraining the other party from molesting a child living with the applicant;
   (c) a provision excluding the other party from the matrimonial home or a part of the matrimonial home or a specified area in which the matrimonial home is included;
   (d) a provision requiring the other party to permit the applicant to enter and remain in the matrimonial home or a part of the matrimonial home; whether or not any other relief is sought in the proceedings.
1(2) Subsection 1 above shall apply to a man and woman who are

living with each other in the same household as husband and wife as it applies to the parties to a marriage and any reference to the matrimonial home shall be construed accordingly."

(i) Procedure: The 1976 Act enables spouses, or "a man and a woman living with each other in the same household as husband and wife" to apply to the county court for an injunction protecting the applicant from his or her partner. Emergency legal aid is usually readily granted, even over the telephone in cases of extreme urgency, providing the practitioner can confirm the merits of the case and that the applicant is within the means limits. In addition, a solicitor's undertaking to lodge the application forms within five days of the grant will be required. The means of the applicant will not be aggregated with those of the violent partner.

Applications for domestic violence injunctions should be made to the court for the district in which the family home is situated, or that in which either the applicant or respondent resides. Proceedings are begun by originating application in county court form N16A, which must state the grounds for bringing the application. An affidavit in support must also be lodged (see O 13, r 6(3) and (3A) County Court Rules ("CCR")). Normally, applications should be made on notice and service should be effected giving at least two clear days notice to the respondent, unless the court grants leave for the proceedings to be served on shorter notice. Previously, four days notice was required. A draft of the injunction order sought should also be lodged with the court.

(ii) Urgent applications: In cases of urgency, applications may be made *ex parte,* although the court will always require justification for the use of the emergency procedure, and the reasons must be explained in the applicant's affidavit. Practice Note [1978] 2 All ER 919 states that an *ex parte* application should not be made or granted unless there is "real immediate danger of serious injury or irreparable damage". It may be felt that all cases of domestic violence are by their very nature urgent. Some courts accept the argument that an applicant genuinely fears that further violence will result from service of the

proceedings upon the violent partner, and where they are still sharing accommodation, *ex parte* protection in the form of a non-molestation order, and possibly a power of arrest, is essential. Where an order is made *ex parte* the court will normally order a short return date, not usually exceeding a week, and service must be effected before the applicant is protected by the order.

In *G v G (Ouster; ex parte applications)* [1990] FLR 395, it was stated that *ex parte* restraining orders should be made only to retain the *status quo* until further hearing, thus confirming the reluctance to grant anything other than non-molestation injunctions *ex parte*. Where there is a need for an urgent ouster injunction, then consideration should be given to an *ex parte* application for leave to abridge the required notice period, with the court granting an early hearing date; although with the reduction of the service period to two days this may be less pertinent than before. Advisors may need to convince the court that they are confident that service upon the respondent can be effected in the abridged period.

(iii) Who can apply? The major obstacle for a cohabitee wishing to take advantage of the protection afforded by the Act is to show that the cohabitees live together in the same household as husband and wife. It is established for the purpose of periods of separation before divorce, that parties can be living under the same roof but in separate households: *Fuller* v *Fuller* [1973] 1 WLR 730 (CA). However, in *Adeoso* v *Adeoso* [1980] 1 WLR 1535, where an unmarried couple lived in one-bedroom accommodation, not speaking to each other, sleeping in separate rooms, washing and cooking separately, sharing payment of the utility bills, the Court of Appeal found that nonetheless they were not living in separate households for the purpose of the 1976 Act. Accordingly, the applicant was not prevented from making an application under the Act for protection against her partner's alleged violence. Thus the requirement has been interpreted liberally and quite differently from the divorce context, although it should be stressed that the court did not rule out a different finding had the parties been living in larger accommodation.

The relevant date at which the parties must have been living together is the date of the incident of violence, and in *O'Neill* v

Williams [1984] FLR 1, the court accepted jurisdiction although cohabitation had ceased six months before the application. However, the court also indicated that the length of time between the parties ceasing to cohabit and the application is a significant factor in determining whether the required degree of urgency is present for the court to exercise its discretion in favour of the applicant. Thus delay is not desirable if it can be avoided.

The injunctions available under the Act are usually described as non-molestation orders and ouster orders. Any or all of these orders can be made by the court regardless of whether or not any other relief is being sought. It should also be noted that the Act affords protection in s 1(1) not only to the applicant but also to "a child living with the applicant" and therefore extends to children who are not necessarily children of the relationship.

Although the workings of the Act have been restrictively interpreted in some instances and have recently been criticised (see Law Commission Working Paper no.113), the Act does provide first aid for heterosexual cohabitees who are suffering at the hands of a violent partner, but it rarely provides long term solutions.

(iv) Non-molestation orders: Such orders restrain a party from molesting his or her partner or any child living with them, and provide protection for children, who need not necessarily be children of the relationship. These orders are granted pursuant to s 1(1)(a) and (b) of the 1976 Act. The phrase "living with" is not defined, and thus if a child is in hospital or at boarding school, there is scope for a restrictive interpretation. However, if an order were refused on this basis, it may be possible to apply for protection ancillary to an application for a residence order under the Children Act 1989 as was previously the case ancillary to custody orders under the Guardianship of Minors 1971. This will be considered below.

"Molestation" has been broadly interpreted to include not just assault or threats of violence but also harassment and pestering, and so affords wider protection than the DPMCA 1978 which, in s 16(2), limits magistrates' powers to circumstances where there has been violence or threat(s) of violence. In *Vaughan* v *Vaughan* [1973] 1 WLR 1159, a man who called upon his wife morning and evening, at home and at work, making a thorough nuisance of himself and knowing his wife was frightened of him, was held to have molested her within the meaning of the Act. Generally, as was indicated in *Spindlow* v *Spindlow* [1979] Ch 52, to justify an order, behaviour constituting molestation needs to have occurred. More recently, it was suggested in *F* v *F* *(Protection from Violence: Continuing Cohabitation)* [1989] 2 FLR 451 that non-molestation orders may not be appropriate where the parties intend to continue to cohabit. Such a development seems unnecessarily restrictive. There may well be situations where it is felt that a non-molestation order may effectively be capable of saving a relationship from further violence. A contrary view is that that contravenes the intentions of the Act to provide an emergency remedy without the need to decide at the same time whether a more permanent or final remedy might be needed in the future. Applications for non-molestation orders alone may be heard by a district judge.

(v) Ouster orders: Section 1(1)(c) DVMPA 1976 empowers the court to exclude a partner from the home, or from a part of it. It can also exclude a person from a specified area in which the home is included. Thus orders can, in appropriate circumstances, relate to a radius of, say, half a mile of the home. In addition, by virtue of s 1(1)(d), the court can make a mandatory order requiring the other party to permit the applicant to enter and remain in the home, or a part of it. It is well established that where such orders are sought and the facts are contested, the court should not rely on affidavits alone, but should hear oral evidence and allow this to be tested by cross examination.

There was no guidance in the 1976 Act as to how this wide discretion should be exercised, but case law has laid down various principles.

First, it was established by the House of Lords in the case of *Davis* v *Johnson* [1979] AC 264, that an ouster order can be made against a respondent who is the sole tenant or owner of the home, notwithstanding that the applicant has no legal or equitable interest in the home. Another House of Lords decision crucial to the working of the Act was *Richards* v *Richards* [1983] 2 All ER 807. This case decided that in making ouster orders the court must have regard to the criteria set out in s 1(3) Matrimonial Homes Act 1983. The case of *Lee* v *Lee*

[1984] FLR 243 extended this principle to cohabitees applying for protection under the 1976 Act notwithstanding that the MHA 1983 did not generally extend to cohabitees. Section 1(3) MHA 1983 provides:

"On an application for an order under this section the court may make such order as it thinks just and reasonable having regard to the conduct of the spouses in relation to each other and otherwise, to their respective needs and financial resources, to the needs of any children and to all the circumstances of the case..."

Richards v *Richards* also established that none of these factors is paramount in an application for an ouster injunction, and expressly rejected the contention that the needs of the children should be considered paramount in accordance with the welfare principle then contained in s 1(1) GMA 1971. The court did, though, accept that there may be situations where it was just and reasonable that the needs of the children should prevail.

In *Lee* v *Lee,* there was no evidence of violence by the man against the woman, although a child of the family alleged sexual abuse by the man and was taken into care. The woman and her son left the home and went to live in accommodation which was judged unsuitable for the other child to move into, and in these circumstances, an ouster order was made. This also illustrates a more unusual situation in which an ouster order was made without proof of serious molestation or threat of violence to the physical or emotional health or well-being of the applicant. In *Wiseman* v *Simpson* [1988] 1 FLR 490, Ralph Gibson LJ observed at page 497:

"It can only be 'just and reasonable' to make an ouster order if the case of the party claiming the order is not only stronger on those matters than the other party's case but is such as to justify the making of an order that a man or woman be ousted from his or her home."

Normally, violence or the threat of violence will be enough to warrant the making of the order. However, refusal by an applicant to live in accommodation with the respondent, without what the court considers reasonable grounds, does itself amount to unreasonable conduct to which the court must have regard within s 1(3) MHA 1983 when determining ouster applications.

Another relevant factor is the availability of alternative accommodation. The court is more likely to grant an ouster injunction if the applicant can show that the respondent can easily find other accommodation with a member of his or her family, or has the means to rent other accommodation (see *Baggott* v *Baggott* [1986] 1 FLR 377). The prospect of any duties owed to either party under part III Housing Act 1985 upon becoming homeless, is another factor to be considered. The court will not, though, grant an order merely because a local authority requires such an order to be obtained before agreeing to rehouse a victim of violence who, although not wanting to return to the property, is the joint tenant of local authority accommodation. This practice by local authorities was deplored by Ormrod LJ in *Warwick* v *Warwick* (1982) 2 FLR 393.

Neither will a court necessarily refuse an order where the applicant but not the respondent has a priority need and would thus be more likely to be rehoused by the local authority. In *Thurley* v *Smith* [1984] FLR 875, a woman was granted an ouster injunction despite the fact that she and her son had a priority need but her partner did not, as she would have had to spend an indefinite period of time in unsatisfactory temporary accommodation. This contrasts with the outcome of the earlier case of *Wooton* v *Wooton* [1984] FLR 871 where an order against a single man who was the sole tenant of accommodation shared as a family home by his partner and four children was refused, the court accepting that he would not be eligible for rehousing. Here, the violent situation, caused by the man's epilepsy, had subsisted for some considerable time and the court took the view that it was inappropriate to grant an emergency remedy in such circumstances.

Given the current acute shortage of local authority accommodation, many authorities feel forced to insist that the accommodation granted to a family as a whole is recovered where possible, although this approach is not always appropriate in domestic violence situations.

(vi) Duration of orders: It is well established that the DVMPA 1976 provides first aid only, not long term solutions on breakdown of relationships (see for example *Davis* v *Johnson* (above)). The general rule is that an ouster injunction should be granted for an initial period of three months only, as stated in the Practice Direction [1978] 1 WLR

1123. Where there are children, as will be seen in Chapters 8, 9 and 10, a court now has power, pursuant to para 1(2) of Sch 1 CA 1989 (re-enacting s 11B Guardianship of Minors Act 1971), to transfer property between parents for the benefit of a child of the parties.

However, where there are no children and the victim cohabitee has no legal or equitable interest in the home, or where there is a non-transferable tenancy or other interest in the property, there is no mechanism for a long term solution after the ouster injunction. Indeed, where the excluded party is the sole tenant, a victim who obtained an ouster injunction but is not in priority need will have no ultimate right to be rehoused. Yet as soon as the ouster injunction lapses, the tenant's rights of occupation revive and the victim can be evicted by possession proceedings.

A victim who has obtained an ouster can always apply to renew the order, and advisors should ensure that dates for renewal do not get forgotten. Conversely, where an order has been made for a specified period of time, a respondent can apply for an earlier discharge, although the court would normally require a change in circumstances to warrant such a step. Courts have in some circumstances been prepared, particularly where the accommodation is rented, to grant injunctions for longer periods of time.

In *Spencer* v *Camacho* (1983) 4 FLR 662 after an ouster injunction had already once been extended for six months and the respondent had breached both this order and a non-molestation injunction, the ouster order was granted until further order. That case involved a joint council tenancy and the parties had a young son who lived with the applicant. The court seemed to think it relevant that at that time the applicant had no mechanism for getting the tenancy transferred into her own sole name. In *Fairweather* v *Kolosine* (1984) 11 HLR 61, the tenancy was in the man's sole name. He left the home and issued proceedings to evict his cohabitee and their children. The court made an order on her counterclaim under the DVMPA 1976 excluding him from the property until the youngest child reached the age of sixteen.

However, both of these cases predated the decision in *Richards* v *Richards* (above), and accordingly should be treated with caution. The question of housing on breakdown of the relationship will be considered more fully in Chapters 9 and 10.

(vii) Powers of arrest and breach of injunction: Where a court is satisfied that the respondent has caused actual bodily harm to the applicant or a child living with them and is likely to do so again, it may
pursuant to s 2(1) DVMPA 1976, attach a power of arrest to any order
it makes restraining violence against the applicant or the child or
excluding the other party from the home or from the area in which the
home is included.

If a power of arrest is attached to the order, it should be lodged at
the police station for the area in which the applicant resides. The
effect of a power of arrest is to enable a constable without warrant to
arrest a person whom he or she reasonably suspects of breaching the
terms of the order. In the event of such an arrest, the person arrested
must be brought before a court within twenty-four hours from the
time of arrest, not including any Sunday, Good Friday or Christmas
Day. A person so arrested cannot be released save at the direction of a
judge, and the police must seek the directions of the court as to the
time and place at which the person is to be brought before the judge.

The judge then deals with the arrested person for contempt of
court, and so may impose a fine or commit to prison. This procedure
is potentially a quick and effective means of punishing a violent partner in breach of the injunction, but a power of arrest should not be
attached routinely to orders; see *Lewis* v *Lewis* [1978] Fam 60 and
Widdowson v *Widdowson* (1983) 4 FLR 121. The judge must give the
reasons why it is considered necessary to attach the power of arrest.
The power of arrest should not normally be attached for a period in
excess of three months; see the Practice Note [1981] 1 WLR 27. A
power of arrest should not usually be granted on an *ex parte* application, and even where there are circumstances warranting such a step,
the power should be attached only until the next hearing on notice
(see *Ansah* v *Ansah* [1977] Fam 138).

Where a non-molestation or ouster order is granted without a
power of arrest attached, then where the respondent breaches the
order, the only way the applicant can seek to punish the breach is by
issuing an application to commit the respondent to prison for contempt. A separate application (on county court form N78), with an
affidavit in support, must issue from the county court and be served
upon the respondent, giving at least two days notice of the committal

hearing, unless the court gives leave for abridgment of the service period. Where the applicant is legally aided, an amendment to the legal aid certificate will be required to cover a committal. The committal application must strictly comply with the procedural requirements as reiterated in the case of *Nguyen* v *Phung* [1984] FLR 773. A very useful article by Judge Fricker QC at [1988] Fam Law 232 is essential reading for any advisor about to apply to commit a party in breach for contempt. The application should set out the exact wording of the injunction, and give clear particulars of the breach alleged. Only then does the court have power to commit the respondent to prison or impose such other penalty as may be appropriate in respect of the breach. Where an ouster injunction is granted and the respondent fails to vacate the home, then a warrant for possession can issue. A letter before action should be sent to the property and then a request for a warrant in county court form N325 should be lodged. The county court bailiffs should then evict the respondent.

(viii) Undertakings: Undertakings may be offered by respondents at court in response to applications for injunctions under DVMPA 1976. The giving of an undertaking does not involve any finding of fact by the court and should not be accepted by the court in lieu of an injunction where a finding has been made (see *McConnell* v *McConnell* (1980) 10 Fam Law 214). Yet because an undertaking does not imply a finding of fact and allows the issues to be heard fully at a later date if necessary, acceptance of an undertaking is often seen as a good compromise between the parties. An undertaking is a binding promise to the court, breach of which is consequently punishable as contempt of court. However, no power of arrest can be attached to an undertaking, as decided in *Carpenter* v *Carpenter* [1988] 1 FLR 121. Thus in the absence of express instructions to the contrary, an undertaking should not be accepted where the applicant or child has suffered actual bodily harm and fears it will happen again.

(b) Injunctions in wardship proceedings or ancillary to the Children Act 1989
Where there are children of the parties, injunctions can be sought ancillary to wardship proceedings. It was also clear that injunctions

could be granted ancillary to proceedings under the Guardianship of Minors Act 1971 ("GMA 1971") for custody or access, to protect the child and the custodial parent. However, as discussed below, non-molestation injunctions alone, not ouster injunctions, could be granted in this way. It is submitted that despite the repeal of the GMA 1971 by the Children Act 1989 ("CA 1989"), the county court can still grant non-molestation injunctions ancillary to an application for a residence order to protect the child and the residential parent as well, by virtue of ss 38 and 39 County Courts Act 1984. Such a method of obtaining a non-molestation injunction is valuable where the parties cannot be said to be living with each other in the same household as husband and wife, which would prevent an application under the DVMPA 1976. The need for an ouster injunction where the parties are not living together would be limited to the need to be readmitted to the premises, or to restrain the respondent from coming to the home or to the area, and the county court's power may extend to this. It has been established by the Court of Appeal in *Re G (Wardship)* (1982) 4 FLR 538 that no power of arrest can be attached to a non-molestation injunction in wardship proceedings. The position would be the same in relation to injunctions granted ancillary to CA 1989 proceedings.

Before the decision in *Richards* v *Richards* (above), it was held in the case of *Re W* [1981] 3 All ER 401 (CA), that there was power to make both non-molestation and ouster orders ancillary to GMA 1971 proceedings. However, because it was decided in *Richards* that all applications for ouster orders must be dealt with under the MHA 1983 and not by virtue of the inherent jurisdiction of the High Court which lies to protect a legal right only, and because it was held (with Lord Scarman dissenting) that the welfare principle found in s 1(1) GMA 1971 is not the determining factor in deciding ouster applications under the DVMPA 1976, it was thought that there was no power to make an ouster order in proceedings brought under the GMA 1971, even if such an order may be in the child's best interests. This view was confirmed by the Court of Appeal in *Ainsbury* v *Millington* [1986] 1 All ER 73, where the parties, who were not married, were joint tenants of a council property and there were children of the relationship. While the respondent was in prison, the applicant married another man and fled the home on the respondent's release, applying for an ouster injunction ancillary to an application for custody under GMA 1971. The ouster application was refused on the basis that, following *Richards,* the court had no jurisdiction to make the order; this was endorsed on appeal. However, some commentators feel that there is scope for distinguishing *Richards* from a situation where the issue of custody was directly before the court under the GMA 1971, and where the welfare principle has therefore necessarily to be applied. Can the court in such a situation find authority for granting an ouster injunction? *Richards* left open the granting of injunctions pursuant to an inherent jurisdiction now found in s 37 Supreme Court Act 1981 in appropriate cases. Arguably it could be appropriate, where protection of children by virtue of an ouster injunction is felt necessary, and could be justified either on the grounds of protecting a legal right of the children not to be assaulted or due to an inherent jurisdiction of the court to protect children *per se*, something to which Lord Scarman refers to in his dissenting judgment in *Richards* (at page 822g). In view of the decision in *Ainsbury* v *Millington* this issue would have to be taken at least to the Court of Appeal.

Section 1(1) CA 1989 has re-enacted the welfare principle and thus it seems the position remains the same in relation to injunctions sought ancillary to applications for residence orders under the new legislative provisions. The position of ouster injunctions in wardship proceedings may be stronger, as the courts' inherent power to protect the welfare of the ward could arguably extend to the exclusion of a party from the home where no means of achieving this end, other than an ouster injunction, is available. This view is supported by recent Court of Appeal decisions endorsing ouster injunctions made after decree absolute where the former spouses and the children of the family continue to occupy the matrimonial home. In this situation, there are no rights under the MHA 1983, nor under the DVMPA 1976. Yet in *Wilde* v *Wilde* [1988] 2 FLR 83, the Court of Appeal granted an injunction ousting the father from the home pursuant to its inherent jurisdiction under s 37(1) Supreme Court Act 1981, stating that the court was entitled to intervene to protect the welfare of the children, and despite the fact that there was no evidence of violence, merely a high degree of tension between the parties at the home that was seen to be adversely affecting the children.

It will be interesting to see how the position is interpreted where injunctions are sought ancillary to proceedings brought under CA 1989 in situations where the provisions of the DVMPA 1976 do not apply as in *Ainsbury* v *Millington* (above). The CA 1989 does not curtail the inherent jurisdiction of the court in this regard.

Where the violent partner has no legal or equitable interest in the home, it may of course be possible to obtain an order restraining him or her from trespassing as will be discussed below.

(c) Injunctions in tort actions

Where there are no children, and the partners do not live together in the same household as husband and wife, the only possibility of protection for a victim of domestic violence is to apply for an injunction ancillary to an action for damages in tort for assault, battery, trespass or nuisance whereby the court can restrain the other party from behaviour which amounts to assault, battery, trespass or nuisance. These are the only remedies available to cohabitees of the same sex and to former cohabitees.

To establish a cause of action, it must be shown that a tortious act has been committed. If there has been violence or threats of violence then this will fall within the torts of assault and battery. However, there is no tort of harassment, and the tort of nuisance applies only where there has been unlawful interference with the enjoyment of a right in land, which will rarely be the case. Thus the remedies available are even more restricted than under the DVMPA 1976. Where there is trespass and a cohabitee refuses to desist, then providing the plaintiff can show that the defendant entered on the land as a trespasser, an action for damages and an injunction must lie. Thus if the victim cohabitee is the tenant or owner of the home, the partner has no legal interest in it, and if he or she refuses to leave, trespass is established. The fact that the value of the action for damages may be nominal does not prevent an injunction from issuing, as was decided by the Court of Appeal in *Hatt* v *Pearce* [1978] 2 All ER 474. Where the parties are joint tenants of property, an action for trespass will be inappropriate, although an action for nuisance, albeit far from straightforward, may be a possibility.

The procedure for applying for protection in this way involves issuing a summons and particulars of claim out of the county court (assuming the level of damages fall within the county court limit), and making an application for an injunction pursuant to s 38 County Courts Act 1984. An injunction may be granted if the other party behaves in an unconscionable manner or threatens to do so, or if an order is necessary to protect a person from the invasion of a legal or equitable right.

Applications may be made *ex parte* on affidavit, and, unlike hearings under the DVMPA 1976 or the CA 1989, the matter will be heard in open court, not in chambers. Two days notice is otherwise required for an injunction application. It is not clear whether an exclusion order can be made other than where there is an action for trespass, and no power of arrest can be attached to these injunctions. Breach of an injunction will again be punishable as contempt and in such a situation, committal proceedings have to be issued and pursued, following the same procedure described above.

3. Emergency accommodation

Often the most urgent need of a victim of domestic violence is a safe place to live, either permanently or temporarily, until court orders affording some protection against violence can be obtained. Many victims are reluctant to go and stay with relatives or friends as these are likely to be the violent partner's first port of call on discovering that they have fled the home. There is now a fairly wide network of women's refuges offering temporary accommodation and the local Women's Aid will provide details of possible refuges. However, such accommodation, whilst safe, often leaves a great deal to be desired and can only ever be temporary. The homelessness legislation now contained in Housing Act 1985 Part III has acknowledged at least to some extent the difficult situation of victims of domestic violence. A general discussion of the workings of this legislation can be found in Chapter 3. However, some specific provisions as they affect victims of domestic violence will be examined here.

Section 65 of the 1985 Act gives local authorities a duty to secure suitable accommodation for applicants who are homeless or threatened with homelessness, in priority need and not intentionally home-less. Thus applicants must jump three hurdles in order to secure accommodation and local authorities must make appropriate enquiries (s 62) to establish whether these criteria have been fulfilled by the applicant. A victim of domestic violence in need of urgent accommo-dation, regardless of whether or not they are the tenant or owner of accommodation, may still be homeless within the meaning of the Act, as s 58(3)(b) specifically states that a person is homeless if they have accommodation but: "it is probable that occupation of it will lead to violence from some other person residing in it or to threats of vio-lence form some other person residing in it and likely to carry out the threats" Section 58(3)(a) also states that such a person is to be regard-ed as homeless if unable to secure entry to his or her accommodation.

The next hurdle requires the applicant to show priority need pur-suant to s 59 of the Act; applicants will fulfil this if they are pregnant; have dependent children residing with them or who might reasonably reside with them; or are vulnerable as a result of old age, mental ill-ness or handicap or physical disability or other special reason, or if such a person might reasonably reside with the applicant. The Homelessness Code of Guidance for Local Authorities 1991, issued by the Secretary of State for the Environment pursuant to s 71 of the Act, for the assistance of local authorities, states at paragraph 6.6 that dependants need not necessarily be residing with the applicant at the time. Residence or custody orders, which may be a starting point, should not be an absolute requirement. This was confirmed by the Divisional Court in the case of *R* v *London Borough of Ealing, ex parte Sidhu* (1983) 2 HLR 41 which also indicated that accommoda-tion available at a women's refuge to the applicant did not prevent her being homeless.

The Code also states at paragraph 6.17 that the phrase "any other special reason" would, for example, make it appropriate for authori-ties to accept battered women without children as vulnerable and therefore in priority need. Authorities should secure accommodation in these circumstances "wherever possible". Some authorities may have policies about the type of people they are likely to regard as vul-nerable and it may be worthwhile checking this in appropriate cases where a client does not automatically have a priority need. The Code

does now refer to battered men in the same situation, unlike its predecessor, although success will doubtless vary according to the policies
of the authority and the availability of housing in the area.

Authorities are bound to have regard to the Code but do not have to
follow it.

Where an authority believes the applicant may be homeless and in
priority need, s 63 provides a duty to secure temporary accommodation pending their more detailed enquiries. Such accommodation is
very often bed and breakfast, which, although also often unsatisfactory, should be provided regardless of whether the applicant has a connection with another authority.

The last hurdle, of showing that the applicant is not intentionally
homeless (s 60), is the most litigated and is the factor which will
determine whether the applicant will be secured permanent accommodation. Readers are referred back to the discussion in Chapter 3.
However, non-tenant cohabitee domestic violence victims who have
no legal interest in another property, should not be regarded as intentionally homeless. They have no enforceable right against their violent partner to be readmitted to the home, other than under the
DVMPA 1976 which, as discussed above (see pages 121 to 122),
should not be used to provide permanent housing solutions. It is felt
that the new provisions permitting the court to make transfer of property orders for the benefit of the children between unmarried parents
should not provide an authority with a reason not to provide permanent accommodation, particularly following domestic violence. Such
litigation would take a long time to reach a final conclusion and the
outcome must always be uncertain. However, some authorities put
pressure on victims of domestic violence to attempt to oust their partners from the home by means of ouster injunctions, threatening that
failure to take such action will lead to a finding of intentionality.
Whilst there may be situations where an authority may reasonably
require an applicant to use their domestic violence remedies (as in *R* v
Eastleigh Borough Council, ex parte Evans (1984) 17 HLR 515), a
policy that *all* such applicants must do so is challengeable. Advisors
should attempt to resist such pressure upon their clients, and particularly where injunctions have been breached in the past or where the
violence is so serious that a further attack should not be risked or

where, perhaps, it can be shown that an injunction with a power of arrest attached will be no deterrent.

In addition, such a course of action can have no basis where the applicant is not a sole or joint tenant or legal owner of the property, as no permanent accommodation will be forthcoming after obtaining an ouster injunction. The only possibility here, of obtaining a transfer of the home to the victim, is where there is a child of the relationship, in which case an application can be made for a transfer or settlement of property order for the benefit of the child under para 1(2) to Sch 1 CA 1989 discussed in Chapters 8, 9 and 10. Given that these provisions are still virtually untested in the courts, there can be no certainty as to the outcome of applications at the present time.

An application for a transfer of property order under para 1(2)(e) to Sch 1 CA 1989 will also be available to a joint tenant or owner. Here the pressure to obtain ouster injunctions may be stronger, although the same reasons for resistance may apply.

It should be noted that if an ouster order is obtained, the violent partner is no longer "a person residing at the property" and thus, if violence recurs, the victim is no longer considered automatically homeless under s 58(3)b). However, the home may then become accommodation which it is not reasonable to continue to occupy, within both s 58(2A) which renders the applicant homeless again, and s 60, by virtue of which the applicant would not be intentionally homeless.

It is likely that the degree of violence will have a great bearing on the authority's approach to a victim who has interest in former accommodation. Even where the three hurdles set out above are successfully overcome, the applicant may be referred to another authority with whom he or she has a local connection pursuant to s 67. Advisors should be aware that where the applicant, or a person reasonably expected to reside with the applicant, runs the risk of domestic violence in that other district, no referral should be made – s 67(2)(c).

Applicants must be advised in writing of the local authority's decision and the reasons for the decision where a duty to secure accommodation is denied pursuant to s 64 of the Act. This letter will form the basis for any challenge by way of judicial review of the decision. A first step will to obtain copies of the information from the local authority's file to which the applicant or the applicant's advisor is entitled pursuant to s 106(5) Housing Act 1985. Such information will be vital to assess whether the decision is open to challenge. Any advisor intending to challenge a local authority decision by way of judicial review pursuant to RSC O 53 is again advised to refer to a specialist text and ensure that the challenge is made without delay and in any event within three months of the decision.

Another option where a violent partner and the victim are joint tenants of public sector rented accommodation is for the victim to give notice to quit the accommodation, as notice by one joint tenant is valid to terminate the tenancy, even though the other joint tenant does not know and would not wish the tenancy to be terminated; this was established by the Court of Appeal in *Greenwich LBC* v *McGrady* (1982) 267 EG 515 and confirmed in *Opoku-Forfieh* v *Haringey LBC* (1988) (unreported Court of Appeal decision). Normally this action may render the notice giver intentionally homeless but it is a device used where the local authority agrees to it in consideration of their providing alternative accommodation in their area. This device, which is likely to be available only to local authority, or possibly housing association, tenants will be discussed further in Chapter 9 where permanent housing solutions for cohabitees will be considered.

Chapter 7

The status of children on relationship breakdown

When a relationship breaks down, any children of the relationship often become a focus for the dispute between their parents. Legal advice is often sought by both parties about their respective positions in relation to the children. In the first place, advisors should suggest the possibility of a conciliation or mediation appointment, to see whether differences can be resolved by reaching an out of court agreement which can if necessary later be translated into an order by consent in court proceedings. Few courts yet have conciliation schemes which include disputes between unmarried parents, but there are many out of court schemes. The appropriateness of conciliation will have to be considered, as well as the willingness of the parties to participate, but the possibility of resolving a dispute concerning children by this means should always be examined at the outset before harmful litigation is launched.

The issue of custody on relationship breakdown has in the past been less disputed in the courts where parents are unmarried than when they are married. All the parental rights vested in the mother from birth and in practice, unless there was evidence of neglect or

133

abuse by the mother, or unless the mother consented, the unmarried father would usually find himself as the non-custodial parent. As was discussed in Chapter 2, even the Children Act 1989 ("CA 1989") does not give parental responsibility automatically to unmarried fathers, although they may acquire it by entering into a parental responsibility agreement with the mother, or by an order of the court pursuant to s 4. However, the law both before and after the coming into force of the relevant provisions of the CA 1989 enables unmarried parents who cannot agree on arrangements for the children to seek an order of the court to resolve matters of what, after the 1989 Act, are terms "residence" and "contact".

1. Before the Children Act 1989

As discussed in Chapter 2, the 1989 Act revolutionises the traditional concepts of parental rights and duties, and custody and access, and replaces them with the new principles of parental responsibility, and residence and contact orders. However, many people will continue to have old-style custody and access orders, and thus the old concepts remain important to advisors, particularly as variations of such orders may be sought. The relevant transitional provisions under the 1989 Act are discussed below and in themselves require an understanding of the old law.

(a) Custody and access orders

Before the coming into force of Part I CA 1989, an unmarried parent had to apply under s 9(1) Guardianship of Minors Act ("GMA 1971") for an order seeking legal custody or access on breakdown of the relationship, in order to resolve any dispute in these areas. If a father was to have custody, he could apply for a parental rights order under s 4 Family Law Reform Act 1987 ("FLRA 1987") as well, but this was not an order that would be automatically made.

Section 1 GMA 1971 related to any application for custody, access or parental rights, and thus the court, in making its decision had to make the welfare of the child its first and paramount consideration. Applications under s 9(1) could be made only by a parent of the child but could be made in either the magistrates' court, the county court, or to the High Court. The CA 1989 has repealed all of these provisions.

When making a custody or access order under s 9(1), the court was not empowered by virtue of s 11A GMA 1971 to make an order for joint custody, but it could order that the non-custodial parent should retain all, or such as the court may specify, of the parental rights and duties comprised in legal custody which were then to be shared with the parent who had legal custody.

Another option open to unmarried parents before the CA 1989, and one which is still open to them, is to make the child a ward of court. This has effect of vesting all parental rights in the High Court, and a parent could then seek care and control or access in those proceedings. Wardship proceedings must be issued in the High Court and are normally used only where the dispute involves a third party, such as a grandparent, or perhaps where there is a difficult issue such as alleged sexual abuse by one parent, or a threat by one parent to take the child permanently out of the jurisdiction without the other's consent.

However, wardship is being actively discouraged by the introduction of the CA 1989. It is envisaged that, whilst it still can be used between unmarried parents in disputes concerning their children, the cost of such proceedings, the fact that legal aid may well be considered inappropriate given the wider ranging alternative remedies now available in the lower courts, and the ability for the lower courts to transfer proceedings to the High Court where appropriate, mean that its use is likely in practice to become increasingly rare.

It was generally acknowledged that all fathers, but especially unmarried fathers, had great difficulty in being awarded custody of their children. Although there was no specific rule of law which stated that this should be the case, it is in most cases, even today, the mother rather than the father who has the primary role in caring for the children and therefore it is in her care that it is usually considered the children's interests will best be served. The GMA 1971 did not identify factors to be taken into account when deciding custody disputes between unmarried (as opposed to married) parents, and each case depended on its merits.

However, some significant factors evolved through the case law which, whilst not being definitive principles, provided the court with a starting point. As the welfare principle found in s 1 GMA 1971 is almost identical to the new welfare principle enacted in s 1(1) CA 1989, it is highly likely that the case law developed before the 1989 Act will continue to be referred to by the courts in deciding cases under the current law.

(i) Age and gender: In *M v M (Custody of Children)* (1983) 4 FLR 603, Cumming-Bruce LJ approved the contention that it was a working rule that in the absence of a substantial reason to the contrary, the appropriate place for young children is with their mother. However, in *A v A (Custody Appeal: Role of Appellate Court)* [1988] 1 FLR 193, the Court of Appeal (per Bingham LJ at page 205 para A) indicated that this did not amount to a legal presumption. Any application for an order involving the separation of a child from its brothers and sisters will be looked upon very carefully by the court, as such a separation is felt to deprive the child of a positive source of emotional support following the break up of the family unit (see for example *Cossey v Cossey* (1980) 11 Fam Law 56). However, of course the older the child is, the more significant its own wishes become to the court's decision in line with the principle laid down in *Gillick v West Norfolk Area Health Authority* [1986] 1 FLR 224. The gender of the child, together with its age, has also been considered a significant factor as in *Cossey v Cossey* (above) where a view was expressed that girls should normally be brought up by their mothers.

(ii) Continuity and quality of care: Perhaps the factor most often considered to be overriding is that of continuity of care. The longer one parent has had the day to day care of a child and the less frequently the other parent has had contact with the child, the more likely it is that the primary carer will be awarded custody. This principle often overlaps with what is known as the *status quo* argument – the assumption that children should remain where they are. Thus an unmarried father who had had care of the children for over eighteen months, during which time the mother had not seen them, was granted custody in *Aldous v Aldous* (1975) 5 Fam Law 152 (CA). However, in *Allington v Allington* (1985) Fam Law 157 (CA), where the mother was separated from her two year old child for only ten weeks and dur-

ing this period had continued to share responsibility for the day to day care of the child through frequent access, she, rather than the father with whom the child had been living during this time, was granted custody.

The quality of the care, as opposed to the material wealth and standard of living of either parent, is significant. Thus the accommodation available to either parent will be highly relevant, and with the advent of the court's power to transfer property between the parents for the benefit of the child pursuant to s 11B GMA 1971, now re-enacted in para 1(2)(e) to Sch 1 CA 1989, it is possible that the desire to remain in, or at least not to lose the benefit of, accommodation, may fuel bitterness in custody (or, now, residence) disputes between unmarried parents as it has done in divorce. The relationship between the child and each parent, and of course any new partner of either parent, will be significant (see for example *Scott v Scott* [1986] 2 FLR 320). Where the parent seeking custody lives with a new partner of the same sex in a homosexual relationship, the courts have been predictably cautious. In the case of *C v C (a Minor) (Custody) (Appeal)* [1991] FLR 223, the Court of Appeal held that although the mother's lesbian relationship did not of itself make the mother unfit to have care and control of the child, it was an important factor in deciding which of two alternative homes the parents could offer was most likely to advance the child's welfare. In fact, it allowed an appeal against the decision awarding the mother care and control. It granted interim care and control to the father (who had remarried), with reasonable access to the mother, pending a rehearing. Interestingly, at the rehearing Booth J awarded care and control to the mother who had had care of the child for some five years before the father's application, despite the fact that her partner had served a twelve month prison sentence for wounding and theft.

The means of caring for the child will also be taken into account. Thus if one parent's hours of work necessitate heavy reliance on a child minder whereas the other parent can give the child more time, the court may well lean towards the latter, providing none of the other factors mentioned above make this inappropriate (see *D v M (Minor: Custody Appeal)* [1983] Fam 83 (CA)).

Conduct by either parent such as would make him or her an unsuitable carer for the child will be taken into account, but refusal of access alone did not mean that custody should not be awarded to a mother who was the most suitable carer in all other respects: *M* v *M* [1980] 1 FLR 77.

(iii) Principles relating to access: Turning to the question of access, it is thought that decided principles relating to access are likely to be applied to disputes concerning contact orders, although contact is a broader concept than access.

It was stated by Wrangham J in *M* v *M (Child: Access)* [1973] 2 All ER 81 (at page 85) that access was the right of the child rather than the right of the parent, although subsequently s 85(1) Children Act 1975 included the right of access in its definition of parental rights and duties. Bevan and Parry suggest in their book *Children Act 1975*, at para 211, that the best way to reconcile this apparent conflict is to treat access as a mutual right of the parent and child to the other's companionship, of which each can be deprived only exceptionally when the paramountcy of the child's welfare so warrants.

There has developed a very strong presumption that access is in the best interests of the child and this, it is considered, is equally applicable to unmarried as to married parents, especially where there has been a stable relationship comparable with marriage (see *S* v *O* [1982] 3 FLR 15 and *M* v *J* [1982] 3 FLR 19). However, where there has been only very limited contact between father and child, and thus there is really only a blood tie, it has been held that the interests of the child are best served by the child's being allowed to settle as a child of the family in the mother's new relationship, as in *Re W (a Minor: Access)* (1989) 19 Fam Law 112 and *Re SM (A Minor) (Natural Father: Access)* [1991] Fam Law 308. Where there is no new partner, however, such an argument, it is submitted, is likely to be far less compelling (see for example *S* v *O*, above). In the recent decision of *Re C (Minor) (Access)* [1991] Fam Law 417, Ewbank J found that it was not normally regarded as in the child's interest to know the non-custodial parent as well as he knew the custodial parent. Accordingly, staying access to the unmarried father, who had never lived with the child, was reduced to alternate weekends.

Once an access order has been made, there may be a problem in enforcing it, if either the child or the other parent is against access taking place. Where it is the child who is unwilling to take up access, attempts to persuade him or her to do so will be made by the court, usually through a court welfare officer on the non-custodial parent's application. If this proves fruitless, the court is finally powerless to enforce the order, and is likely to terminate it (see *B* v *B* [1971] 3 All ER 682). A child will not be liable for contempt of court in this situation.

If the other parent prevents access, either physically or by turning the children against the non-custodial parent, the former, and possibly the latter, is, at least in theory, behaviour punishable as contempt of court. However, the welfare principle means that as it can rarely be in the child's best interests for the custodial parent to be committed to prison or fined, so the court's powers are unlikely to be invoked (see *Thomason* v *Thomason* (1985) FLR 214). In some situations, particularly where the non-custodial parent could be considered the full-time carer of the child, a review of the custody position could be contemplated by the court.

(b) Other orders available to the court

On considering an application for custody or access, the court had at its disposal various other orders which it could make in appropriate circumstances.

Firstly, it could order a parent to provide financial relief for the benefit of the child. This power remains unchanged following the coming into force of the CA 1989 and are considered in Chapter 8.

Secondly, the court had power, on the application of either party to the proceedings, where making an order for legal custody or subsequently whilst the custody order was still in force, to order that the child not be taken out of the jurisdiction of the United Kingdom or a specified part thereof without leave of the court pursuant to s 13A GMA 1971. In addition, the court had power in these proceedings to order a supervision order or care order pursuant to s 2(2)(a) and (b), although the exercise of these powers in such proceedings has been confined to exceptional circumstances. A supervision order would be made where the court felt supervision by a local authority was desirable in the interests of the child. This involved a social worker or probation officer meeting the child and custodial parent regularly to ensure that the child was receiving appropriate parental care. A care order could be made instead of a custody order in favour of either parent, but only where the care of the child could not in the opinion of the court be entrusted to either parent. Where a care order was made, the court had no power to order access to either parent, but once the child was in care then a separate application for access could be made under the Child Care Act 1980. However, the CA 1989 changes the courts' powers with regard to supervision and care orders in proceedings between parents, as will be discussed below.

2. The Children Act 1989

(a) Parental responsibility

Following the implementation of Parts I and II of the Children Act 1989, parents, whether unmarried or married, can no longer apply for custody of or access to their children. Indeed, the Act has repealed *inter alia* the whole of the GMAs 1971 and 1973 and s 4 FLRA 1987. As discussed in more detail in Chapter 2, the Act introduces a new concept of "parental responsibility" which replaces the idea of parental rights and duties. Parental responsibility is defined in s 2 as "all the rights, duties, powers, responsibilities and authority which by law a parent of a child has in relation to a child and his or her property". It is given automatically on the birth of a child, jointly to both parents where they are married to each other, but only to the mother where they are unmarried. However, an unmarried father can acquire parental responsibility jointly with the mother by entering into a parental responsibility agreement in the prescribed form with the mother (s 4(1)(b) CA 1989). It is no longer necessary for unmarried parents to issue proceedings to achieve this end where there is agreement, although a parental responsibility order can be made by the court on the father's application in the same way as it could under s 4 FLRA 1987. By virtue of Sch 14 para 4 CA 1989, old style parental rights orders made under the FLRA 1987 will be treated as if they were parental responsibility orders made pursuant to s 4 CA 1989. As discussed in Chapter 2, the presence or absence of a parental responsibility order or agreement may influence the court's approach to resolving disputes between parents regarding their children on relationship breakdown.

Interestingly, where an unmarried father now obtains a "residence order" whereby the child lives with him following breakdown of the relationship, the court must now make a s 4 order giving him parental responsibility (s 12(1)), and this cannot be brought to an end whilst the residence order remains in force (s 12(4)).

Perhaps the most striking and possibly controversial aspect of Part I of the 1989 Act (at least from the perspective of custodial or "residential" parents) is that, following breakdown of the relationship, where both parents have "parental responsibility" arising out of marriage, they retain it, even though a residence order is made in favour of one parent alone. In the case of married parents, it seems that parental responsibility cannot be withdrawn from either parent, although it can be restricted by the making of residence, contact, specific issue or prohibited steps orders. In the case of unmarried parents, this is also true of the mother. Thus even where an unmarried father becomes the sole residential parent and a s 4 order is accordingly also made, the mother will retain parental responsibility, which cannot, by virtue of s 2(9), be surrendered or transferred. However, as the unmarried father can acquire parental responsibility only by virtue of s 4, his parental responsibility can, subject to s 12(4), be terminated in accordance with s 4(3), upon the application of himself or of any other person who has parental responsibility for the child or, with leave of the court, on the application of the child. It should also be stressed that s 2(8) states that the fact that a person has parental responsibility for a child shall not entitle them to act in any way which would be incompatible with any order made under the Act. Thus, although a non-residential parent may retain parental responsibility and thus may approach the child's school, or consent to medical treatment, it does not entitle him or her to take the child to live with him or her where there is a residence order in favour of the child's other parent.

(b) General philosophy
Part I of the 1989 Act is an attempt to translate into practice the philosophy expressed in the Law Commission's Report *Guardianship*

and Custody (Law Commission no. 172). The main guiding principles are contained in s 1.

It is thought that, despite a slight difference in wording, s 1 CA 1989 restates the welfare principle contained in s 1 GMA 1971. It says that the child's welfare shall be the court's "paramount consideration" when determining any question regarding the upbringing of a child or the administration of a child's property, but it does not retain the old words "first and paramount". The omission of the word "first" has been said by the Lord Chancellor not to be significant, and so it seems the welfare principle has been left intact. Accordingly, much of the case law developed under the old law will remain important providing it does not conflict with the other guiding principles expressed in Part I of the 1989 Act. It should be noted that "upbringing" includes the care of the child, but not his maintenance (s 105(1)).

Section 1(5) breaks with tradition in stating that a court should not make any order under the Act with respect to a child unless it considers that doing so would be better for the child than making no order at all. It remains to be seen how the courts will apply this "no order" presumption. However, it could be used to support the contention that an unmarried father with parental responsibility who is not to be the residential parent on breakdown, but who wishes to retain parental responsibility obtained pursuant to s 4, should do so.

On the breakdown of a formerly stable and long relationship between unmarried parents, where the mother has consented to a parental responsibility agreement or order, it could be argued that the situation is akin to that on divorce. Therefore, although it may be accepted that the mother should be granted a residence order, nevertheless, the father should retain parental responsibility in the same way as would a married father, because an order on the mother's application bringing parental responsibility to an end would not be better for the child than making no order at all.

Thus there is a welfare principle contained in s 1(1) and a presumption of non-interference unless there is a positive advantage for the child in s 1(5). Section 1(2) requires the court to have regard to the general principle that delay in determining a question relating to the upbringing of a child is likely to prejudice the welfare of the child. Again, this is a most welcome restatement of an established principle, but it remains to be seen how the courts will react. Requests for adjournments may now be dismissed more readily, and advisors and representatives are likely to be strongly criticised if they are the cause of delay. However, where delay is caused by, for example, the slow processing of a legal aid application, the court will have a difficult decision to make. Delays preparing court welfare reports which have always been much criticised, are often due to lack of resources. The court will have to balance whether the child's interests are best served by proceeding on the basis of incomplete evidence or by yet further delay.

Before looking at s 8 orders in more detail, attention should be drawn to the checklist, set out in s 1(3) of the Act, of matters to which the court shall have regard when making s 8 orders. This is an attempt to clarify priorities:

"1(3). In the the circumstances mentioned in subsection (4), a court shall have regard in particular to –

(a) the ascertainable wishes and feelings of the child concerned (considered in the light of his age and understanding);

(b) his physical, emotional and educational needs;

(c) the likely effect on him of any change in his circumstances;

(d) his age, sex, background and any characteristics of his that the court considers relevant;

(e) any harm which he has suffered or is at risk of suffering;

(f) how capable each of his parents, and any other person in relation to whom the court considers the question to be relevant, is of meeting his needs;

(g) the range of powers available to the court under this Act in the proceedings in question."

Subsection 4 firstly applies the checklist considerations where a court is considering whether to make, vary or discharge a s 8 order, and such making, variation or discharge is opposed by any party to the proceedings. If the parties are agreed and the application is unopposed, then it seems that the court is not directed to have regard to the checklist. Subject to the welfare principle and s 1(5), it cannot automatically intervene and reject the proposals in the light of the checklist considerations.

Secondly, the checklist applies where the court is considering whether to make a care or supervision order under Part IV of the Act. Here, agreement cannot oust the court's power to intervene and apply the checklist. However, care and supervision orders can now be made only on application to the court by a local authority or other authorised person such as the NSPCC. Section 37 enables the court to order an investigation of the child's circumstances by the local authority where it feels it may be appropriate for a care or supervision order to be made, but the court has lost its power to make a care or supervision order of its own motion in family proceedings where it is troubled by the unsatisfactory nature of the arrangements proposed by the parents. Although an application can be made for a care or supervision order, either as an end in itself or in other family proceedings (s 31), the court's loss of power to intervene in this way is a sign of the shift towards leaving responsibility for children much more with their parents and free from state interference.

What, then will a court do if it is concerned about the arrangements and making no order at all does not resolve the situation? Section 7 does give the court power, of its own motion, when considering any question with respect to a child under the Act, to seek welfare reports from a probation officer or a local authority on specified matters relating to the welfare of the child. Thus, if a court was dissatisfied about the agreed arrangements in respect of which s 8 orders were being sought by the child's parents, the court has power to order a report with a view, if appropriate, to the local authority's then applying for a care or supervision order. Alternatively, as will be discussed below, the court can in exceptional circumstances make a "family assistance order" pursuant to s 16 of the Act, requiring a probation or local authority officer to advise, assist or befriend any person named in the order providing the adult parties agree. Finally, as mentioned above, where they feel a care or supervision order may be appropriate, the court can order a s 37 investigation by the local authority.

3. Residence, contact and other orders under s 8 Children Act 1989

Section 8 CA 1989 sets out the orders that can be made with respect to children in family proceedings. It introduces residence and contact orders, which replace orders for custody and access both under s 9 GMA 1971 and in matrimonial proceedings. Thus all disputes relating to children will be dealt with under the 1989 Act regardless of the marital status of their parents. In addition, s 8 provides for prohibited steps and specific issue orders, which it is envisaged will be used to control where necessary the steps which can and cannot be taken by a parent in relation to a child following breakdown of the parents' relationship.

On breakdown of an unmarried relationship where there are children, in order to clarify any arrangements and ensure they are as far as possible acknowledged in law and enforceable, it may still be necessary for the parents to seek an order pursuant to s 8 CA 1989. This section defines the orders that can be made with respect to children in "family proceedings", which, by virtue of subs 3, means wardship proceedings and proceedings under Parts I, II and IV of the 1989 Act; the Matrimonial Causes Act 1973; the Domestic Violence and Matrimonial Proceedings Act 1976; the Adoption Act 1976; the Domestic Proceedings and Magistrates' Court Act 1978; ss 1 and 9 of the Matrimonial Homes Act 1983; and Part III of the Matrimonial and Family Proceedings Act 1984. Section 30(8) Human Fertilization and Embryology Act 1990 ("HFEA 1990") adds to this list proceedings under s 30 HFEA 1990.

Of these, only the DVMPA 1976 and orders under the CA 1989 are likely to be of direct relevance on the breakdown of an unmarried relationship. In particular, as was explained in the preceding chapter, where an unmarried couple is involved in proceedings under the DVMPA 1976 and where there are children of the relationship, in addition to granting injunctions, the court can of its own motion make orders under s 8 if a question arises with respect to the welfare of a child and the court considers the order should be made, even if there has been no application (s 10(1)(b)).

Section 8 orders comprise the following, as defined by s 8(1):

"a contact order" means an order requiring the person with whom a child lives, or is to live, to allow the child to visit or stay with the person named in the order, or for that person and the child otherwise to have contact with each other;

"a prohibited steps order" means an order that no step which could be taken by a parent in meeting his parental responsibility for a child, and which is of a kind specified in the order, shall be taken by any person without the consent of the court;

"a residence order" means an order settling the arrangements to be made as to the person with whom a child is to live; and

"a specific issue order" means an order giving directions for the purpose of determining a specific question which has arisen, or which may arise, in connection with any aspect of parental responsibility for a child.

(a) Applicants

Unlike orders under s 9 GMA 1971, applications for s 8 orders are not restricted to parents. In addition to any parent or guardian of the child, the following may apply as of right for a s 8 order (s 10(5) & (6)):

"Any person in whose favour a residence order has been granted;
Any party to a marriage in respect of which the child is a child of the family;

Any person with whom the child has lived for three out of the past five years, providing that period of time has not ended more than three months prior to making the application; and

Any person who has the consent of each of the persons who does have a residence order or has parental responsibility where there is no residence order, or, where the child is in care, the consent of the relevant local authority. "

Any person not included in these categories, including the child him/herself, providing the court considers he or she has sufficient understanding, may also apply with the court's leave. Section 8 orders can be sought or made by the court of its own motion in any family proceedings (s 10(1)), as defined above, or where there are no family proceedings, on the application of any person who is entitled to apply for a s 8 order or who has been granted leave to do so (s 10(2)). These provisions are subject to s 9, which prevents a court making a s 8 order, other than a residence order, with respect to a child who is in the care of a local authority; prevents a local authority from applying for a residence or contact order; and prevents such an order being made in favour of an authority. Normally, a person seeking to remove a child from care would apply to discharge the care order pursuant to s 39. However, an unmarried father without parental responsibility is not eligible to make such an application. Thus his only course would be to apply for a s 8 residence order, for, once a residence order is made in relation to a child who is in care, this automatically discharges the care order (s 91(1)).

(b) Residence orders

Residence orders will be used to settle where and with whom a child should live, usually, but not exclusively, on the breakdown of a child's parents' relationship. As has been seen above, although in the context of the unmarried family it is likely to be the child's parents who will be the parties to the proceedings and who will be seeking the order, applications for s 8 orders are open to a wide range of people. Where parents agree the arrangements, the court does not, it seems, have to have regard to the checklist set out in s 1(3). However, where the court feels there is cause for concern, welfare reports or a s 37 investigation can be ordered, or a family assistance order made under s 16. This power should not be exercised unless the court is satisfied that the circumstances are exceptional. The effect of such an order is discussed below (see page 155).

Interestingly, since earlier case law was generally not in favour of granting joint custody to divorcing parents, except where there was evident willingness to co-operate (see for example *Caffell* v *Caffell* (1984) 14 Fam Law 83 (CA)), the 1989 Act leaves parental responsibility with both married parents after the making of a residence order. Where an unmarried father becomes the residential parent on breakdown, s 12(1) directs that the court shall also make a s 4 order giving him parental responsibility. As the court cannot take away a mother's parental responsibility, both parents will in this situation have parental responsibility for the child subject to the s 8 orders. Where a s 4 order has been made granting the father parental responsibility, it is open to the mother (or, with leave, the child) to apply to discharge the s 4 order on breakdown. However, as discussed above it seems that the court should not automatically discharge the order but consider the application in the light of the principles set out in s 1. Any person who is not a parent but in whose favour a residence order is made, is automatically given parental responsibility while the residence order remains in force by virtue of s 12(2). However, their parental responsibility is limited to the extent that they are specifically denied power to consent or refuse to consent to adoption, and cannot appoint a guardian for the child (s 12(3)). Another break with the principles established under previous case law is the acknowledgment in s 11(4) that a court may under s 8 make a residence order in favour of two or more persons who do not live together.

Previously, joint custody, care and control orders were even rarer than joint custody orders in divorce cases and it was not possible to make joint orders in the case of unmarried families. However, s 11(4) provides that where more than one person is granted a residence order, the order may specify, although this is not a requirement, the periods during which the child is to live in the households concerned. Thus, an order may now be made granting one parent residence during term time and the other residence for the duration of the school holidays, or that the child spends Monday to Thursday with one parent and Friday to Sunday with the other. Such orders have become popular in the USA, but even where parents here have agreed such an arrangement, the courts have in the past sometimes been reluctant to approve them, even where, as in *Riley* v *Riley* [1986] 2 FLR 429 (CA), such an arrangement had been in existence for some five years without any apparent adverse effect on the child. However, a recent Court of Appeal decision did endorse an arrangement for joint custody, care and control stating that although in the majority of cases such an order would mean a child did not know where their home was, in this case the child was left in no doubt where she was going to be (see *J* v *J* *(Minor)* *(Joint care and control)* [1991] 2 FLR 385.

It is felt that, providing it is better for the child than making no order at all, where there is agreement, the court cannot refuse a joint residence order unless there is serious concern for the child's welfare. In this case welfare reports or an investigation of the child's circumstances at the court's direction pursuant to s 37 will be ordered with a view to a family assistance order or care proceedings. These are likely to be exceptions rather than the rule. However, given the existing case law, which recognises the unsettling effect of such an order on the child, and the degree of co-operation between the parents that is likely to be required, the courts are perhaps unlikely to impose a joint residence arrangement on parents who are in dispute. Should the child express a wish for such an arrangement, and should it be practical in terms of the parents' ability to look after the child, the locations of the parents' homes and the child's school, the Act may have paved the way for such orders to be made more frequently. In this situation each parent will have to retain or acquire parental responsibility but cannot exercise it in a way that is incompatible with the residence or other s 8 order(s), notwithstanding that he or she is a residential parent (s 2(8)).

Should a child's parents resume cohabitation for a period exceeding six months, then any residence order that has been made will lapse.

When a residence order is in force, no person may cause the child to become known by a different surname, or remove the child from the UK, without either the written consent of every person who has parental responsibility for the child, or leave of the court. However, a residential parent may now take the child out of the UK for a period of up to one month (s 13(2)) without consent or leave; and the court may grant leave for other proposed visits out of the UK, either generally or for specified periods or places, when making the residence order (s 13(3)). Thus s 13 has made welcome modifications to the existing law but has in fact imposed on unmarried parents restrictions in these two respects which were not previously automatically imposed with orders for custody or access. Although these requirements now apply to children of unmarried, as well as married, parents, the anomalous need for leave to be sought to take the child to Scotland or other parts of the UK, not a part of the jurisdiction of England and Wales, – a restriction that many parents did not realise in any event – has at least been removed. Holidays abroad for a period of up to one month where the child is to travel with the residential parent are now possible, but it seems that school holidays abroad will require the consent of every person who has parental responsibility. Advisors might give thought to whether a blanket consent for such trips should be sought at the time a residence order is being made.

Section 14(1) provides a sanction where a residence order is in force and any person, including a person in whose favour there is also a residence order, breaches the terms of the order. Providing the person has been served with a copy of the residence order, then the offended residential parent may enforce the residence order as if it were an order requiring the other person to produce the child to them under s 63(3) Magistrates' Courts Act 1980. This enables justices to impose a fine of £50 per day up to a maximum of £2,000 whilst the breach continues, or to sentence the person to imprisonment of a maximum of two months or until the breach is remedied. This is the only remedy available where the residence order was made in the magistrates' courts, but where the order was made in the county court or High Court, it can be enforced in the usual way for contempt of court (see Chapter 6).

It remains to be seen whether the new style residence order, which is more flexible and less possessory (at least in name) than its predecessor, will ease the bitterness of disputes between separating parents.

(c) Contact orders

Contact orders are the successors to access orders, but are more wide-ranging as they specifically contemplate contact other than visits. Contact can include letters and telephone calls, as well as visits and stays with the other parent, although it was recently held in *W* v *B* The Times 26 March 1991, that justices had power under s 9 GMA 1971 to make an order granting the right to correspond with, and make telephone calls to, a child, even though physical access was not possible due to the father was serving a term of imprisonment.

Whilst the child is with the contact parent, if the parent does not also have parental responsibility, the parent may nevertheless do what is reasonable to promote or safeguard the welfare of the child (s 3(5)); a contact parent with parental responsibility may do anything that a parent may do provided it is not inconsistent with any residence or other order under the Act (s 2(8)).

Perhaps surprisingly, the Act leaves the question of contact with the non-residential parent entirely to the court's discretion, and does not enshrine the child's right to have contact with the other parent. Accordingly, the old case law is likely to influence decisions about contact orders, at least as between parents.

Providing he or she can obtain leave, a grandparent can now apply for a contact order, as the Act does not restrict to parents applications for this or any of the s 8 orders. Previously, wardship was the only forum in which grandparents had *locus standi,* and where access was the only issue, the cost of such proceedings and the unwillingness of the legal aid authorities to grant legal aid for the purpose left most grandparents who were being denied access without a remedy.

The court may define contact in the order, but it is likely that the standard order will provide for "reasonable contact". Thought should be given to whether any further definition which could be in the child's best interests, is desired by either parent, although the general principle that no order should be made unless it it is better for the child than making no order at all will apply (s 1(5)), and may prove an obstacle.

Contact orders will not of course be made in relation to parents with the benefit of a joint residence order.

As with residence orders, contact orders cease to have effect if the child's parents live together for a period of more than six months. Clients should be advised that if a reconciliation takes place, the whole procedure for residence and contact orders will have to be gone through again should the reconciliation last for more than six months but prove not to be permanent.

(d) Prohibited steps orders, specific issue orders and wardship
The two new orders, prohibited steps orders and specific issue orders, are defined as follows:

"a prohibited steps order" means an order that no step which could be taken by a parent in meeting his parental responsibility for a child, and which is of a kind specified in the order, shall be taken by any person without the consent of the court;

"a specific issue order" means an order giving directions for the purpose of determining a specific question which has arisen, or which may arise, in connection with any aspect of parental responsibility for a child."

One of the aims in introducing these new orders was, according to the Law Commission, to incorporate into the statutory code the most valuable features of the wardship jurisdiction (see Law Com no. 172, 4.20). The definitions of the two new orders seem to allow the court to give negative and positive directions to any person in relation to the exercise of aspects of parental responsibility. Thus it seems that the court can prohibit a person without parental responsibility from doing any act which could be done by a person with parental responsibility. For example, an unmarried father without parental responsibility could, it seems, be prevented from contacting the child's school even though, strictly, this is an act that only a parent with parental responsibility should do. Wardship however has not been abolished and remains available for use by individuals, in contrast to local authorities whose use of the inherent jurisdiction has been severely curtailed.

In wardship, parental responsibility is vested in the court, so that no important step can be taken in relation to the child without leave of the court. Although there is no general embargo as in wardship, by using these new orders the court can define matters upon which it wishes to be consulted before action is taken. This can be achieved by imposing a prohibited steps order and/or giving directions on any matter in dispute by means of a specific issue order.

Although neither of these orders should be imposed with a view to achieving a result which could be obtained by making a residence or contact order (s 9(5)(a)), they may be made where no residence or contact order is being sought. Thus a prohibited steps order could be made preventing the child being taken out of the jurisdiction by a non-parent where there is no residence order; and a specific issue order could be made in relation to the appropriate schooling or religious education for a child where there is no agreement between the parents. These orders can also be made supplemental to residence and contact orders and can be applied for not only by parents but by any other person eligible to apply for a s 8 order pursuant to s 10(2), although they may need leave of the court to make the application.

At the present time it is difficult to see how the relationship between these orders and conditional residence and contact orders will develop. Section 11(7) enables the court to impose conditions when making a s 8 order on, *inter alia*, any parent or person with parental responsibility, and to "make such incidental, supplemental or consequential provision as the court thinks fit". It is difficult to think of a wider discretion for attaching conditions, and it seems that where a residence and/or contact order is being made, any result desired by the making of a prohibited steps or specific issue order, could probably also be achieved by attaching conditions to the residence or contact order and thus separate orders need not be made – in line with s 9(5). Perhaps these orders are therefore most likely to be sought other than in the context of relationship breakdown, or possibly where disputes arise some time after breakdown, when the issues of contact and residence have already been resolved.

The court can again make these orders of its own volition in any "family proceedings" (s 10(1)). However, the Act specifically prevents their being used in any way that is denied to the High Court by s 100(2) in the exercise of its inherent jurisdiction. Section 100(2) essentially prohibits the court using the wardship jurisdiction for the purpose of placing a child in the care or under the supervision of a local authority, or in relation to a child already in care. Neither can it be used to confer on a local authority power to determine any question relating to parental responsibility for a child. Thus specific issue and prohibited steps orders cannot be used to circumvent the deliberate restriction of a local authority's powers in this regard. It should also be noted that no local authority may seek to invoke the wardship jurisdiction without leave of the court (s 100(3)), ensuring that authorities are largely confined to the powers specified in Part III of the Act relating to care proceedings and emergency protection of children – matters outside the scope of this book.

Where a child is not in care, however, wardship remains an option both for parents and non-parents in relation to specific matters concerning the child's upbringing. The prohibitive cost has already been mentioned, but one advantage where a non-parent is seeking the assistance of the court is that no application for leave will be required in order to ward the child. As regards matters between parents themselves, the new s 8 orders may be applied for without leave, and in most cases, there need be no thought of wardship proceedings.

(e) Duration of s 8 orders
Interim s 8 orders may be made as the Act states that where the court has power to make such an order it may do so regardless of the fact that it is not in a position finally to dispose of the proceedings. Thus an order can be made until the date of the next hearing or a specified

event. It has also been seen that contact and residence orders cease upon the child's parents resuming cohabitation for a period of six months. Section 9(6) provides that no court shall make any s 8 order which will continue to be effective after the child is sixteen unless it is satisfied that the circumstances are exceptional. Thus normally residence and contact orders will be expressed to continue until the child attains the age of sixteen. After this, the *Gillick* principle, that young people of this age are well able to make up their own minds on these issues, comes into play under the Act. Section 9(7) goes on to say that no s 8 order, other than one varying or discharging an existing order shall be made in relation to a child who is already sixteen unless the court is satisfied that the circumstances are exceptional. It is thought that exceptional circumstances would certainly include a child who is mentally handicapped, for example. Similarly where unorthodox medical treatment with potentially serious repercussions is being considered for or by a seventeen year old, it may still be appropriate to make a specific issue order.

Where a s 8 order does continue in respect of a child beyond the age of sixteen, it shall then cease on the child's reaching the age of eighteen (s 91(11)). If a care order is made in respect of a child, this automatically discharges any s 8 orders relating to the child (s 91(2)).

(f) Directions and conditions

In proceedings where the question of making a s 8 order arises, the court must draw up a timetable with a view to determining the question, and give appropriate directions to ensure adherence to that timetable (s 11(1)). Rules of court may specify appropriate periods for particular steps, but this power has not been used to date. As noted above, the court is given very wide discretion, when making s 8 orders to impose conditions on any parent or person with parental responsibility or with whom the child lives (see s 11(7)).

4. Appointment of guardians, parental responsibility and residence orders

The inter-relation of parental responsibility and residence orders has already been canvassed in Chapter 2. It should be noted that, once a residence order has been made, where the non-residential parent retains parental responsibility, this does not postpone the effectiveness of the appointment by the residential parent of a testamentary guardian in the event of death (s 5(7)). However, the guardian would have parental responsibility jointly with the surviving non-residential parent. Any appointment of a testamentary guardian by a parent where the surviving parent has parental responsibility and no residence order has been made, or where a residence order has been made in favour of the deceased parent and the surviving parent jointly, will not take effect until after the death of the surviving parent.

5. Family assistance orders

The Act introduces a new family assistance order, which can be distinguished from supervision orders previously available to the court on making orders for custody, and from supervision orders under the 1989 Act discussed below. As shall be seen, supervision orders can now be made only upon the application of the local authority and not of the court's own motion. Section 16 gives the court power in any family proceedings, where the court has power to make a s 8 order and regardless of whether or not it does make such an order, to make a family assistance order requiring a probation officer or local authority officer to advise, assist and (where appropriate) befriend any person named in the order. Such orders can be made only where the court is satisfied that the circumstances are exceptional and where every party named in the order, other than the child, consents.

Such orders may require a person named in the order to keep the officer informed of the address of any person named in the order and to allow them to visit. An order will last for a maximum of six months. It enables the officer to refer to the court the question of a variation or discharge of a subsisting s 8 order.

It is perhaps surprising that the consent of older children is not required before such an order is made, particularly as the main distinction between this order and a supervision order is the voluntary nature of the new order. However, advisors should be aware that clients do not have to consent to these orders, although it may be that the consequence of refusing to consent will be for welfare reports to be ordered if this has not already been done and the appropriate local authority applying for a supervision or care order pursuant to s 31, following a direction from the court to investigate the child's circumstances pursuant to its power under s 37.

6. Welfare reports and care and supervision orders

As has been seen above, s 7 gives the court power of its own motion, and at its absolute discretion, when considering any question with respect to a child under the Act, to seek welfare reports from a probation officer or a local authority on specified matters relating to the welfare of the child. Regulations are to be made by the Lord Chancellor specifying matters which must be dealt with in any report unless the court orders otherwise. However, care and supervision orders can now be made only on application to the court by a local authority or other authorised person such as the NSPCC (s 31); and such an order can no longer be imposed by the court of its own motion. The only course open to the court is a family assistance order, which is dependent upon the consent of the relevant parties. Where the court feels a care or supervision order may be appropriate it can order a local authority to carry out an investigation of the child's circumstances pursuant to s 37.

Although an application can be made by a local authority or authorised person for a care or supervision order, either as an application on its own or in other family proceedings (s 31), the court's inability to act on its own embodies the shift towards leaving responsibility for children with their parents and free from state interference.

7. Jurisdiction and procedure

By virtue of s 92 of the Act, the magistrates' court, county court and High Court all have concurrent jurisdiction in proceedings under the Act, and domestic proceedings in the magistrates' court are renamed "family proceedings".

The procedure applicable in relation to Children Act proceedings in all three courts is now almost uniform. Unlike some of the public law proceedings under the Act, the Children (Allocation of Proceedings) Order 1991 (SI 1991 No 1677), which details which proceedings are to be commenced in particular courts as well as the rules relating to transfer of proceedings between different courts, does not place any restriction on the court in which private law Children Act proceedings should be commenced. Thus an applicant and his or her legal adviser have a free choice (subject to any legal aid difficulties) as to where to commence an application for a s 8 order or a s 4 parental responsibility order, although any application for variation or discharge of an order under the Act should normally be made to the court which made the order (art 4).

In addition, the courts have power to transfer proceedings between the three jurisdictions (Sch 11 para 2 CA 1989) but the Order only provides for "upward and downward" transfers as between magistrates' and county courts and county courts and the High Court. Thus the magistrates' court cannot transfer a case directly to the High Court, which itself is limited to a downward transfer to the county court. The Order sets out the criteria to be taken into account by the court when considering any such transfer; a transfer may be effected only if it is in the best interests of the child.

New court rules now provide details of the procedure to be followed in relation to applications under the Act, which have both changed and harmonised the procedure in all three jurisdictions. Part IV Family Proceedings Rules 1991 (SI 1991 No 1247) ("FPR") contain the details of the procedure to be followed in the county court and High Court, and Part II of the Family Proceedings Courts (Children Act 1989) Rules (SI 1991 No 1395) ("FPCR") set out the magistrates' courts procedure, which is broadly the same.

Proceedings are issued by completing the appropriate form (for example, Form CHA 10 for a s 8 application). No affidavit evidence is required in any of the three jurisdictions but the application form requires fairly detailed information about the applicant, the child, the child's family and the respondent. Service on the respondent, giving notice of the hearing, is required as specified in the rules and is now effected in all cases by the applicant, not by the court. It should be noted that in urgent cases only applications for a prohibited steps or specific issue order under s 8, but not for a residence or contact order, may be made *ex parte* (r 4.4 of FPR 1991 and r 4 of FPCR). Appendix 3 FPR and Sch 2 FPCR specify persons whom the applicant is required to serve with, or to whom the applicant must give, notice of the application.

Any further evidence can be filed in the form of a statement which is signed and dated by the maker and contains a declaration by him or her that the contents of the statement are believed to be true and that it is understood that the statement may be placed before the court. This is now the case in all three jurisdictions and no affidavit evidence is required in the county court or High Court in relation to Children Act proceedings. The respondent must file an answer to the application, within the period specified by the rules, on the appropriate form where there is one. In the case of s 8 proceedings, the period is fourteen days of service and the appropriate form is Form CHA 10A. All the forms appear in the appendices to the two sets of rules.

The court then draws up a timetable and gives any necessary directions to ensure the timetable is adhered to. No rules yet specify periods in which particular steps must be taken, other than service on the respondent at least twenty-one days prior to the hearing.

Where a person requires leave to apply for an order under the Act, a written request setting out the reasons for the application should be made to the court, and a draft of the appropriate substantive application form, with sufficient copies for service, should be filed. The court then considers whether or not to grant leave immediately; if so, the applicant is notified and the matter proceeds. If the court cannot grant leave immediately, it must fix a date for the hearing of the application and notify the applicant and other appropriate persons. The major difference in the procedure from that applicable to old-style custody and access or parental rights proceedings is that the complaint and summons procedure in the magistrates' court has been abolished, and written evidence is now filed in statement form and not on oath in all three courts. The new uniformity of procedure throughout the family jurisdiction is to be greatly welcomed.

8. Existing orders for custody and access and the transitional provisions

Where proceedings for custody or access were commenced under s 9 GMA 1971 before the 1989 Act came into force, these will be decided under the old law and will not therefore be immediately affected. Orders for custody and access under the old law are preserved, although some modifications have been made to reconcile them with the new 1989 Act scheme. As has already been noted, parental rights order made under the FLRA 1987 will be treated as if they were made under the 1989 Act, and will thus confer parental responsibility. Any unmarried father who has been awarded legal custody of his child will be deemed to have the benefit of a s 4 order and thus will acquire parental responsibility which cannot be terminated whilst the existing custody order continues in force (Sch 14, para 6 (4)). A person with access under an existing order may apply for a contact order, and such a person is broadly treated for the other purposes of the Act in the same way as a person with a contact order (see Sch 14, para 9) and thus, for example, may be named with consent in a family assistance order.

The making of a residence order in respect of a child who is the subject of an existing order discharges the existing order, and where any other type of s 8 order is made, the existing order remains in force subject to the s 8 order (para 11). Thus if a mother has been granted custody under the old provisions and the child's father subsequently applies for and is granted a contact order pursuant to s 8, then the mother's custody order will continue in force subject to the contact order.

However, if a residence order is granted to a grandmother, where previously orders had been granted giving custody to the mother and access to the father, the father's access order will be automatically discharged notwithstanding the grandmother's agreement to his continued contact with the child and he would therefore need to apply for a new-style contact order to preserve his right to see his child.

Generally, the court is given power to discharge an existing order (or part thereof) in any family proceedings where any question relating to the child's welfare arises, or on the application of any parent or guardian of the child or other person named in the existing order, or, with the leave of the court, the child him/herself. Where an application is opposed, then the court must have regard to the checklist of considerations set out in s 1(3).

Chapter 8

Financial provision for children

The provisions for financial relief for children in unmarried families, previously contained in ss 11A to 12C GMA 1971 as introduced by the FLRA 1987, have been largely re-enacted by the CA 1989 and are to be found in Schedule 1. The 1987 amendments, which also abolished affiliation proceedings, brought the principles for financial relief for children of unmarried parents more into line with those found in the Matrimonial Causes Act 1973, which were and remain available on relationship breakdown to children of married parents only. Although significant differences remain, both the orders available and the criteria for making the orders under the Schedule can be seen to have descended from the MCA 1973.

Schedule 1 to the Children Act 1989, which derives its authority from s 15 of the Act, is not restricted to financial relief for children on the breakdown of unmarried relationships. However, given the continuation of the relevant provisions of the MCA 1973 and the DPMCA 1978, enabling orders for financial relief for children of married families to be made under perhaps more generous criteria, it seems the schedule will mostly be used by unmarried parents and is certainly of great importance to them. Married parents may prefer to use its provisions where there has been a separation and they are unsure whether divorce or judicial separation proceedings will ensue, but again the DPMCA 1978 is an alternative for periodical payments and lump sum orders, although only in the magistrates' court. It is therefore likely that unmarried parents only will use the provisions of Schedule 1 to obtain final orders for financial provision for their children as, for them, it is the only course.

Applications for financial relief for children can be made in their own right irrespective of whether any application for residence or contact orders are or have been before the court. However, as applications for financial provision come within the definition of "family proceedings" in the Act, a court can make any s 8 order, or order a local authority to investigate a child's circumstances pursuant to s 37, during the course of the financial provision proceedings in the absence of any application. Thus, should an unmarried mother who has sole parental responsibility apply for maintenance, the court can make orders for residence and contact, providing it thinks that doing so is better for the child than making no order at all. If it feels a care or supervision order may be appropriate, then it can order a s 37 investigation.

1. Orders available

All paragraph numbers cited in this section refer to Sch 1 CA 1989. Paragraph 1(2) lists the orders available as follows:
"a) an order requiring either or both parents of a child –
   i) to make to the applicant for the benefit of the child; or
   ii) to make to the child himself, such periodical payments, for such term, as may be specified in the order;
b) an order requiring either or both parents of a child -
   i) to secure to the applicant for the benefit of the child; or
   ii) to secure to the child himself, such periodical payments, for such term, as may be specified in the order;
c) an order requiring either or both parents of a child -
   i) to pay to the applicant for the benefit of the child; or

ii) to pay to the child himself, such lump sum as may be so specified;

d) an order requiring a settlement to be made for the benefit of the child, and to the satisfaction of the court, of property -

i) to which either parent is entitled (either in possession or reversion); and

ii) which is specified in the order;

e) an order requiring either or both parents of a child -

i) to transfer to the applicant for the benefit of the child; or

ii) to transfer to the child himself, such property to which the parent is entitled (either in possession or reversion) as may be specified in the order".

In addition para 2 of the schedule provides for applications to be made by a person over eighteen for periodical payments or a lump sum order providing the applicant's parents are not living together in the same household and the applicant did not have the benefit of a periodical payments order in force when he or she reached the age of sixteen. However, as discussed on page 167, this is appropriate only where the person is or will be undergoing full-time education or training, or where there are other special circumstances which justify the making of an order.

Paragraph 6 permits the variation or discharge, including the temporary suspension, of an order for secured or unsecured periodical payments. Interim orders for periodical payments and giving appropriate directions may be made pursuant to para 9. On variation or discharge of an order under paras 1 or 2, the court has power at that stage to order the paying parent to pay a lump sum (para 5(3)).

Orders for periodical payments can be made for any appropriate amount as decided by the court having taken into account the matters set out in para 4. These factors (see page 170) must be considered in relation to any application made under paras 1 and 2 and are also referred to in relation to applications for variation and discharge.

Lump sum orders under paras 1 and 2 made in the magistrates' court are subject to a ceiling of £1,000 but are unlimited in the county and High Courts. They may also be made in consideration of liabilities or expenses reasonably incurred before the making of the order in connection with the birth or in maintaining the child (para 5(1)). Thus if a court feels a lump sum should be made in respect of a child's future needs under para 1(2)(c), and in addition accepts that expenses have been incurred in maintaining the child prior to the application, this sum may be added to the former. This situation is most likely to arise where the parties have not been cohabiting and thus such earlier expenses have not been shared or met by the paying parent. The court can also order the lump sum to be paid by instalments, and has power to vary such an order, to change the number of instalments or the amount payable in respect of any instalment and also the date on which any instalment is payable. The total amount of the lump sum cannot be varied (see sub-paras 5(5) and (6)). There is no limit on the number of applications for a lump sum that can be made and thus where circumstances change a further application is now possible in appropriate circumstances.

The 1987 Act introduced for the first time, and Sch 1 preserves, the possibility of orders requiring the settlement or transfer of property for the benefit of a child of unmarried parents, as well as secured periodical payments. Unsecured periodical maintenance payments and lump sum orders were available even in affiliation proceedings, albeit in more limited circumstances. Unlike lump sum payments only one application can be made for orders under sub-paras (d) and (e).

Settlement of property may require specialist advice, including advice on the tax implications, which is outside the scope of this book, although the possibility of settlement of the family home will be considered in Chapter 10. Broadly, the same considerations apply as for children of married parents in divorce proceedings, subject to some significant differences apparent in the drafting of Sch 1 discussed below. It is thought that settlements will generally be appropriate only where there are substantial assets available for the benefit of the child. It is submitted though that where property which was the family home is owned solely by one parent who is not to be the residential parent following breakdown, settlement of the property for the benefit of a child until the age of eighteen or some other appropriate event, rather than transfer of the property to the residential parent for the benefit of the child which could lead to persons other than the child and the residential parent benefiting, may be thought to be more appropriate. If this is so, then settlements may become more frequently used in relation to families of less substantial means to establish an equivalent of the *Mesher* and *Martin* orders developed in the matrimonial jurisdiction. This may also be appropriate where both parents have contributed to the purchase of the home and both have legal and/or equitable interests in the property, but it is not possible to achieve a clean break.

Transfer of property orders are thus likely to be increasingly sought by unmarried parents and it is thought that very often it will be the family home which is in dispute. The court has power to order the transfer of *any* property to which the parents are entitled, to either the applicant, which will usually be the other parent, for the benefit of the child; or to the child him/herself. "Property" includes both real and personal property and the court can order, for example, the transfer of stocks and shares. However, it is usual to realise as far as possible resources to be directed to the child in the form of periodical payments or lump sum orders. Indeed the courts in proceedings ancillary to divorce have been reluctant to make capital awards or transfer of property orders directly to the child (see for example *Chamberlain* v *Chamberlain* [1974] 1 All ER 33). However, it may well be that a different approach will be seen in relation to the unmarried family, where the court does not have a direct jurisdiction to adjust the assets between the unmarried parents, but only between parent and child.

The transfer of property provision may conceivably be used where there is an unresolved dispute relating to personal property vested jointly in the parents (such as shares or even a building society or bank account) which the court can order should be transferred to the residential parent for the benefit of the child. However, it is thought that applications under this sub-paragraph are likely often to concern the family home.

As has been noted, there is no family jurisdiction whereby the court can redistribute family property between the parties on breakdown of relationships between cohabitees where there are no children. However, para 1(2)(d) and (e) now enable some redistribution, but only for the benefit of the child where there are children in an unmarried relationship. It seems that an order transferring property can be made in respect of at least some tenancies where the home is rented, as well as empowering a court to make such an order where the home is owned by one or both of the parents. This provision has significant consequences for the housing of the unmarried family on relationship breakdown and will be discussed in Chapter 9. As discussed below, the criteria to be applied by the courts when making these orders is, arguably, less generous to the child than those applied in orders made under the MCA 1973, although there is as yet little case law. The reader is, however, referred to the recent decision of *H* v *M* [1991] Fam Law 473, in which Waite J gives some guidance as to the appropriate procedure to be followed in resolving multi-faceted financial provision disputes concerning the unmarried family.

2. Applicants and venue

Either parent or a guardian of a child, or any person in whose favour a residence order has been granted may apply for the financial provision set out in Sch 1, para 1 of the CA 1989. An application can be made to any of the three courts (magistrates', county or High Court) for order(s) requiring either or both parents to make periodical maintenance payments (para 1(2)(a)) or a lump sum (para 1(2)(b)) to the applicant for the benefit of the child or directly to the child. However, magistrates' courts are limited to a prescribed maximum lump sum, presently £1,000. An application for any order under the schedule can be made by either parent irrespective of whether the parents are living together at the time of the application, but periodical payments cease if the parents live together for more than six months. Applications can be made to the county court or High Court only where secured periodical payments under para 1(2)(c), settlement of property on, or transfer of property to or for the benefit of, the child is sought under paras 1(2)(c) and (d) respectively against either or both parents (Sch 1, para 1(1)).

In addition, when making, varying or discharging a residence order, the court may exercise any of its powers under Sch 1, even though no application has been made for financial provision for the child (Sch 1 para 1(6)) and thus the court can decide to look at the financial needs of the child at this stage of its own motion.

As was noted above, para 2 permits a person over eighteen whose parents are not living together in the same household to apply for periodical payments and a lump sum order in special circumstances. The time limits and criteria for making such an application are discussed below.

Generally speaking, the greater the resources of the intended paying party, the more important it is to apply to the High Court or the county court rather than to the magistrates' court, which has limited powers, although the courts are able to transfer cases to other courts where appropriate. Where it is known at the outset that periodical payments and/or a small lump sum only can be obtained, then the magistrates' or county court will be most appropriate. Consideration should also be given to whether any other relief, such as an injunction under the DVMPA 1976, is to be sought, as this is available to cohabitees in the county court only, and would make that court the most appropriate forum.

Where either or both parents own a property and where there are contemplated concurrent proceedings relating to a dispute between the parents under s 30 Law of Property Act 1925 ("LPA 1925"), it may be advantageous for both sets of proceedings to be consolidated. Previously this would have involved transferring them to the Family Division of the High Court, but the county court now has unlimited jurisdiction to hear s 30 proceedings. Consolidation enables the issues relating to the respective interests in the property and the financial provision appropriate for the child to be looked at in the round. This is the nearest unmarried parents can come to having their own financial situation and those of their children dealt with in the same manner as divorcing parents.

3. Time for applying and duration of orders

The court may exercise its powers to make any of the orders under the schedule at any time whilst the child is under the age of eighteen, although normally an order for periodical payments, whether or not secured, will not be made to extend beyond the child's seventeenth birthday. An extension beyond this is possible if it appears to the court that the child will continue beyond that time in full-time education or training (whether or not in gainful employment), or there are other special circumstances, such as a physical or mental handicap. Generally, though, there are no specific time limits in which an application for financial provision for the benefit of the child must be made, providing it is made before the child becomes of age.

In para 2 there is provision for separate applications for periodical payments and/or lump sum orders by persons over eighteen who remain in full-time education or training for a trade, profession or vocation, or where there are other special circumstances. However, this applies only where a periodical payments order had not been in force immediately before the child reached the age of sixteen. This provision seems to apply where parents separate after the child is eighteen or where for some reason there has not been a previous order. If it is known that a child is likely to require the order to continue, the child's parent can apply at any time before the child's eighteenth birthday for the order to be extended until his or her education or training is completed. On the other hand, where there was an order in force when the child reached sixteen and which subsequently ceased, if the child later decides to return to full-time education or training after the age of eighteen, it is not possible for the eighteen-year-old then to apply under para 2 for further periodical maintenance. However, if such a decision is taken, or other special circumstances arise after the order has ceased but before the child's eighteenth birthday, an application may be made by the child to revive the order pursuant to para 6(5).

The court has power to make interim orders for periodical payments (para 9) in relation to any application under either para 1 or 2, and this order can be backdated to the date of the application. It can be an order on such terms and for such period as the court thinks fit. It will of course cease on the final disposition of the application.

Only one order can be made in relation to settlement or transfer of property to or for the benefit of the child. However, the number of applications for periodical payments, secured periodical payments and lump sum orders is not limited. All orders for periodical payments may be varied or discharged upon the application of the payer or the recipient (para 1(4)) and there is also provision for temporary suspension (para 6(2)). Once the child has reached sixteen, the child as well as the parents can apply for variation (para 6(4)).

An application for financial provision under the schedule can be made by either parent irrespective of whether the parents are living together at the time of the application. It may also be appropriate for applications to be made by both parents where there is a joint residence order. Where one parent, say, owns two homes but has a low income, and the other has a larger income but no accommodation, it would be possible, where care of the child was effectively shared, for there to be a maintenance order in favour of the first parent and a transfer of property order in favour of the other.

However, an order for periodical maintenance payments, whether secured or unsecured, made in favour of a parent for the benefit of a child, ceases to have effect if the child's parents live together for a period longer than six months (para 3(4)).

In contrast, an order payable directly to a child does not cease to be payable in this situation and so although there is now no income tax advantage following the changes introduced in the Budget of 1988, it is possible for an order to be made and to continue, despite the fact that the child's parents are cohabiting. All periodical maintenance payments are now treated as tax free in the hands of the recipient, but there is no tax relief for an unmarried parent making maintenance payments. It is not even now possible for the additional personal allowance to be claimed by more than one parent in relation to a child where the care of the child is shared.

Unsecured periodical payments made pursuant to para 1(2)(a) or 2(2)(a) cease automatically on the death of the paying party, notwithstanding anything in the order. Herein lies one of the advantages of secured periodical payments, but a child would of course have the right to apply for provision pursuant to the Inheritance (Provision for Family and Dependants) Act 1975 as discussed in Chapter 5. Although secured periodical payments do not cease on death, it is open to the personal representatives of the deceased paying party to apply for variation or discharge, having regard to the same criteria as apply on making the order and the change in circumstances resulting from the death of the parent. Such an application must be made within six months of the taking out of a grant of probate or letters of administration, although leave may be given for a late application (para 7).

4. Transitional provisions

Paragraph 8 provides that where a residence order is made in relation to a child in respect of whom a financial relief order made under another enactment is in force, then on the application by the paying party or the person in whose favour the residence order has been made, the court may revoke or vary the existing order; the court's powers include the substitution of the applicant as the new payee if appropriate. Otherwise, as Sch 1 is a re-enactment of the financial provision sections of the GMA 1971, existing orders will be treated as if they were made under the 1989 Act and can be varied in accordance with the criteria discussed below.

5. Alteration of maintenance agreements

Where parents have made a maintenance agreement in writing, whether before or after the commencement of the paragraph, which makes financial provision for a child, Sch 1, para 10 provides that the court has power to vary the agreement if it is satisfied either that it should be varied in the light of changed circumstances, or that the agreement does not contain proper financial arrangements for the child.

6. Criteria for making the orders

Paragraph 4(1) of Sch 1 directs the court on considerations to be taken into account in making, varying or discharging orders for financial provision for a child, prefaced by the indication that the court shall have regard to all the circumstances of the case. These considerations can be summarised as follows:
  (a) the income, earning capacity, property and other financial resources which each parent has or is likely to have in the foreseeable future;
  (b) the financial needs, obligations and responsibilities which each parent has or is likely to have in the foreseeable future;

(c) the financial needs of the child;

(d) the income, earning capacity (if any), property and other financial resources of the child;

(e) any physical or mental disability of the child;

(f) the manner in which the child was being, or was expected to be,
educated or trained.

Where it is envisaged that an order is to be made against a non-parent (which means a step-parent in this context (see para 16(2)), then
additional considerations apply (see para 4(2)). However, this is
unlikely to affect the unmarried family directly, as marriage is the
mechanism by which an adult becomes a step-parent.

The criteria can be seen to owe a great deal to s 25 MCA 1973,
although important distinctions remain. Firstly, para 4 does not
require the welfare of the child to be the "first consideration" as is
specifically stated in s 25 MCA 1973. Although the court must take
the child's welfare into account as a part of "all the circumstances of
the case", this is not the first consideration, simply one of the factors
to be taken into account. The general welfare principle does not apply
to applications for financial provision as they do not concern the
upbringing of the child (s 105(1)).

Thus it is open to the court to give greater priority to, say, a father's
difficult financial position than to the benefit to the child of remaining
in a home which happens to be a property owned solely by the father.
It remains to be seen how the courts will react to the different provisions, but it is thought that there is scope for orders to be less generous than those made on divorce, partly of course because the court
will not usually be dealing with a maintenance application for the residential parent, as there is no provision for the maintenance of cohabitees by each other. This factor could in some circumstances benefit a
child, as it will leave the departing parent with more disposable
income than if he or she also had a duty to maintain the former partner. Another omission from the criteria is the standard of living of the
family unit or of the child before the order. Obviously, the family may
never have lived as a unit, but where they have, this would seem to be
a highly relevant factor which should be drawn to the court's attention
as an important circumstance of the case. Another distinction is that
any future earning capacity the court feels either parent could reason-

ably be expected to take steps to acquire is not expressed to be a factor, in contrast with the MCA provisions.

The fact that the residential parent's financial needs, as well as those of the child, is a factor to be taken into account may open the door to orders which effectively help maintain the mother (who is most often the residential parent) as well as the child. This seems to be the correct approach as of course the care of the child will affect the mother's earning capacity, particularly where the child or children are young; effectively there is scope to increase the appropriate amount payable to take account of the reality of the situation.

In the case of *Haroutunian* v *Jennings* [1980] 1 FLR 62 (Fam Div), a decision relating to an old-style affiliation order, Balcombe LJ said "There is no reason why the maintenance for a child should not afford a proper sum towards the services rendered by the mother to that child". Later in the same case, Sir George Baker reinforced this:

"The maintenance must not only be for food, clothing, heat, light, housing and so on, but also for care for a young child. And the fact that the money goes to the child and may eventually find its way into the pocket of the mother, paying for her caring of the child, seems to me to be something which the father cannot pray in aid to bring down the amount of the order."

If a mother works and has to pay another to look after her child, then this forms a financial need of the mother that the court must take into account in considering the appropriate order against the unmarried father, where the child is to live with her. Accordingly, it is arguable that where the father has sufficient resources, the notional cost of the care carried out by a mother should similarly be a factor to weigh in the equation, and one which may result in a higher order being made. Any transfer of property by the court for the benefit of a child will normally go hand in hand with the other parent's continuing to live with the child, which again gives a former cohabitee a benefit which is a side effect of the benefit intended for a child. Thus, whilst not formally recognising that a cohabitee in this situation has any duty to maintain his or her former partner, even where there are children of the relationship, the seed of such an obligation has been planted. Only time will tell how far the courts will be prepared to let it grow.

Where there has been a long period of cohabitation as a family unit, it should be argued that a solution similar to that which would have been made on divorce should be achieved in the circumstances of the case, notwithstanding the lack of specific powers to adjust the assets between the adults themselves. Where there is joint parental responsibility between unmarried parents by virtue of a s 4 order or agreement, it can be more strongly argued that the situation is akin to divorce and the financial consequences should therefore follow in the same way.

However, the public policy argument referred to in Chapter 1 is perhaps likely to ensure that the courts reinforce the view that adults seeking maximum protection on relationship breakdown should either marry, or at least enter into binding legal agreements relating to the ownership of their property where possible.

7. Maintenance and State benefits

As discussed in Chapter 4, any maintenance ordered to be paid to or for the benefit of a child will be deducted from the resident parent's income support, and taken into account in relation to a claim for family credit or housing or community charge benefit.

The non-resident parent will be a liable relative whom the DSS may pursue for maintenance where none is being paid, to recover the sums expended by the State in maintaining, in whole or in part, the child. When the provisions of the Child Support Act 1991 are in force, the resident parent will be obliged to divulge the whereabouts of the liable relative or risk losing benefit. The Act will also introduce a statutory formula for calculating maintenance and will severely limit the court's role in relation to periodical maintenance payments (see page 90).

Where an order for periodical maintenance has been made for the benefit of a child but is being paid only erratically, it is usually advantageous for the order to be assigned to the DSS to ensure that the claimant and child receive their full entitlement to benefit regularly regardless of whether the maintenance is paid. This of course applies only where the amount of benefit payable exceeds the sum of maintenance due.

8. Enforcement of orders

Broadly, orders are enforceable in the same way as the equivalent financial orders made in matrimonial proceedings or in the magistrates' courts in the past, and are well documented in standard texts on family law.

9. Procedure

Applications for financial provision for a child under Sch 1 CA 1989 are now governed by the new procedure applicable to all Children Act proceedings. As explained in Chapter 7, new rules govern procedure, although the procedure in the three family jurisdictions has been harmonised. Part IV Family Proceedings Rules 1991 (SI 1991 No 1247) ("FPR") contains the details of the procedure to be followed in the county court and High Court, and Part II of the Family Proceedings Courts (Children Act 1989) Rules 1991 (SI 1991 No 1395 ("FPCR") sets out the magistrates' court procedure, which is broadly the same. However, applications for transfer of property orders and settlement of property for the benefit of a child can be made to the county court or High Court only. Form CHA 13 needs to be completed by the applicant; it requires information relating to the applicant, the child, the child's parents, any other relevant proceedings and the child's financial needs and resources. A statement of means form (CHA 14) must also be completed by the applicant and served with the application form on the respondent. The respondent must file an answer on Form CHA 14A, together with a statement of means form, within fourteen days. The first hearing will be a directions hearing, when matters such as discovery and the attendance of the parties at the hearing will be dealt with in accordance with the court rules.

10. Legal aid and the statutory charge

Legal advice under the green form scheme is available to those whose income and capital come within its ungenerous financial limits.

Generally, civil legal aid, with its wider eligibility criteria, should be granted to those who are financially eligible to bring any of the applications under CA 1989 where merit can be shown. It would be rare for legal aid to be refused on grounds of merit, certainly where residence and contact are in dispute, given the significance of the orders for those concerned. The child may now apply for legal aid in his or her own right, and this may mean that legal aid is more accessible to resolve disputes relating to financial provision within the unmarried family, as the means of residential parents will not be taken into account where the child is the sole applicant and thus, unquestionably, the assisted person.

The caveat in this respect is of course the statutory charge which will apply to any property "recovered or preserved", to the extent of the legal costs incurred under the legal aid certificate, and the green form. Any person applying for legal aid must now be advised in writing by his or her solicitor of the effects of the statutory charge. The charge does not apply to periodical maintenance payments but it does apply to lump sum payments, although there is an exemption for the first £2,500 (reg 94(d)(vii) and 94(c)). Thus an applicant will always receive the first £2,500 of a lump sum order but the charge will apply to any amount over and above this. There is now power to postpone enforcement of the charge in relation to a home or money recovered for purchase of a home, pursuant to regs 96 & 97 Civil Legal Aid (General) Regulations 1989 where such orders are made under Sch 1 CA 1989, as costs do not normally follow the event in these proceedings. The effect of the charge should be borne in mind in negotiations, as must the duty to the legal aid fund.

Indeed, the statutory charge may provide a cogent reason for property to be settled on the child rather than transferred directly to him or her, as this may avoid the statutory charge. Where a property is jointly owned by the mother and father, and an application is made by the child, an order imposing a trust providing for the occupation of the home by the child and postponing the sale until the child is eighteen, during which time the mother and child have sole rights of occupation, may avoid the statutory charge as the child has obtained an interest in possession only. Although the child, who is the assisted party, has preserved the right of occupation, there is no beneficial interest in the child's favour to which the charge can attach and so the home escapes the charge. Nonetheless, this would not succeed in avoiding the charge if the parents are also disputing their respective beneficial interests in s 30 LPA 1925 proceedings where one or other of them is legally aided. Here the charge will attach to the preserved legally aided partner's share to the extent of their legal costs, and here the effect of the charge cannot be postponed.

The orders that can be made in relation to the family home on relationship breakdown, pursuant to paras 1(2)(d) and (e) Sch 1, will be considered in Chapters 9 and 10.

Chapter 9

The family home on relationship breakdown: rented property

1. Introduction

On relationship breakdown jointly owned or shared property commonly becomes a focus for dispute, and it is at this time that many cohabitees belatedly regret not having made advance provision for such an eventuality. The family home, whether rented or purchased, is often both the couple's most valuable asset and the place where one or both of them wish to continue to live. Other jointly acquired property may also become an issue when parties are separating.

In contrast with divorce, the court does not always have power to intervene to resolve a dispute, particularly where it involves rented accommodation. This means that agreement or total stalemate may be a couple's only courses. Furthermore, even where the court does have power to decide issues, the law does not formally distinguish between separating cohabitees and other co-owners in dispute. Thus principles of property law are applied by the courts and, with the limited exception of recently introduced remedies available where there are children, family law considerations do not specifically apply. Whether the home is rented or purchased, the relevant law is complex and in places uncertain, making legal advice both imperative, yet difficult. This chapter will attempt to identify and clarify the legal issues to be addressed in relation to rented homes; Chapter 10 concentrates on owner-occupied property. In Chapter 3, the various types of tenure of a family home were discussed. On breakdown, the first issue is to identify the tenure and consequent legal rights. Any advice to cohabitees on their housing position following breakdown is governed by the legal implications of their arrangements during cohabitation. The rules relating to assignment of tenancies, the options exercised by cohabitees who have jointly purchased a property, and homelessness legislation discussed earlier, are all relevant. It is always wise to consider the possibility of conciliation or mediation before litigation. There are now many agencies offering professional mediation and conciliation in relation to property disputes on relationship breakdown.

Particularly in relation to property disputes, the cost of legal proceedings and, where appropriate, the effect of the Legal Aid Board's statutory charge, must be at the forefront of a practitioner's mind and makes the possibility of compromise an important avenue to explore. It can indeed be one which a client may literally not be able to afford to ignore, although the statutory charge will not apply to rented accommodation which is recovered or preserved (see *Curling* v *The Law Society* [1985] 1 All ER 705).

Many cohabitees live in rented accommodation. Where the home is rented and there are no children of the relationship, there is often little option on breakdown but for one partner to concede the home to the other, as the court does not have jurisdiction to resolve any dispute. Even if there is agreement, only where a tenancy is capable of assignment can a straightforward resolution of the situation be guaranteed. Whether or not a tenancy is assignable depends on the terms of the tenancy agreement and the security of tenure afforded by the type of tenancy in question.

Where there are children, the court may be able to intervene and order that the tenancy be transferred to one parent for the benefit of the child pursuant to para 1, Sch 1 Children Act 1989 ("CA 1989"), which has re-enacted s 11B Guardianship of Minors Act 1971 ("GMA

1971"). Here again, much may depend on the nature and terms of the tenancy. Alternatively, it may be possible for one partner to be excluded for the benefit of the children by virtue of the court's inherent jurisdiction to protect children. The additional remedies limited to cohabitees with children will be discussed separately in the following sections.

The court has no power to intervene where the home is rented and there are no children, unless there is domestic violence which justifies the exclusion of the violent partner, pursuant to the Domestic Violence and Matrimonial Proceedings Act 1976 ("DVMPA 1976"), as discussed in Chapter 6. The position of cohabitees without children in rented accommodation is governed by the law of landlord and tenant which cannot be mitigated in any way on relationship breakdown. There will be different consequences depending on whether breakdown has produced agreement between the parties in relation to the home, desertion or non-co-operation by one partner; or a dispute where both partners wish to remain in the home. Given that the law currently permits a number of different types of tenancy to co-exist, and given the complexity of the law, the rules relating to assignment and surrender are considered in relation to each type of tenancy in turn.

2. Joint tenancies – the general position

Any form of joint tenancy gives each joint tenant the right to occupy the accommodation let, and renders each jointly and severally liable to pay the rent regardless of whether or not in occupation. These factors raise obvious problems on breakdown of a relationship, even where there is broad agreement as to who should remain in the home. One partner will wish to remain in occupation without the other partner exercising the right to occupy, and the departing partner will not want to remain liable to the landlord for the rent in the event of non-payment by the former partner.

Overcoming these problems may depend on the assignability of the tenancy. Where the joint tenancy permits assignment, there is little difficulty if the parties agree a solution. Where there is agreement, but the tenancy cannot be assigned, perhaps the best protection that can be achieved is for the parties to enter into a deed of indemnity. The remaining partner will agree to indemnify the departing partner against any liability in respect of the rent, the departing partner agreeing in turn not to exercise his or her rights of occupation. In this way, the landlord does not have to know that one partner has left and the remaining partner remains a tenant. However, notwithstanding the indemnity, the departing partner will still be liable to the landlord for the rent in the event of non-payment. Also, it is not clear whether the courts would uphold an agreement to suspend legal rights of occupation. As shall be seen, where there is no agreement, one joint tenant may unilaterally terminate a periodic tenancy regardless of whether or not the former partner wishes to remain, with varying effects on the remaining partner.

3. Rent Act tenancies

(a) Joint contractual tenancies (excluding protected shortholds)
Where the parties agree who should continue to occupy the home, the situation is relatively simple. If there is no covenant against assignment or where there is a qualified covenant but the landlord consents, (and consent should not be unreasonably withheld – s 19 Landlord and Tenant Act 1927), the departing partner can assign his or her interest in the joint tenancy to the former partner, who will then become the sole contractual tenant. Assignment should be in writing, in the form of a deed, witnessed in the normal way to comply with s 52 LPA 1925.

Where assignment is not possible and there is a periodic tenancy, the departing partner can serve notice to quit on the landlord. Providing the notice is in the form required by the agreement and complies with s 5 Protection from Eviction Act 1977, giving a minimum of four weeks notice in writing, it operates to determine the contractual tenancy in accordance with the decision in *Greenwich* v *McGrady* (1983) 81 LGR 28. However, in contrast to the periodic secure or periodic assured tenant's position, it does not operate to terminate the remaining partner's right of occupation. Instead the latter becomes the statutory tenant of the premises, providing he or she continues to occupy the home as his/her only or principal residence (see *Lloyd* v *Sadler* [1978] 2 All ER 529). At the same time, the notice determines the departing partner's liability to pay the rent and, of course, the right to occupy. The remaining partner will only be the statutory, and not the contractual, tenant of the premises, which can have certain disadvantages.

A fixed term tenancy cannot be surrendered by one joint tenant alone, but only by all the joint tenants acting together (*Leek and Moorlands Building Society* v *Clark* [1952] 2 All ER 492 (CA)) and thus effective assignment to the remaining joint tenant is dependent upon the terms of the tenancy permitting assignment.

Where the parties do not agree, or where the departing partner has deserted the remaining partner, there are various options. Where one partner has left the premises, the remaining periodic joint tenant can himself or herself give notice to quit to the landlord, and providing he/she then continues in occupation of the home, the remaining partner becomes the sole statutory tenant of the premises. By this action the departing partner loses the right to occupy and liability to pay rent, but the remaining partner unfortunately thereby gives the landlord a discretionary ground for possession under Case 5 of Sch 5, Part I Rent Act 1977. The landlord would have to prove not only that the remaining partner gave notice to quit, but also that it is reasonable to make a possession order (s 98(1)). Given that Rent Act tenancies are generally unattractive to landlords, they may be keen to attempt to obtain possession in such a situation and advisors must warn of the possible consequences of a tenant's notice.

Where there are no children and joint tenant cohabitees cannot agree who should remain, the only means the court has to exclude one partner is an ouster order granted pursuant to DVMPA 1976 if there are grounds. This possibility has been discussed in Chapter 6 (see pages 119 to 121). It is a remedy likely to provide only a temporary solution unless the circumstances are exceptional. Such orders are usually granted for a period of up to three months only, although an application can be made to renew the order.

Where there is violence and an ouster order has been granted, the *McGrady* notice to quit device could be used to terminate the excluded partner's occupation rights, subject to a note of caution. It is arguable that for one joint tenant unilaterally to give notice to quit constitutes a breach of trust for which the other joint tenant may seek to be compensated, as discussed below.

If neither assignment nor exclusion under the DVMPA 1976 is possible, notwithstanding the relationship breakdown, both joint tenants continue to have occupation rights. Unless one of them leaves voluntarily, the parties may have to remain living under the same roof. This highlights the main problem of a joint tenancy on relationship breakdown – where there are no children, there is simply no mechanism for resolving a dispute.

(b) Joint statutory tenancies

In this situation, where there is agreement as to who should remain, no problem arises. Both joint statutory tenants have occupation rights, but once the departing tenant ceases to occupy the premises as his or her residence and abandons any intention to return, then that person ceases to be a statutory tenant and ceases to have rights of occupation (see s 2(1)(a) Rent Act 1977). A notification by either tenant to the landlord that one but not both of them has ceased to reside in the premises should ensure that the liability of the departing partner to pay rent ceases, and falls solely on the remaining partner, who becomes the sole statutory tenant of the home and whose occupation rights are unaffected.

However, should both joint statutory tenants wish to remain in occupation, then unless there are children or there is violence, again, no mechanism exists to resolve the dispute. Where there is violence, an ouster order may be obtained, but this is usually for a period of three months only. An intention to return on the part of the excluded partner keeps the statutory tenancy alive, but an indefinite period of exclusion by court order seems to ensure the tenancy is effectively transferred to the occupying partner.

(c) Sole contractual Rent Act tenancies

Whether a non-tenant cohabitee, whom the parties agree should stay, can lawfully remain in occupation depends on the terms of the tenancy agreement. There is no difficulty where the tenancy agreement does not contain a covenant against assignment, as a deed of assignment in the proper form will be effective to transfer the tenancy. An oral tenancy where no notice to quit has been served will remain contractual and will therefore usually be assignable.

Where there is a covenant against assignment, even if the sole tenant wishes his or her former partner to remain in occupation, this may not be possible. If the tenant, after departure, having made a *de facto* assignment of the tenancy, were to continue to pay the rent to the landlord, this would constitute breach of the tenancy agreement and give the landlord grounds for possession. However, if the landlord, with knowledge of the facts, continues to accept the rent, then it is arguable that he has waived the breach and accepted the cohabitee as a new tenant. If at any point the landlord serves notice to quit, then, unless it can be argued that a new tenancy has been granted, on expiry, the contractual tenancy comes to an end. A statutory tenancy arises only if the tenant occupies the home as his/her only or principal residence or can show they have not relinquished possession despite a temporary absence and there is a definite intention to return. The longer the tenant is away, the less likely it is that such an argument will be convincing.

Once there is a statutory rather than a contractual tenancy, neither the absent tenant nor the non-tenant partner remaining in the property has a defence to possession proceedings. Unfortunately, in contrast with the position of spouses, occupation by a cohabitee is not sufficient to create or keep alive a statutory tenancy (*Colin Smith Music Ltd* v *Ridge* [1975] 1 WLR 463 (CA)), nor does a cohabitee have any right to pay the rent on behalf of the tenant, which is a particular problem where the non-tenant partner has been deserted.

If a non-tenant partner remains in occupation with the landlord's knowledge and rent paid by that partner is accepted, then, as noted above, it is arguable that a new tenancy has been granted. If this arose before 15 January 1989, it will be a Rent Act protected tenancy. If it arose after that date, then an assured tenancy has been granted, which will entitle the landlord to charge a market rent, but will afford the new tenant security of tenure in accordance with the provisions of the Housing Act 1988. If a landlord is approached for consent to a new tenancy, the likely outcome is at best an offer of an assured shorthold tenancy, which will give security for a minimum six months, but is thereafter determinable by the landlord without need for grounds for possession other than the expiry of the initial fixed term and compliance with the statutory procedures.

Where there is a dispute between the parties, if the cohabitee who is the tenant wishes to remain, then where there are no children and there are no grounds for an ouster order under the DVMPA 1976, the former partner has no right to remain in the home. Indeed, the tenant cohabitee can force the estranged partner to leave by means of possession proceedings, as he or she is no more than a licensee who has no right of occupation once the licence to occupy is revoked. The situation where there is violence has been explored in Chapter 6. Where there are grounds for an ouster order but there are no children, this remedy is likely to give them temporary respite only. Another problem is that the remaining cohabitee cannot force the landlord to accept rent, and the DVMPA 1976, unlike the Matrimonial Homes Act 1983 ("MHA 1983"), does not make specific provision for payment of rent in such circumstances. Non-payment may of course lead a landlord to terminate the contractual tenancy and commence possession proceedings, which the ousted partner may not wish to defend. Neither can the landlord be forced to accept rent from the occupying non-tenant partner, notwithstanding the ouster order. However, the court must be satisfied that a landlord in that situation has proved that it is also reasonable to make a possession order as required by s 98(1) RA 1977.

In addition, a vengeful ousted partner may give notice to quit to the landlord. This will be in breach of the order made under the DVMPA 1976 and thus contempt of court where the order is expressed to allow the applicant to enter and remain. Nonetheless it may lose the applicant the right to reside there as possession can then be obtained by the landlord and no statutory tenancy will arise.

(d) Sole statutory tenancies

Statutory tenancies are a personal right and cannot be assigned unless the landlord consents and is a party to the deed of assignment (see Sch 1, para13 Rent Act 1977). Given the protection and rent restriction which a Rent Act tenancy affords, the landlord's consent is most unlikely to be forthcoming. The statutory tenancy is wholly dependent upon the tenant's occupying the premises as his or her only or principal residence. Thus it seems that any right to continued occupation by the non-tenant partner depends either upon the statutory tenant partner's having an intention to return (which is not likely to be found in the context of breakdown), or upon the landlord's expressly or impliedly creating a new tenancy in favour of the remaining partner, who has no right as such to pay the rent as discussed in the preceding section. A tenancy arising after 15 January 1989 will be assured rather than Rent Act protected in any event.

Occupation by a cohabitee has not yet been accepted as equivalent to occupation by a spouse which, by virtue of MHA 1983, is deemed to be occupation by the tenant for these purposes (see *Colin Smith Music Ltd* v *Ridge,* above). Where there is a fixed term ouster injunction excluding the statutory tenant, it is not thought this would prejudice the statutory tenancy. However, the partner of a statutory tenant, even where there are children (see further below), will be unable to remain in the accommodation in the long term, and can be forced to leave by his or her partner or, if deserted and alone in the premises, by the landlord.

4. Tenancies governed by the Housing Act 1988

Assured tenancies will be found most commonly in the independent sector, and will be granted mainly by housing associations. Although they can be granted in the private sector, it is thought that most private sector landlords prefer assured shorthold tenancies which afford tenants very little security, although during the initial fixed term period are treated as fixed term assured tenancies with regard to assignability.

(a) Joint assured tenancies
On breakdown, the joint tenants each retain the right to occupy, and remain jointly and severally liable to pay rent; once again, in the absence of violence or children, the court cannot adjust the occupation rights.

In the case of a fixed term tenancy, assignment is permitted where the terms of the tenancy agreement do not prohibit it. Thus if there is agreement between the cohabitees and assignment is possible, the situation is simple. All that is required is a deed of assignment in proper form.

However, in the case of periodic tenancies, regardless of whether they are periodic from the outset or are statutory periodic tenancies which arise on expiry of the fixed term, a covenant against assignment without the landlord's express consent is implied by s 15 Housing Act 1988 ("HA 1988") (unless, in the case of an expressly periodic tenancy, the agreement provides otherwise, or a premium is payable on the grant or renewal of the tenancy). The statutory proviso that consent cannot unreasonably be withheld is specifically excluded. Thus, in direct contrast to the Rent Act position, an oral periodic assured tenancy where nothing at all is said about assignment, is unassignable without the landlord's express consent. This is also the case with statutory periodic tenancies arising after the expiry of the fixed term, even though the original fixed term tenancy permitted assignment. The only way to achieve certainty is therefore to obtain the landlord's consent. It is thought that many housing association assured tenancies will provide for consent to assignment between joint tenants and/or cohabitees on relationship breakdown where there is agreement between the parties. A private sector assured tenant is likely to encounter more difficulty.

Again in contrast to the Rent Act position, a notice to quit given by one of two joint tenants will bind all, and thus bring a periodic assured tenancy to an end in accordance with the principle confirmed in *Greenwich* v *McGrady* [1983] 81 LGR 288 (CA). No statutory tenancy arises by operation of law as in the Rent Act situation, and accordingly the landlord will be entitled to possession. However, it seems that a notice to quit by one joint tenant will not operate to determine a fixed term assured tenancy (see s 5(2)(b) and s 45(2) HA 1988 which, read together, confirm the common law rule that it requires all the joint tenants to determine the fixed term tenancy).

Where one cohabitee deserts a joint tenant partner, the tenancy remains an assured joint tenancy, as s 1(1)(b) HA 1988 requires that just one of the joint tenants occupies the premises as his only or principal home to qualify for protection. A housing association landlord may agree to accept a notice to quit from the deserted joint tenant and to grant him or her a new sole assured tenancy. This has come to be known as the *McGrady* device, and is the only means of determining the deserter's occupation rights where there are no children. However, a joint tenant who does this may risk an action by the former partner for breach of trust, in respect of which damages could be awarded. Thus, although this device holds attractions for the deserted or battered partner who has obtained an ouster order, there is a risk of litigation. However, as it would be an action in equity, any remedy is discretionary and subject to equitable principles, which it is hoped would assist a "deserving" remaining partner.

(b) Sole assured tenancies
Assignability of a sole assured tenancy depends on the landlord's express consent, and where the non-tenant wishes to remain in occupation, the landlord must be approached.

Residence by the tenant is required to continue security, and at the present time residence by a cohabitee is not sufficient (*Colin Smith Music Ltd* v *Ridge,* above). Thus once the sole tenant leaves, the protection afforded by the Act falls, as the tenant's leaving must amount to a "surrender or other action" by the tenant which brings the tenancy to an end (s 5(1)(b)). The landlord, on discovery of the situation, can obtain possession. Alternatively, the landlord may be prepared to grant the remaining partner a new tenancy, quite possibly, in the private sector, at an increased rent.

Once a notice to quit is served by the tenant, then again the tenancy is surrendered and there can be no defence to possession proceedings. Acceptance of rent from the remaining partner, who has no right to pay the rent may constitute evidence that a new tenancy has been granted, which in turn may assist the remaining partner's position.

(c) Assured shorthold
Assured shortholds are possibly the most popular form of private sector tenancy, as on the expiry of the initial fixed term of a minimum of six months, a landlord can obtain possession by complying with the statutory notice provisions and needs no ground for possession (see ss 20 & 21 HA 1988). In this situation, other than the protection afford-

ed for the initial fixed term, neither the tenant nor a non-tenant wishing to remain has any security of tenure, although a departing tenant remains liable for the rent. Only an indemnity to pay the rent and any legal costs incurred by the departing tenant as a result of the partner's continued occupation can assist the position between the parties, but there is no protection from ultimate eviction by the landlord.

5. Secure tenancies

A local authority tenant will usually have a periodic secure tenancy, now governed by the Housing Act 1985. Housing association tenancies granted before 15 January 1989 will also be secure tenancies, but those granted after this date will be assured tenancies and are subject to the provisions of HA 1988 as described above.

(a) Joint secure tenancies

As with all other types of joint tenancy, secure joint tenancies confer rights of occupation and liability to pay the rent on both joint tenants. Again, security of tenure is preserved if just one of the joint tenants occupies the premises as his or her residence. Thus, where a joint tenant is deserted, he or she continues to have security and the right to remain.

However, where a partner who has left the accommodation, serves a notice to quit upon the local authority, it will terminate the periodic tenancy even though the partner wishes to remain; this is in accordance with the decision in *Greenwich* v *McGrady* (above). Thus a deserted joint tenant partner is in a vulnerable position. A remaining partner, having obtained the local authority's promise subsequently to grant a new tenancy, can himself or herself give notice to quit, but as discussed above in relation to assured tenancies, may then be open to an action for breach of trust by the former partner.

Where there are no children, nothing can be done other than persuade the outgoing partner or the landlord to agree to an assignment or new tenancy before a notice is served. Advisors should be aware of the remaining partner's vulnerability and take preventative action where possible. It is thought that an injunction restraining the deserting partner from determining the tenancy may be possible. Alternatively, an ouster injunction excluding the deserting partner and allowing the remaining partner to enter and remain in the premises may have the desired effect, but problems of service on the deserting partner may arise. Arguably, if the local authority were given notice of the ouster or restraining order, this may persuade it to grant a new tenancy if a notice to quit were served in breach of either order. Once the notice has been served, all that can be done is to ask the council to grant the remaining partner a new tenancy – a matter entirely within its discretion. However, if no duty would otherwise fall on the council to house the remaining partner, it may not be easy to persuade; ironically, a cohabitee who would be entitled to succeed to the tenancy on death may have no right to remain in the property if deserted.

Where there is agreement, the secure tenancy can be assigned to the remaining joint tenant cohabitee. Section 92 HA 1985 permits assignments to a person who would have succeeded to the tenancy on death, which includes a joint tenant, and security of tenure will be retained. However, this counts as one succession on death, as discussed in Chapter 3 (see page 57). An assignment of this nature will be achieved by both parties notifying the local authority, who will have a form for the purpose, although there is no reason why the assignment should not be achieved by means of a deed executed in accordance with s 52 LPA 1925.

(b) Sole secure tenancies

Sole secure tenancies can be assigned between cohabitees by agreement, where permitted by the terms of the tenancy, but security of tenure will be retained only if, immediately before the assignment, the remaining partner could have succeeded to the tenancy on the death of the outgoing tenant partner. Thus cohabitees who are not joint tenants but have lived together for the preceding twelve months as husband or wife can agree an assignment to the non-tenant partner (s 91(3)(c) HA 1985).

As discussed in Chapter 3 in the context of succession to tenancies on death (see pages 57 to 58), although a cohabitee does not qualify as a "spouse" (in contrast to the wording in HA 1988 Act relating to assured tenancies), he or she comes within the definition of "a member of the tenant's family", but must satisfy the twelve month residence qualification. *In Peabody Donation Fund Governors v Higgins* [1983] 1 WLR 1091, it was held that such an assignment was permissible even though the tenancy agreement contained an absolute covenant against assignment.

This provision does not permit assignment to a non-tenant cohabitee of the same sex, who cannot be regarded as a member of the tenant's family (see page 57). The benefits of a joint tenancy in this situation are more than apparent.

Similarly, in the absence of children or domestic violence which would found an ouster order, or agreement, nothing can be done to assist a non-tenant cohabitee of the opposite sex who would not qualify as a successor. The only other possibility is to see whether they are in priority need and thus owed a duty as a homeless person pursuant to the provisions of HA 1985, Part III, as discussed in Chapter 3 (see pages 65 to 74).

6. Children

Where there are children of a relationship, the court does now have power to intervene on relationship breakdown with regard to a rented family home. Where appropriate, it can make a transfer of property order to one of the parents for the benefit of the child of the relationship (para 1(2)(e) of Sch 1 CA 1989). It can also transfer property to, or settle it on, the child. It should be noted that any transfer of property to the other parent must be "for the benefit of the child". Thus it is not a mechanism that is universally applicable to all separating cohabitees with children who are in dispute over their property, but may be particularly pertinent where the family home is concerned. How widely the courts will be prepared to extend the notion of benefiting the child remains to be seen. Another limitation is that where there are children not of the relationship, the court cannot intervene; these cases depend solely on the law of landlord and tenant set out above in the context of cohabitees without children. However, the court may be willing to exercise its inherent jurisdiction to protect children. Where there is an otherwise insoluble situation between cohabitees in relation to their housing situation, it is possible, but by no means certain, that the court will exclude one parent from the home indefinitely. This remedy cannot be relied upon and will depend very much on the facts of the case; see pages 124 to 127.

(a) Transfer of property orders

As was seen in Chapter 8, the FLRA 1987 amended the GMA 1971 to enable property to be transferred for the benefit of a child of an unmarried family for the first time. Paragraph 1 of Sch 1 has re-enacted s 11B GMA 1971 and gives the court discretion, on the application of a parent to, *inter alia*, make an order pursuant to para1(2)(e) transferring "property" from one parent to the other for the benefit of the child, or to the child him/herself. It was seen in Chapter 8 that the courts have not been keen in the matrimonial jurisdiction to transfer property directly to a child. However, it is possible that different considerations will be applied where the parents are unmarried. It is not thought, though, that a court would order the transfer of a tenancy to a child under eighteen.

The considerations to which the court must have regard are set out in para 4 and are detailed in Chapter 8 above. Broadly, they comprise the income, earning capacity, needs, obligations and responsibilities of the parents; the financial needs and resources if any of the child; any disability of the child and the manner in which the child was intended to be educated or trained. In addition, all the circumstances of the case must be considered. However, the duration of the relationship and its stability will not be specifically examined, nor will the conduct of either party.

Perhaps surprisingly, the welfare of the child is not the first consideration as it is in the matrimonial jurisdiction, and thus it seems that there is room for a court to take the view that the father's property rights outweigh other considerations. Section 1 CA 1989, which contains the welfare principle, does not apply in relation to applications for financial provision.

The first problem that may arise in relation to the rented family home is whether or not it comes within the definition of "property" and thus whether the court has jurisdiction to transfer it. Although the wording of para 1 mirrors that of s 24 MCA 1973, most property transfers on divorce or judicial separation are effected under the MHA 1983 which specifically gives the court power to transfer all types of tenancy, and such a transfer takes place not following an assignment pursuant to the order but "by virtue of the order and without further assurance" (Sch 1, para 2(1) MHA 1983). This avoids any problem where there is an absolute covenant against assignment.

A further problem is avoided by s 1 MHA 1983 which gives a spouse occupation rights, a right to occupy on behalf of their tenant spouse and the right to pay the rent for the matrimonial home until decree absolute. Furthermore, the court may direct during the marriage that such occupation rights may continue after decree absolute pursuant to s 2(1). None of these provisions applies to cohabitees who, even where there are children, may remain vulnerable to the partner's determining the tenancy, failing to pay the rent, or losing statutory protection where they no longer reside in the home, as has been discussed.

It is therefore necessary to look closely at the position of cohabitees with children in rented accommodation where the partner with whom it is proposed the children will live (the residential parent), seeks a transfer of property order for the benefit of the child. Whether or not the resident parent is able to preserve the home for the benefit of the child will often depend, even where there is agreement between the parties, on the nature and terms of the tenancy of the family home and the court's interpretation of its new-found powers in relation to former cohabitees with children. Once again the assignability of the tenancy may be critical as the order will require one parent to assign his/her interest to the other. Fortunately, some guidance can be found in cases where transfer of property orders have been sought under s 24 MCA 1973 in which the MHA 1983 jurisdiction was not invoked.

(i) Is a tenancy "property"? Hale v Hale [1975] 2 All ER 1090 (CA) concerned a wife's application for transfer of the matrimonial home which was a weekly contractual Rent Act tenancy granted to the husband alone; it was argued that such a tenancy did not constitute property. However, the court did not agree. It was said by Megaw LJ at p. 1094e: "I regard the position as really being clear, substantially beyond argument. Where there is a tenancy, whether it be a weekly

tenancy or any other tenancy, that tenancy is property;". Stephenson LJ endorsed this view at p.1095a:

"Is this weekly tenancy property which can be transferred ... under s 24(1)(a) MCA 1973? 'Property' in that Act is left undefined. We only know from the terms of the subsection that it may be 'either in possession or reversion'. I see no reason to restrict it to exclude anything which would in ordinary language be described as property, real or personal, except that it must be transferable."

Accordingly, as the relevant provision in Sch 1 para 1(2)(e) CA 1989 follows the wording of s 24(1)(a) MCA 1973 exactly, it is submitted that it can be safely assumed that all tenancies are property and are capable of being the subject of an order between unmarried parents for the benefit of their child.

However, another more difficult question follows.

(ii) Which tenancies can be transferred? It seems clear that those tenancies which are capable of assignment by agreement between the parties as discussed above, could undoubtedly also be transferred pursuant to a transfer of property order. Where the only difficulty has been the absence of agreement as to who should remain in the home with the child, the court can now make a decision and order the non-residential parent to transfer the tenancy to the former partner for the benefit of the child. Thus any tenancy, whether vested in joint names or the sole name of the non-resident parent, whether assured or Rent Act protected, which does not contain an express or implied covenant against assignment, can be the subject of a transfer of property order. However, as the actual transfer will take place by virtue of a deed of assignment pursuant to the court order, and will not vest automatically following the making of the order (in contrast to orders made under the MHA 1983), it is open to question whether a tenancy which does contain an express or implied covenant against assignment can be transferred under Sch 1 para 1(2)(e).

In the case of secure tenancies, although assignment is generally prohibited, assignment to a person who is qualified to succeed the tenant if the tenant had died immediately before assignment is permitted under s 91 HA 1985. Thus where the parents were joint tenants or where they had lived in the home as husband and wife for twelve months preceding the application, a transfer of property order compelling such an assignment under the CA 1989 will be possible.

In all other cases, the consent of the landlord will be required to be certain that the court will exercise its power to order transfer. In the case of statutory tenancies in the sole name of the non-resident parent, as assignment can be effected with the express consent of the landlord only, the court will certainly not make an order without proof of such consent. In other cases not concerning a Rent Act statutory tenancy where there is an express or implied covenant against assignment, it may be possible to persuade the court that there are good reasons for making the order notwithstanding the absence of the landlord's consent; see below.

In the case of joint tenants a landlord may be more willing to consent to the transfer to one of them, and it is wise to attempt to obtain the landlord's consent to the proposed transfer. The courts may in any event, before considering the matter further, require approaches to have been made, but where this may prejudice the position of a non-tenant parent, there are clear reasons not to put the landlord on notice, particularly where it is a private sector tenancy.

Where there is a qualified or absolute covenant against assignment and where the tenancy is not a Rent Act statutory tenancy, it seems it is still worthwhile for the proposed resident joint or non-tenant parent to make an application without the landlord's consent having been sought, or even where it has been refused, for a transfer of property order for the benefit of the child.

A court may be reluctant to make an order where the landlord has not consented and there is a covenant against assignment, because of the risk that the transfer would be ineffective and all that would be achieved would be to render both tenant and non-tenant parents, not to speak of the child, homeless. However, as Hoath (*Public Housing Law*, Sweet & Maxwell,1989, pages 265-267) argues convincingly in relation to the transfer of secure tenancies under s 24 MCA 1973, this may not in fact be the case. An assignment pursuant to the court order would place the tenant in breach of the terms of the tenancy agreement. Thus although such an assignment may give a landlord a ground for possession, it does not operate to determine the tenancy and render it ineffective, as decided in *Manor Farm Ltd* v *Seymour Plant Sales and Hire Ltd (No. 2)* [1979] 1 WLR 379, where it was held that an assignment in breach of a covenant caused the interest to pass nonetheless. This reasoning was accepted in *Peabody Donation Fund Governors* v *Higgins* (above) where a secure tenancy assigned in breach of the terms of the tenancy agreement was held to be effective.

The next question is whether the landlord would be successful in an action for possession following assignment pursuant to a court order, for, if so, nothing will have been achieved. In the case of contractual Rent Act tenancies, assured tenancies and secure tenancies the relevant statutes make breach of a term of the tenancy agreement a discretionary (not a mandatory) ground for possession, and the landlord would have to prove both that the ground for possession exists, and that it is reasonable to make a possession order. It is thought that, given the assignment was effected due to a court order, that there are very strong arguments to say that it is not reasonable to make an order for possession, but this has yet to be tested in the courts. If this argument is successful, then where there are children this could prove an effective means of transferring all types of tenancy between cohabitees on breakdown, except statutory tenancies in the sole name of the non-resident parent where the landlord refuses to consent. Thus even where the parties agree but where there is a joint or sole tenancy with a covenant against assignment, it would be possible to overcome the problems by obtaining a transfer order by consent to the resident parent for the benefit of the child.

However, where there is a private landlord in particular, the courts may be reluctant to force a new tenant upon a landlord, and may even feel it inappropriate to place the welfare of the child above the property rights of the tenant parent. It is submitted that where there has been a joint tenancy, the courts are likely to be readier to order a transfer of property order. Much will depend on the individual facts of a case, but where a non-tenant resident parent is likely to be rehoused by the local authority if homeless, and where, for example, staying contact is envisaged to the non-resident parent, it may not be felt appropriate to divest that parent of their property rights, particularly if he or she has nowhere else to live.

(iii) Procedure and timing: Applications for transfer of property orders can be made to the county court or High Court only, by completing the appropriate form introduced by the Family Proceedings Rules 1991. Any additional evidence should be in the form of a dated and signed statement containing the appropriate declaration as to the maker's belief in its truth.

A problem arises where a respondent is a sole tenant (statutory, secure or assured) and has left the home. For as soon as the tenant cohabitee leaves and is no longer occupying the accommodation as his or her residence, the security of tenure falls and the tenancy ceases to exist. However, it seems that it is enough for the tenancy to have been in existence at the time of the application rather than at the hearing date. In the House of Lords decision in *Lewis* v *Lewis* [1985] 2 All ER 449, it was held that the court had jurisdiction to transfer a statutory tenancy which was subsisting at the date of the application under the MHA 1983, despite its having been determined before the date of the hearing. This reasoning was followed by the Court of Appeal in the case of a secure tenancy in *Thompson* v *Elmbridge BC* [1987] 1 WLR 1425. It is submitted that there is no reason why this cannot be extended to applications for property transfer orders between cohabitees for the benefit of a child. It is clear that an application for a transfer of property order in this situation must be lodged without delay to protect the remaining cohabitee's position.

In addition, where it is feared that a joint or sole tenant respondent may intend to determine the tenancy by notice to quit, which would leave the court without any property capable of transfer and the applicant homeless, an *ex parte* application for an order restraining the service of a notice to quit by the respondent pending the hearing should be urgently considered, and, where granted, served promptly upon the respondent. An application for emergency legal aid would be appropriate. For once the tenancy is determined, there can be no possibility of preserving the home. There are of course no provisions equivalent to those contained in s 1 MHA 1983 enabling the court to order that a cohabitee has occupation rights of the family home. Where it is not possible to preserve the tenancy, the applicant would be homeless, in priority need and in no way intentionally homeless. The local housing authority would therefore be obliged to secure accommodation in accordance with the provisions of HA 1985 Part III (see page 74).

Desertion by a sole tenant cohabitee who does not give the landlord notice may cause an insuperable problem. As s 1 MHA 1983 does not extend to cohabitees, a non-tenant has no occupation rights nor any right to pay the rent to the landlord. A deserted non-tenant partner may not be able to make an application under the CA 1989 provisions, as he/she may not be aware of the necessity to do so until after the tenant partner has left, at which point, if occupation as a residence is a requirement of the continued existence of the tenancy, the tenancy has already ceased to exist. The position in relation to the deserted partner of a statutory tenant seeking a transfer of property order was left open in *Lewis,* and it seems the point remains to be decided.

Where it will not prejudice the applicant, and where there is an absolute or qualified covenant against assignment, the landlord's consent to the transfer, subject to the court order being made, should be sought, although there is no requirement in the Act to seek the landlord's consent. Unlike divorce proceedings, where a decree *nisi* must be obtained before applying for a transfer of property order, here there is no reason to delay an application. Particularly where it is known who will be the residential parent, an application can and should be made, to protect the resident parent's position, as soon as it is apparent that there may be a dispute about the home. There have not yet been any reported cases relating to applications for transfer of property orders concerning the rented family home. Many of the problems outlined above could, it is submitted, be best resolved by extending the relevant provisions of the MHA 1983 to cohabitees with pending transfer of property applications. Following the House of Lords decision in *Richards* v *Richards* (above, page 119), which made clear that the criteria set out in s 1(3) MHA 1983 were to be applied in deciding the merits of ouster applications under the DVMPA 1976, the Court of Appeal in *Lee* v *Lee* (above, page 119) confirmed that the MHA criteria similarly extended to applications under the 1976 Act made by cohabitees. However, it is thought that any further extension of the 1983 Act to cohabitees will require legislative intervention.

(b) Exclusion orders and the inherent jurisdiction to protect children
Where it is not possible to make an application for a transfer of property order under Sch 1 CA 1989, the court may possibly agree to use its inherent jurisdiction to protect children referred to in *Richards,* and make an ouster order for the benefit of the child ancillary to a residence order under CA 1989 (and formerly a custody order under the GMA 1971), even though there is no violence. This course is likely to be one of last resort, but there is authority for the court to do this by virtue of exercising its inherent jurisdiction to promote the welfare of the child and to protect the resident parent's rights under the joint tenancy. It is unclear whether such an order is consistent with the decision in *Richards* v *Richards* (see page 126), but may be the court's only possible course of action, if it considers it appropriate to intervene. For if, where there are children, a joint tenant refuses to leave and the court cannot compel him or her to leave by a transfer of property order under Sch 1, para 1(2) CA 1989, then nothing can resolve the stalemate. The parties must remain living under the same roof unless there are grounds for an ouster order under the DVMPA or the court sees fit to exercise its inherent jurisdiction. Were the resident parent to leave the home in this situation, he or she is likely to be found intentionally homeless. Thus no remedy can be found in this way. As has been seen (page 171), however, the welfare of the child is not the court's first or paramount consideration in relation to applications for transfer of property orders, and thus it may be that the court will not provide a remedy to resolve the situation even where there are children.

Where there is violence, then the provisions of DVMPA 1976 apply, as discussed in Chapter 6. Where there are children in a violent home and no possibility of obtaining a transfer of property order for the benefit of the child, this may be an appropriate situation for the court to grant an extended ouster order. However, again, unless the order specifically states that the applicant be permitted to enter and remain at the premises, there seems to be nothing to prevent the ousted tenant partner from giving the landlord notice to quit the premises, which in many situations would determine the tenancy. The remaining partner should not be deemed here to be intentionally homeless and should be rehoused.

The exercise of the court's inherent jurisdiction is not of course limited to the rented family home. However, it is thought that it is most likely to be used in this situation, if at all, for where the home has been purchased the court has wider powers to intervene, as will be seen in the next chapter.

Chapter 10

The home on relationship breakdown: owner-occupied property and other arrangements

1. Introduction

Where the home is owned by one or both cohabitees, the court will always have jurisdiction to resolve a dispute by ordering the immediate or postponed sale of the property and the division of the proceeds of sale in a specified way (s 30 LPA 1925). Thus the stalemate which can arise in relation to the rented family home does not occur. That is not to say that ownership disputes between cohabitees are best decided by the courts; as always, negotiation and agreement are preferable to litigation.

If there is a cohabitation contract in the form of a deed, dealing with beneficial ownership of the home and the division of property on breakdown, the courts will probably give effect to it, as discussed in Chapter 1. It there is a declaration of trust, either in the conveyance or in a separate document executed as a deed, setting out the beneficial interests, the courts will, in the absence of fraud or mistake, treat this as conclusive. With the possible exception of cases where there are children of the relationship, there will be little reason for the parties to go to court, as their interests will have been clearly defined. As home ownership increases, financial considerations make it expedient for cohabiting couples to pool their resources and buy jointly, and legal advisors have a critical role to play in establishing at the outset a couple's intentions when they purchase the property and ensure that the title deeds clearly reflect this. Not to do so is clearly negligent (see *Walker* v *Hall,* and *Taylor and Harman* v *Warner* discussed below). Whilst it is difficult for couples and their legal advisors to foresee every eventuality, it is perfectly possible for declarations of trust to establish beneficial interests contingent upon the size of future contributions to a mortgage, as well as to reflect unequal contributions to the capital deposit, requiring only arithmetical calculations to be made on breakdown to realise each party's share. Cohabitation contracts can also set out proposed agreements for the division of property on separation, and for the effect on the beneficial interests in the property of temporary inability of either party to contribute to the mortgage due.

Where there is a declaration of trust or binding agreement relating to the beneficial ownership of the home, this does not of course prevent an application being made, where there are children, for a transfer of property order for the benefit of a child under para 1(2)(e) of Sch 1 CA 1989. The jurisdiction of the court to order transfer of property cannot be ousted, but the property capable of transfer can at least be made readily identifiable by virtue of an express agreement between the parties and will save the court having to establish the interests for itself.

Where there is no conclusive express declaration of trust or cohabitation agreement relating to the cohabitees' beneficial interests, the rights of the respective parties on breakdown depend in the first instance on the legal and equitable ownership of the family home as established by the title deeds. However, these are subject to any resulting or constructive trusts, or claim to equitable proprietary estoppel, which a court deems to have been created by the parties in relation to the property. Thus where the parties have lived in a property of which the legal and equitable estate is on the face of it vested in the sole name of one of them, this is not necessarily conclusive. Conversely, unequal contributions to a property vested in joint names

of the parties without further declaration as to their respective interests, may lead to a conclusive presumption that the property is beneficially owned in equal shares, as discussed below. The rights of third
parties, particularly mortgagees, are also likely to be significant on
breakdown and steps to be taken in this regard must also be considered.

However, the first task on breakdown is to establish the legal ownership of the family home. Secondly, any steps necessary to protect
the client's interest in that property should be identified.

2. Establishing legal ownership

Most clients are aware of the details of ownership of the family home,
but this is not always the case. Where the title is registered, a Land
Registry search of any title, to discover the registered proprietor, can
now be made by virtue of the provisions of the Land Registration Act
1988. If the title number is not known the search should be combined
with an index map search.

If the mortgagee is known, it can be approached for details of ownership, or for the deeds, upon the usual undertaking as to safe custody
and return. Refusal to release the deeds can only be on the grounds
that the client is not a legal owner of the property, or that they have
been released for another purpose. It is usually a good idea to inform
the mortgagee of a dispute between co-owners and to obtain its undertaking to give notice to the legal adviser before issuing any possession
proceedings if there are mortgage arrears. Where the property is lease-
hold, enquiries should be made about any arrears of ground rent or
service charges, and advice must be given in relation to the risk of
forfeiture for non-payment.

The next stage will depend on whether or not the client cohabitee is
a legal owner. Joint owners will be jointly and severally liable for
payment of mortgage instalments and of ground rent and service
charge due under a jointly owned lease, and it may be possible to
claim income support, or increased income support, to cover these
payments where the estranged co-owner is failing to do so. The property cannot be sold without the co-owner's consent or an order from

the court. Beneficial joint tenants may also need to sever the joint tenancy, and another urgent enquiry will relate to the need to revise any Will that has been made.

Where the title documents reveal that the client's partner is the sole legal owner of the home, the client does not have the protection of a right of occupation afforded to spouses under the MHA 1983. If in actual occupation of the home, the absent partner is unlikely to be able to sell the property without the occupying partner's agreement. In the case of registered land, the occupying partner will have an overriding interest, which will bind a purchaser, but this cannot be protected by placing a caution on the register. However, it is for a purchaser to make enquiries of overriding interests (see *William & Glyn's Bank* v *Boland* (Chapter 3 above)).

In the case of unregistered land a person in actual occupation is in a more precarious situation, as it is not possible to register any land charge protecting occupation, yet only a purchaser with actual or constructive knowledge of the occupation will be bound. In *Caunce* v *Caunce* [1969] 1 WLR 286, occupation itself did not fix a purchaser with constructive notice of a wife's occupation and it seems that this would extend to other occupants. Actual occupation has been interpreted quite broadly. In *Kingsnorth Finance Co* v *Tizard* [1986] 1 WLR 783, a wife who no longer slept at the matrimonial home but attended every day to look after the children and had left many of her belongings there was held to be in actual occupation.

However, the cohabitee will have no claim against the home unless he or she can show some form of equitable interest under a resulting or constructive trust or due to the equitable doctrine of proprietary estoppel. Even so, such an interest will not *per se* give any right of occupation, but only an interest in the proceeds of sale. In practice, where there is a beneficial interest of a party who is no longer in actual occupation and the land is unregistered, it is usually advisable to issue proceedings under s 41 Trustee Act 1925 for the appointment of another trustee if the legal owner refuses to do so. Proceedings under s 30 LPA 1925 can follow where an order for sale is required in respect of the claim to an equitable interest. An application can be made under s 30 by a party claiming a beneficial interest under a trust in the home regardless of whether the applicant is a legal owner, and the court has power to order either an immediate or postponed sale of the home. A caution or land charge on the basis of a pending land action should immediately be lodged; this will give any purchaser actual notice of the non-owner's beneficial interest, achieving indirectly that which cannot be done directly. Where the land is registered, a beneficial interest can be protected as a minor interest by way of caution, restriction or notice and this should be done without delay where the non-legal owner is not in occupation. Any prospective purchaser on notice of the claim is unlikely to complete the purchase at least until the proceedings have been concluded.

As will be seen, the courts have vacillated in their preparedness to use the law of trusts to intervene in disputes between former cohabitees relating to the family home. Although recent decisions have clarified the law to some extent, it is still fair to say that a non-owner cohabitee who does not have hard evidence of having made a monetary contribution to the purchase of a property has no guarantee of having earned an equitable interest in the property, no matter how long the period of cohabitation. The case law reveals that much depends on the individual circumstances and motivation for the arrangements between the parties. Legal advisors will therefore need, at an early stage, a comprehensive proof of evidence giving the history of the relationship; the stated intentions and contributions in money or money's worth of the parties; when the property was purchased or improved; and the cohabitees' periods of residence therein.

3. Joint legal ownership

Joint owners must hold a property as joint tenants of the legal estate, but as either joint tenants or tenants in common in equity. Normally the conveyance or transfer contains a declaration of the beneficial interests. A declaration may be made subsequently or in a separate document providing it complies with the requirements of s 53 LPA 1925. In the absence of fraud or mistake, an express declaration by joint legal owners as to their respective beneficial interests in the property will be conclusive (see *Pettitt* v *Pettitt* [1970] AC 777, *Goodman* v *Gallant* [1986] 1 All ER 311). Normally, the beneficial interests will crystallise on purchase of the property in accordance with the express declaration and notwithstanding the actual contributions to the purchase price and can be altered only by proof of a subsequent express declaration or agreement.

A joint owner may at any time apply for an order for sale of the property where their co-owner fails to agree to sell, pursuant to s 30 LPA 1925. From 1 July 1991, there is unlimited county court jurisdiction for all s 30 claims. Proceedings are commenced in the county court by way of originating application and affidavit in support. Ultimately, the court may order an immediate or postponed sale as will be discussed below.

The court's role in s 30 proceedings is to determine the respective beneficial interests of the parties in the property or the proceeds of sale and the principles of equity will be applied. The starting point will be how the property is expressed to be held in the title documents. Where there is an express declaration, the position is relatively straightforward. Where there is no declaration, the joint legal ownership will usually raise a strong presumption that the parties were each intended to be beneficially entitled, unless the property was put into joint names by mistake or for a completely different purpose (see for example *Thames Guaranty Ltd* v *Campbell* [1985] QB 210). Normally the court will look to the parties' contributions to establish their intention regarding their respective beneficial interests at the date of purchase (see for example the Court of Appeal decisions of *Bernard* v *Josephs* [1982] Ch 391 and *Walker* v *Hall* [1984] FLR 126). However, as will be discussed below, a declaration on a registered land transfer that the survivor of joint purchasers can or cannot give a valid receipt for monies arising on sale, may raise a strong presumption of the existence of a beneficial joint tenancy or tenancy in common as appropriate. Where there is no evidence to show the intended extent of the parties' respective beneficial interests then the principle that equity follows the law will apply, and a beneficial joint tenancy will be deemed to have been created.

4. Joint tenants in equity

A declaration that co-owners hold property as beneficial joint tenants has the effect of attributing to each of them an identical interest in the whole of the land until the joint tenancy is severed. If the property is sold, that interest is transferred to the proceeds of sale and each joint owner will take one half. Severance of the joint tenancy can be effected by either joint tenant giving written notice to the other pursuant to s 36(2) LPA 1925 and they will then hold as beneficial tenants in common in equal shares, notwithstanding their actual contributions to the property, unless the original declaration specified that unequal shares would arise on severance *(Goodman* v *Gallant* above). It should be noted that acting in a way inconsistent with a joint tenancy may also sever it without notice being served, as in *Ahmed* v *Kendrick* [1988] 2 FLR 22 which involved the unilateral sale of the property; and *Re Draper's Conveyance* [1969] Ch 486 where the issuing of proceedings under s 30 LPA 1925 was deemed to be sufficient.

Another important effect of a beneficial joint tenancy is the right of survivorship whereby on the death of one joint tenant, the deceased's share of the property passes automatically to the surviving joint tenant. This contrasts with the position of beneficial tenants in common where the interest of the joint owner passes with his or her estate and not necessarily to the co-owner. In unregistered land, there will always be a declaration of the beneficial interest in the conveyance, and legal advisors must make enquires, and give advice to their clients about the effect of a beneficial joint tenancy before completion of the transaction. Not to do so is negligent *(Walker* v *Hall* [1984] FLR 126). Another case where the role of legal advisors has been held to be even more arduous is *Taylor and Harman* v *Warner* (1988) LSG no. 25 page 26. A woman entering her second marriage bought a farm with her new husband and she provided most of the purchase price. The property was put into joint names and, being registered, there was no express declaration of the beneficial interests, but the transfer did contain a declaration that the survivor of the joint purchasers could give a valid receipt for the property. When the woman died, her children by her first marriage believed her share of the farm would come to them under her will, but instead it passed to the husband by the right of survivorship. Warner J held that the solicitor who had explained the effect of joint tenancies and tenancies in common on purchase was negligent in that he had a duty to address his mind and the client's mind, to the source of the purchase money, and should have stressed that the joint tenancy would effectively disinherit the children.

Thus cohabitees who have purchased as beneficial joint tenants where there is an express declaration, or probably, it is submitted, even where they have in respect of registered land declared that the survivor of them can give a valid receipt for the property, are likely to be entitled to the net proceeds of sale in equal shares. The position in the latter situation is not completely certain, although a declaration as to the survivor's ability to provide a valid receipt is a strong presumption in favour of a beneficial joint tenancy. In *Bernard* v *Josephs* (above) property was transferred jointly to cohabitees without any reference to the beneficial ownership. On relationship breakdown it was held that there was no automatic presumption that the parties held the property in equal shares, but the court decided it should look at the evidence to see whether it supported an intention of the parties to hold the property other than in equal shares. In that case, broadly equal contributions showed an intention to hold the property in equal shares.

The case law is to the effect that practitioners should make sure that clear advice is given concerning the implications of a beneficial joint tenancy and that instructions are followed. Clear advice at this stage will avoid both a finding of negligence, and, perhaps, a dispute between co-owners on subsequent breakdown of their relationship, where only in limited circumstances will it be possible to avoid the effects of an express declaration.

When consulted on breakdown, the effect of severance of the joint tenancy must be explored and explained immediately. It may be that a declaration has been made providing for the property to be held on severance as tenants in common in unequal shares; this was specifically regarded as a possibility in *Goodman* v *Gallant* above. Usually, severance will be appropriate, as it will mean that the right of survivorship will cease to apply, which will accord with the wishes of most (but not all) clients on breakdown. However, although the shares of the property will no longer pass automatically to the co-owner on death, conversely, in the absence of a Will in favour of the co-owner, his or her share of the home will also devolve elsewhere.

Instructions should also be taken with regard to the need for new Wills.

5. Tenants in common in equity

Although the legal estate must be held by co-owners as joint tenants, the beneficial interests may be held as tenants in common. The effect of this is that the co-owners each have a specified share in the equity, usually determined at the date of purchase. Such share does not pass automatically to the co-owner on death, but instead devolves to the beneficiaries of the estate. Thus if a co-owner who holds as tenant in common wishes to leave his or her share of the home to his/her cohabitee on death, it is necessary to make a Will to that effect, as the cohabitee would not benefit on intestacy.

A tenancy in common is particularly appropriate where there have been unequal contributions to the purchase price and where the joint owners wish to preserve their interests in the property in unequal shares, although a tenancy in common can, if required, specify that the shares are held equally. A solicitor who, in a conveyance, declares a beneficial tenancy in common but does not go on to specify the shares is negligent *(Walker* v *Hall* above). Once a declaration as to the beneficial interests has been made, it is again conclusive, in the absence of fraud, mistake or a subsequent express agreement.

Thus if cohabitees on purchase declare that they hold the property beneficially as tenants in common in shares of three quarters to one quarter, on breakdown of the relationship when the property is sold, the net proceeds of sale will be divided in these proportions. If, before breakdown of the relationship, one partner has paid for improvements to the property, in the absence of express agreement to the contrary, this does not alter the beneficial interests in the property and the proceeds of sale will still be divided according to the original ratio. It is therefore necessary to advise joint purchasers to consider making a fresh declaration of trust if future contributions render their original agreement unfair. Alternatively a clause could, and arguably should, be inserted in the original declaration providing for this and other contingencies such as revised contributions to any joint mortgage.

6. Fraud or mistake

An express declaration as to the beneficial ownership is conclusive in the absence of fraud or mistake. If it was induced by fraud, it will be set aside. If it was entered into as a result of a mistake in that it fails to reflect the parties' common intentions, rectification may be sought, although this will not be granted where it would prejudice a *bona fide* purchaser for value who was not on notice of the mistake. In *City of London Building Society* v *Flegg* [1987] 2 WLR 1266, it was held that an express declaration by purchasers that they held as beneficial joint tenants was not conclusive where their parents had contributed to the purchase price with the intention that they should retain a beneficial interest.

7. Quantification of shares on breakdown

Whether co-owners hold the home as joint tenants or tenants in common in equity, once the appropriate share due to each has been established, an arithmetical calculation is necessary to translate this into the correct share of the proceeds of sale. It may well be that on breakdown the property is not actually sold, but rather one co-owner buys the former partner and co-owner's share, but the principles remain the same. Whether or not the property is sold, it is still necessary to establish the correct method of quantifying the share in cash terms. Where there is no mortgage, the calculation is often simple. The net proceeds of sale are the sale price, less the costs incidental to the sale such as estate agents' fees and legal costs. The balance is then divided in accordance with the established shares of the equity. Alternatively, it is possible to divide the gross proceeds of sale between the co-owners in the agreed ratio, each paying towards the incidental costs in the same proportions out of their share of the proceeds of sale. In fact the same figure will be arrived at, but as a matter of practice, the net proceeds of sale are usually taken as the total equity available for distribution and the courts have tended to follow this method.

Where the property is subject to a mortgage the situation may be less straightforward. As Sparkes (*The Quantification of Beneficial Interests etc*, Oxford Journal of Legal Studies, Spring 1991) has highlighted in relation to establishing beneficial ownership in the absence of an express declaration, there has been no specific investigation by the courts of the correct method of quantifying interests arising from contributions by way of mortgage, despite the frequency with which properties are purchased in this way. Should the proportions arrived at be assessed in relation to the net equity after the outstanding mortgage as well as costs incidental to the sale have been deducted from the proceeds of sale? Or should they be assessed in relation to the gross proceeds of sale and the mortgage redemption figure be deducted proportionately from each party's share? Where a separate declaration of trust or a cohabitation contract has been entered into, that document should provide the answer.

Where there is only a simple declaration of beneficial ownership in the conveyance, the situation may not be clear, particularly if one party has contributed mainly to the deposit and the other chiefly by capital borrowed on mortgage. Where each party has contributed consistent proportions to both the capital and mortgage repayments, then either method of calculation will achieve the same result, as was the case in *Bernard* v *Josephs* (above). However, this is not the case where the proportions contributed to capital and mortgage are not consistent, and the most anomalous situation is where these proportionate contributions are inverted.

There seems to be no single correct approach, as much will depend on whether or not the parties contributed to the deposit and/or mortgage equally, with the result that legal advisors need to press for the method which is most advantageous to their client, or that which can be recommended as the fairest in all the circumstances. Where one party has contributed by way of capital and the other by way of mortgage, assessment of the shares from the net, rather than the gross, proceeds of sale can produce inequitable results. In this situation, it is fairer to deduce the shares from the gross proceeds of sale and to deduct the mortgage solely from the share of the party whose contribution was by way of mortgage.

Where there is an endowment mortgage payments of interest only will have been made to the mortgagee, with premiums being paid under a policy which guarantees to repay the capital borrowed under the mortgage at the end of the term, or on death. On breakdown, the sum needed to redeem the mortgage will be greater than the policy will then provide, although there will usually be a surrender value of a joint endowment policy which needs to be taken into account. It may be possible for each party to transfer the accrued benefits to new policies in sole names, or the policy may be surrendered. Where the mortgage is in joint names and the parties have contributed to both the payment of interest to the mortgagee and to the endowment policy premiums, the surrender value should normally be divided in accordance with the contributions to the policy.

The date for valuation of the shares and calculation of the sums due out of the proceeds of sale presents another problem. Where there is an express trust the shares will be valued at the date of acquisition of the property, but following breakdown the date on which the sum to be paid over is calculated, should be the date of realisation, that is, the date of sale or deemed sale, and not the date of separation. This was established in *Turton* v *Turton* [1988] Ch 542. When house prices are the subject of rapid increases, or indeed decreases, the date of calculation of the shares in the proceeds of sale can make an enormous difference and this should be borne in mind when negotiations take place or valuations are agreed.

In view of this approach, both parties may be expected to contribute to the cost of repairs, improvements and mortgage repayments until sale. Where one party has failed to contribute after separation, the sums payable will be adjusted to reflect it, and this process is known as equitable accounting. In *Bernard* v *Josephs* above, equitable accounting was employed to make a fair adjustment in the light of contributions after the date of separation. In that case one half of the mortgage repayments was held to be a fair monetary allowance. Furthermore, in some situations, it has been held where one co-owner is involuntarily no longer in occupation of the home and the former partner thereby has the sole benefit of occupation of the property but is making the whole of the mortgage repayments, that these payments are balanced by an "occupation rent" payable to the absent co-owner. This was also considered in *Bernard* v *Josephs* (per Kerr LJ).

As Sparkes (see above) details, case law is inconsistent as to whether this principle should apply to a co-owner who has left his or her partner (see *Cracknell* v *Cracknell* [1971] P 356, *Eves* v *Eves* [1975] 1 WLR 1338 and *Dennis* v *McDonald* [1981] 1 WLR 810). It seems where a co-owner continues to have the right of occupation and have left voluntarily, occupation rent is not appropriate (*Jones* v *Jones* [1977] 1 WLR 438). Interest, but not capital payments, under a mortgage were held to be paid as equivalent to occupation rent in *Suttil* v *Graham* [1977] 1 WLR 819. If an occupation rent is not considered applicable, then the paying party will be given credit for such interest payments together with any capital payments made under the mortgage following separation.

If the approach in *Turton* v *Turton* above is followed, and the respective interests are valued at the date of realisation, adverse effects of house price increases or decreases will be minimised for both parties. This will not avoid the need for equitable accounting in relation to events following separation even though the actual valuation of the shares will not take place until realisation. Issues of payment of subsequent mortgage instalments, or improvements and occupation rent, remain relevant and need to be assessed to determine the actual sum payable on realisation.

8. Sole legal ownership

It is where the home is owned by one partner alone that the most difficulty on the breakdown of relationships between cohabitees arises, and it is here that the non-owner partner must rely on the law of trusts or the doctrine of proprietary estoppel if they are to establish any equitable interest in the home. Where a property is purchased in the sole name of one partner during the currency of the relationship, or where one partner moves into a property which was purchased by the other previously, on breakdown of the relationship, the non-owner partner is in a vulnerable position.

No rights of occupation accrue to a non-owner cohabitee and the best that can be done is to establish that he or she has a beneficial interest in the property ostensibly owned solely by the partner, either under an express trust or, more usually, a resulting, implied or constructive trust as recognised by s 53(2) LPA 1925.

(a) Express trusts
If on purchasing or moving to a property, the sole legal owner makes a valid express declaration of trust that he or she holds the property beneficially for himself or herself and for a their partner, then the parties' respective shares on breakdown of the relationship will be determined in accordance with that express declaration, which will be conclusive as has already been discussed in the context of joint legal owners. For the declaration to be valid, it must conform to the requirements of s 53(1)(b) LPA 1925, but any written agreement will be evidence of the parties' intentions at the date of acquisition and may be of great significance where a party is attempting to show a common intention as to the beneficial ownership of the property.

(b) Resulting, implied and constructive trusts
Case law is still in the process of clarifying the distinctions between the effects of the above types of trust, which, in contrast to express trusts, arise without being evidenced in writing. It seems that these trusts break down into two rather than three categories and although the term "implied trust" has on occasions been used, it is necessary to explain and distinguish between resulting and constructive trusts.

(i) Resulting trusts: A resulting trust gives effect to the parties' presumed common intention at the date the property was acquired. It will arise where a non legal owner contributes in money or money's worth to the purchase of the property which will be held on trust in shares relative to their contributions. Equity presumes that where two parties contribute to the purchase that they intend to share the property beneficially in proportion to their contributions, although such a presumption can be rebutted by proof that the contribution was intended as a loan, a gift or rent. The presumption of advancement applies between cohabitees who were engaged to be married at the time the property

was purchased in the sole name of one of them, however, and this may override the presumption of a resulting trust.

In *Sekhon* v *Alissa* [1989] 2 FLR 94 Ch D, the presumption of a resulting trust had not been rebutted where a mother had contributed £22,500 to her daughter's purchase of a house as there was no evidence that it was intended as a gift or a loan. Another example is *Richards* v *Dove* [1974] 1 All ER 888 Ch D where a woman's contribution to a deposit was held to have been intended as a loan.

Where the contribution has been made in money, the valuation of the respective shares is relatively simple, although the problem of quantification where there are disproportionate contributions to the capital and mortgage with which a purchase was effected, as discussed above, also feature here.

Further difficulties arise where it is alleged that the contribution was made in money's worth rather than money. The courts themselves can be seen to have blurred the distinction between resulting and constructive trusts in that in some cases actual physical work by a non-owner partner which has improved the property has been held to give rise to a resulting trust, whilst in others it has been considered only as conduct relevant to establishing whether or not the requisite intention for a constructive trust was present. The case law is considered below.

(ii) Constructive trusts: Constructive trusts similarly depend on a common intention, but require further elements to be present.

The leading exposition on constructive trusts can now be found in the judgment of Mustill LJ in the Court of Appeal decision of *Grant* v *Edwards* [1986] Ch 638 at p 652. He identified four situations on acquisition (or later in appropriate circumstances) which could give rise to a common intention constructive trust, providing the non-owner claimant subsequently conducted himself or herself in a manner which was both to his/her detriment and referable to the promise or common intention established on acquisition:

"a) An express bargain whereby the proprietor promises the claimant an interest in the property in return for an explicit undertaking of the claimant to act in a certain way.

b) An express but incomplete bargain whereby the proprietor promises the claimant an interest in the property, on the basis that

the claimant will do something in return. The parties do not themselves make explicit what the claimant is to do. The court therefore has to complete the bargain for them by means of implica-
tion, when it comes to decide whether the proprietor's promise
has been matched by conduct falling within whatever undertaking
the claimant must be taken to have given *sub silento*.

c) An explicit promise by the proprietor that the claimant will
have an interest in the property unaccompanied by any express or
tacit agreement as to a *quid pro quo*.

d) A common intention not made explicit to the effect that the
claimant will have an interest in the property, if she subsequently
acts in a particular way."

In situations a, b and d, once the non-legal owner acts in a way which
is to his or her detriment and is referable to the legal owner's promise,
in that it can be explained only by a belief that they had a beneficial
interest in the property, the bargain is complete and a beneficial interest is established. The court must then go on to quantify the non legal
owner's share of the equity. In situation (c), the position is still not
clear, although in *Gissing* v *Gissing* [1971] AC 886, Diplock LJ stated *obiter* that if this category of claimant had then acted to his/her
detriment in reliance on such a promise, a beneficial interest would
thereby be conferred.

In *Rossett* v *Lloyds Bank PLC* [1990] 2 WLR 867 HL (discussed
below) Lord Bridge drew attention to a critical distinction between an
express common intention based on evidence of express discussions
between the parties, and an inferred common intention based on conduct. In the former situation, he stated:

"... it will only be necessary for the the partner asserting a claim
to a beneficial interest against the partner entitled to the legal
estate to show that he or she acted to his or her detriment or significantly altered his or her position in reliance on the agreement
in order to give rise to a constructive trust or proprietary estoppel."

In the latter situation, he went on,

"... direct contributions to the purchase price by the partner who is
not the legal owner, whether initially or by payment of mortgage
instalments, will readily justify the inference necessary to the cre-

ation of a constructive trust. But as I read the authorities, it is at least extremely doubtful whether anything less will do."

This last category may in any event fall within the definition of a presumed resulting trust by virtue of a monetary contribution on acquisition of the property, unless the presumption can be rebutted as discussed above.

A common intention to share the beneficial ownership without a written declaration of trust, and in the absence of any detrimental conduct or contribution to the purchase price, will not be enough to give a non-legal owner a beneficial interest, as was the case in *Midland Bank* v *Dobson* [1986] 1 FLR 171.

Apart from common intention or a promise by the legal owner, the relevant factors needed to establish shared beneficial ownership comprise acts which are detrimental to the claimant, although there are no set rules about the nature and degree of detriment required; and a causal link between the common intention or promise and the detrimental act. It is felt that the best way to assess the impact of these additional requirements is to attempt a review in summary of the case law. Factors relevant to establishing common intention will also be considered, although it should be recognised that there are issues yet to be decided by the courts.

(c) The case law
(i) Common intention: In the case of *Cooke* v *Head* [1972] 1 WLR 518, the Court of Appeal, headed by Lord Denning, agreed unanimously that Ms Cooke was entitled to a beneficial interest amounting to one third of the proceeds of sale. The facts of the case were that the parties who, it was accepted, had an intention to marry, purchased a plot of land in Mr. Head's sole name. Ms Cooke then assisted him in building a bungalow on the land which was intended to be the family home. She assisted him by way of hard physical labour, which impressed the court as work over and above that which was expected of a wife, and she assisted in the mortgage repayments which were made from their pooled resources. Before the parties moved into the property the relationship broke down and Ms Cooke claimed a beneficial interest. Lord Denning asserted, without attempting to clarify the distinction between the different types of trust, "...Whenever two par-

ties by their joint efforts acquire property for their joint benefit, the courts may impose or impute a constructive or resulting trust."

In this case there was an express common intention which gave rise either to a presumed resulting trust consequent upon Ms Cooke's contribution to the acquisition of the property in both money and money's worth, or a constructive trust whereby the beneficial interest was established by Ms Cooke's acting to her detriment, as evidenced by her labour and monetary contribution on the basis of the common intention.

This case can be directly contrasted with the more recent Court of Appeal decision in *Thomas* v *Fuller-Brown* [1988] 1 FLR 237. Here, the parties lived together in a house purchased in the sole name of the woman without any financial contribution from the man claimant whom she supported. However, she subsequently obtained an improvement grant and she agreed that the man, who was unemployed but skilled in building work, should carry out the necessary repair and improvement works in return for her providing him with accommodation and his keep plus "pocket money". The work involved was of a substantial nature but shortly after it was completed the relationship broke down. The Court of Appeal upheld the trial judge's decision that on the facts the only reasonable inference was not that the parties intended joint beneficial ownership. On the contrary, it was accepted that she had never led him to believe that he would acquire an interest in the property and accordingly he remained no more than her licensee. The woman's explanation of the arrangement was preferred and neither a resulting nor a constructive trust was imputed. These two cases also illustrate the difficulty of establishing an indirect contribution to the acquisition of a property.

The Court of Appeal decisions of *Eves* v *Eves* [1975] 1 WLR 1388 and *Grant* v *Edwards* (see page 214) can also be contrasted with *Thomas* v *Fuller-Brown*. In both these cases, the women cohabitees were misled by their partners about why the family home had not been purchased in joint names. In *Eves*, the man told her that she was too young to appear on the title of the property which was not true. She subsequently carried out repair works and improvements to the house to prepare it for joint occupation but then the relationship broke down. The court unanimously held that she was entitled to a quarter of the equity, but Lord Denning differed in his reasoning from the other two members of the court. He felt that the court had power to impose a constructive trust regardless of the presence or absence of a common intention to share the beneficial ownership. However, the majority of the court considered that the woman's work on the property could be explained only by a common intention that she had a beneficial interest in the property. Her conduct evidenced both the common intention and her contribution in money's worth and thus the property was held on a resulting trust. More recent cases have not adopted Lord Denning's approach of imposing a trust which will produce an equitable result and, as will be seen, there has been a return to a more orthodox trust law approach.

In *Grant* v *Edwards* the parties lived together and had a child. The man purchased a property in the name of himself and his brother (whom it was accepted, had no beneficial interest in the property). The man told his partner that the reason the property was not bought in their joint names was to avoid complications in relation to the matrimonial proceedings in which she was involved at that time. The court held that this ostensible reason raised the clear inference of a common intention that the woman should have an interest in the house. She subsequently contributed to the household and mortgage expenses in a substantial way, and without such a contribution the man could not have afforded to purchase the house. Accordingly she had acted to her detriment in an appropriate way and a constructive trust was found to exist under which she was beneficially entitled to a half interest in the property. It is questionable whether the deceptions in both *Eves* and *Grant* v *Edwards* could realistically be evidence of a common intention to share beneficial ownership. Indeed, the men in both cases were attempting to avoid beneficial joint ownership. Their conduct, particularly in the light of the subsequent detrimental acts of their partners, was clearly inequitable and justified the court's intervention. It is submitted that the courts are in this type of situation readier to follow Lord Denning's approach.

However, a common intention is not always easy to establish. In *Howard* v *Jones* (1989) 19 Fam Law 231, a man who was cohabiting with a woman purchased a property in his sole name whilst they continued to live in rented accommodation. She maintained that her payment for most of the household expenses enabled the man to purchase the property but the Court of Appeal found that she had no beneficial interest as she had failed to establish any common intention. In *Windeler* v *Whitehall* [1990] 2 FLR 505 Ch D, Millett J held that a woman cohabitee who had contributed nothing to the acquisition of the property but had lived with the defendant for six years, during which period she did not work and was supported by the man, could not establish a common intention that she was to have a beneficial interest by virtue of the man's having previously left the property to her in his Will. There was no evidence that she had been led to believe that whatever happened she would inherit the property, or that she did believe this.

(ii) Detriment and contributions: The cases cited above in relation to common intention can similarly be used to illustrate what the courts have considered to be a sufficiently detrimental act by the non-owner, and there is some overlap between the issues. Direct or indirect contributions can also be seen to be a detrimental act by the non-owner in some circumstances and detriment referable to the common intention or promise is indispensible where there are indirect rather than direct contributions.

Thus in *Eves* v *Eves* and *Cooke* v *Head* physical labour in building or improving the home was considered both a detrimental act and a direct contribution in money's worth to the properties. However, in *Thomas* v *Fuller-Brown* the same type of hard physical work was not a sufficient contribution and was not considered detrimental given that the claimant was receiving his keep and some pocket money.

The detriment must always relate to the common intention and not to any other purpose. In *Rossett* v *Lloyds Bank PLC*, the matrimonial home was purchased in the husband's sole name because of the terms of the trust under which he was entitled to the money which he used to purchase the property. Unbeknown to his wife, a mortgage on the property was taken out to fund renovation works. The wife, who was an interior designer, supervised the building works, worked extremely hard in assisting the progress of the renovation works, but the husband paid for the materials and workmen. It was accepted that there was a common intention that the property was to be occupied by the parties and their daughter as the matrimonial home, but no express common intention was found that the wife was to have any beneficial interest in it. The court therefore had to look at the wife's contributions to the property to see whether this evidenced a resulting or constructive trust in her favour. There were no direct monetary contributions, only her decoration work and supervision of the renovation works, but these were adjudged to be *de minimus* relative to the overall cost of the property and the works. Lord Bridge said:

"Mrs. Rossett was anxious to have the property ready for Xmas. In these circumstances, it would seem the most natural thing in the world for any wife, in the absence of her husband abroad, to spend all the time she could spare and to employ any skills she may have, such as the ability to decorate a room, in doing all she could to accelerate progress of the work, quite irrespective of any expectation she might have of enjoying a beneficial interest in the property. The judge's view that some of this work was work 'on which she could not have reasonably expected to embark unless she was to have an interest in the house' seems to me ... to be quite untenable ... On any view, the monetary value of Mrs. Rossett's work expressed as a contribution to a property at a cost of £70,000 must have been so trifling to be *de minimus*"

The court felt that Mrs Rossett's work was not a sufficiently substantial detrimental act, and may not in any event have been referable to the belief in having a beneficial share. Rather it was no more than the fulfilment of natural wifely duties. Perhaps in such a situation a cohabitee would have fared better than a wife, although the leading decision of *Burns* v *Burns* [1984] 1 All ER 244 involving cohabitees makes it clear that it is no longer sufficient to look after children and run the family home to earn an interest in the property.

Lord Denning's broad brush approach, in which he allowed a contribution to the household by means of domestic services to be taken into account in assessing the parties' respective beneficial shares in much the same way as happens on divorce, was specifically rejected in *Burns*. Lord May provides a useful summary of his assessment of the various situations where a beneficial interest can be identified, despite one partner's being the sole legal owner. A contribution to the initial deposit will on resulting trust principles give rise to a beneficial interest for the non-owner, and this share will be increased by subsequent contributions to mortgage repayments. Similarly if, having contributed to the deposit, the non-owner partner meets other household expenses without which the legal owner would be unable, or find it more difficult, to pay the mortgage, this also increases the non-owner's share. Thus a contribution by indirect means is a possibility.

Both in *Burns* and in *Gissing* the court recognised that as a matter of convenience, one partner's salary may be used to meet the mortgage repayments and the other salary to meet other household expenses, with the intention that both parties would thereby be entitled to share in the property to the extent that their overall contributions, whether direct or indirect, merited. However, these contributions must be made with the intention of assisting in the purchase of the property and not for any other purpose. If they are made with a view to sharing day to day expenses only, this will not be considered a sufficient indirect contribution as they lack referability to the intention to acquire an interest in the property (see Lord Diplock in *Gissing*). It is vital to establish referability or, as in both these cases, the non-owner will fail to establish any beneficial interest in the property, despite having devoted many years to looking after the home and family. Where there are indirect contributions through household expenses, without any contribution to the initial deposit, an interest may be acquired if the non-owner's contribution were essential to enable the legal owner to meet the mortgage repayments, although the position has not been made clear (see *Hazell* v *Hazell* [1972] 1 WLR 301). Again, it seems that such indirect contributions can produce a beneficial interest only if they were made with the intention of assisting in the acquisition of the property in any event. In *Burns* the couple had lived together for nineteen years and had two children of whom the woman was the primary carer. The family home had been purchased in the man's sole name after they had been cohabiting for two years without any contribution from the woman to the deposit or mortgage. She later went out to work and her earnings were used for general household expenses but were not crucial to the man's ability to pay the mortgage. The court held that she had no beneficial interest in the property as no common intention or direct or indirect contribution to the acquisition of the property could be found on the facts. Had the parties been married, the result would have been different indeed, and this case is a dramatic illustration of the disadvantage to which a non-owner cohabitee can be put.

However, the new provisions in the para 1(2) to Sch 1 CA 1989, permitting applications for transfer of property orders to or for the benefit of the child and settlement of property on the child, may ameliorate the position of the woman cohabitee in a *Burns* situation, providing the application is made before the children are independent or over eighteen.

Where one partner moves into a property already purchased by the other, it is possible, providing there is sufficient evidence, for the non-owner cohabitee to earn a beneficial interest in the property. It seems that evidence of a complete recasting of the financial arrangements of the parties, disclosing direct or indirect contributions to the mortgage or, say, improvement works, accompanied by a referable intention that the non-owner would acquire an interest would be necessary; this was discussed in *Gissing*, where a change in intention was specifically canvassed as a possibility. Thus, the more recent authorities lean towards a more onerous interpretation of the nature and level of contribution needed to acquire a beneficial interest in a property in the absence of either a provable common intention or inequitable behaviour by the legal owner of the property such as inspires the court to step in and infer a common intention where arguably there is none.

9. Transfer and settlement of property orders for children

As was discussed in relation to tenancies and in Chapter 8, para 1(2)(e) to Sch 1 to the CA 1989 enables the court to order the transfer of property between parents for the benefit of the child. Any beneficial interest in the home, or any other property owned by one parent, may be transferred either to the child or to the other parent for the benefit of the child. This opens up the possibility of the court's effectively ordering the transfer of the home to the residential parent. Paragraph 1(2)(d) empowers the court to order the settlement of property owned by one parent for the benefit of the child.

In both cases, only one such order can be made against a parent in respect of the same child. To date there are few reported cases on how these new provisions, originally introduced by the FLRA 1987 amendments to the GMA 1971, will be used by the courts. The criteria set out in para 4 of the schedule discussed above and in Chapter 8, identify the factors to be taken into account by the court. As discussed in Chapter 8, courts have been reluctant to transfer property to children directly in matrimonial cases (see *Chamberlain* v *Chamberlain* [1974] 1 All ER 33). In the recent case of *H* v *M* [1991] Fam Law 473, capital provision for children of an unmarried couple under s 12 GMA 1971 was deemed inappropriate and only periodical maintenance payments were ordered in favour of the children. This may indicate a reluctance to use their powers more liberally where parents are unmarried. Yet where the parents are unmarried there is to be no adjustment of the property rights as between the parents by the court under Sch 1 CA 1989. Courts may therefore feel it appropriate to effect some redistribution, particularly where the residential parents' resources are far less substantial than those of the other parent, by transferring property either to or for the benefit of the child. Much will of course depend on the assets available and whether there are any s 30 LPA proceedings, but it is to be hoped that Sch 1 CA 1989 orders could be used to preserve a home for the child either by means of transferring one parent's interest to the other to achieve a clean break, or by settling the property on the child.

How these will translate into practice, given that the welfare of the child is not paramount, remains to be seen. It is felt that courts are likely to be less generous in their approach than in relation to similar situations on marriage breakdown, as there will not be any element relating to maintenance for the other parent. This factor may also make courts reluctant to transfer property for the benefit of the child as if will inevitably benefit the residential parent as well as the child, an outcome the courts may not wish to encourage.

There is no power in the schedule to order the sale of the property and thus it may often be appropriate, where the property is jointly owned or the non-owner claims a beneficial interest in it, to combine the application for a transfer or settlement of property order with an application for an order for sale under s 30 LPA 1925. All such applications may now be heard by the county court. This is as near as it is possible to get to achieving a family law based consideration by the courts of a property dispute between cohabitees. The case of *H* v *M* (above) gives guidance as to how multifarious claims incidental upon unmarried family breakdown should be dealt with procedurally. All possible issues, including maintenance for the children, should be raised at the earliest stage so that the appropriate forum and procedure, leading to the quickest and most effective outcome, can be decided.

It seems clear that under the provisions of para 1(2) to Sch 1 CA 1989, the court could achieve a *Mesher* order, whereby the home is settled for the benefit of the children until they reach eighteen, and it is hoped that the new powers will be exercised in the same way as on divorce, particularly where the relationship between the cohabitees has been stable and long and it is clearly appropriate for the assets of both parties to be used for the benefit of the child in this way. Such orders have been much criticised in divorce proceedings but may be the only way of ensuring a home is provided for a child of unmarried parents where the parties' assets do not permit a clean break.

Transfer and settlement of property orders extend to any property owned by a parent in possession or reversion and therefore, as discussed in Chapter 8, are not limited to use in respect of the family home. However, as the home is usually the largest asset and the most crucial for the child, it is thought that they will be most used in this domain. It should be noted that there is no power to order sale.

A child may now apply in his or her own right for legal aid and this may have certain consequences. If the child is the legally aided party in respect of the transfer of property application, then if the property is transferred to the parent for the child's benefit, this seems to avoid the statutory charge. If the property is transferred to the child however, the charge will attach to all but the first £2,500 (reg 94 Civil Legal Aid (General) Regulations 1989), as for these purposes an application for financial relief under these provisions is classified with similar applications in matrimonial proceedings. If the property is the family home, or is to be used to purchase a family home, then there is power to postpone the operation of the charge under Regulations 96 and 97, as is also the case with an order made in matrimonial proceedings.

This now avoids having to sell the property to satisfy the charge, providing the order clearly states that the property is to be used as, or to purchase, a family home.

If the property is settled on the child and the child derives only a right to occupy the home, then the charge again will be avoided. In s 30 proceedings, the charge will attach to the property without even the benefit of the £2,500 exemption or the power to postpone the sale; the effect of the legal aid regulations must be borne in mind, communicated to and fully discussed with the client before deciding to use s 30 if the same result may be achieved by means of a settlement or transfer of property order in favour of the child. However, given the lack of the power to order sale and the current uncertainty as to whether the courts will enable these orders to provide a complete remedy as between cohabitees with children, s 30 may indeed be appropriate. Where the parties' respective interests in the property are clear, and a transfer without sale is being sought, it may not be needed. However, the other party may seek a sale pursuant to s 30 in any event, which may mean the residential parent needs legal aid to defend the application, and then the effect of the charge cannot be avoided or indeed postponed.

10. Proprietary estoppel

Another principle under which beneficial interests can be established by non-legal owners is that of proprietary estoppel. The crucial distinction between this doctrine and that of the constructive trust has been identified by Hayton (*Equitable Rights of Cohabitees*, The Conveyancer, vol 54, 1990). He asserts that the common intention constructive trust requires a bilateral understanding or agreement that if the non-owner acts in a particular and detrimental way, they will obtain a fair share in the family home. To succeed in a claim for proprietary estoppel, however, there need be only unilateral conduct by the legal owner which leads the partner to believe that he or she has an equitable interest in the home. Should that partner subsequently act to his or her detriment in reliance upon that conduct, it then becomes unconscionable for the legal owner to insist upon total ownership of the property. The court then intervenes to prevent the unconscionable conduct affecting the non owner detrimentally. It will not necessarily perfect the gift, but rather decide what is the minimum equity to do justice. The non-owner will not necessarily obtain a realisable interest in the proceeds of sale of the property but may be deemed to be entitled to a personal right of occupation only until the children are eighteen, or an equitable life interest.

In fact, it can be argued that there is a good deal of overlap between the situations in which these two doctrines apply, and from a practical point of view it may well be appropriate to use both lines of argument in the alternative where the facts warrant such an approach. In *Grant* v *Edwards* (above), Sir Nicholas Browne-Wilkinson remarked that in other cases of that kind, useful guidance might in the future be obtained from the principles underlying the law of proprietary estoppel which are closely akin to the constructive trust approach laid down in *Gissing* v *Gissing* (above). He went on to say that although the two principles had developed separately without cross fertilisation, they rest on the same foundation and have on all other matters reached the same conclusion.

The doctrine is of greatest use where it is not clear whether or not the non-owner would have done the detrimental acts relied upon in the absence of a common intention that a beneficial interest had been acquired, rather than for other reasons, such as mutual love and affection, not specifically referable to the house. In contrast to the constructive trust approach, the doctrine of proprietary estoppel does not require the detrimental acts to be specifically referable in this way, although reliance on the inducement must be shown. However, once there is evidence of an inducement and some detrimental act, the burden then falls on the legal owner to show that the non-owner did not do the act in reliance upon the inducement.

In *Pascoe* v *Turner* [1979] 1 WLR 431 (CA), a woman who relied on the man's assurance given after breakdown of the relationship that "the house and everything in it is yours" to the extent of spending a large proportion of her capital on the property successfully defended possession proceedings later brought by the man. The Court of Appeal found that although there was insufficient evidence to justify a trust, the man was estopped from revoking his imperfect gift of the house to the woman. The court then ordered that the gift be perfected by the transfer of the house to the woman.

A more restrictive approach was taken in the later case of *Coombes* v *Smith* [1986] 1 WLR 808 Ch D. Here a woman who found herself pregnant by her lover, left her husband and job and moved into a property owned by her lover. He never moved in to live with her but she was assured by him that he would always look after her. She failed to establish proprietary estoppel on the grounds that the assurance did not lead her to believe she was acquiring an interest in the property and she had not acted to her detriment in leaving her husband and job and having the baby. This can be seen to be an ungenerous approach to the definition of "detriment" which illustrates the precarious nature of relying solely upon this doctrine.

In *Greasley* v *Cooke* [1980] 1 WLR 1306, although a proprietary estoppel was established, it was held to give rise only to a right to occupy the property rent free for life and not to the right for the property to be transferred to the non-owner as in *Pascoe* v *Turner* (above). Where proved, the nature of the remedy is at the court's discretion and may therefore result in an award of monetary compensation.

11. Alternative occupation rights

A non-owner cohabitee will at the very least have a bare licence to occupy the home of the partner. However, such a licence amounts to little more than permission to occupy the home, and is determinable upon reasonable notice. On breakdown of the relationship, the licence will usually be revoked, and in the absence of any defence to possession proceedings by virtue of any of the matters discussed in this chapter, the licensee will have to leave. However, in some cases, even if it is not possible to establish a beneficial interest or use the doctrine of proprietary estoppel, it may be possible to show an alternative right of occupation.

(a) Contractual licences
Although it is usually not possible for a cohabitee to show that he or she was the tenant of the partner, there have been cases where a con-

tractual licence to occupy has been established. Most notable is the case of *Tanner* v *Tanner* [1975] 1 WLR 1346. Here, the woman gave up her rent controlled flat and moved into a property owned by the father of her two children, although the parties never cohabited. The Court of Appeal held that giving up her flat and looking after the children amounted to good consideration for an inferred contractual licence that she should be allowed to occupy the property until the children left school. However, this remedy has not been liked by the courts in more recent cases. In *Coombes* v *Smith,* discussed above in relation to proprietary estoppel, the court specifically rejected the argument that a licence had been created in not dissimilar circumstances, in that the woman's acts of leaving her husband and moving into the property did not amount to sufficient consideration.

(b) Licence by estoppel

Where the legal owner induces in the partner a belief that he or she has a right to long term occupation of the property rather than a beneficial interest in it, then a licence by estoppel rather than proprietary estoppel will arise, whereby the court will hold that the legal owner is estopped from denying that right of occupation. This argument succeeded in *Greasley* v *Cooke* (above) where the woman who had originally come to live with the man as his housekeeper but subsequently lived with him as his wife had been led to believe, following breakdown of the relationship, that she could continue to live in the property for as long as she wished. As the successors in title were unable to prove that she had not acted to her detriment in reliance on the inducement, and had indeed continued to care for a member of the family who was ill without any payment, the court took the view that they were estopped from denying that she had such a right of occupation.

(c) Occupation pursuant to the Settled Land Act 1925

The decision in *Tanner* v *Tanner* (above) specifically avoided a finding that the woman's right of occupation amounted to an exclusive irrevocable licence to occupy land which would have made her the tenant for life under the Settled Land Act 1925. However, the recent decision of the Vinelott J in the Chancery Division in *Ungurian* v

Lesnoff [1989] 3 WLR 840 indicates that the courts may be prepared to invoke another mechanism to give what is felt to be an equitable resolution where there is insufficient evidence to infer a beneficial interest under a constructive trust. In this case the woman who was a Polish academic, gave up her career and the valuable tenancy of her flat in Poland. She came with her sons to live in a property in London purchased by the man in his sole name for joint occupation by them and her children. His children, who were being educated in England, were also to live there from time to time. He purchased the property and she and her sons did some repair and renovation work to the property. It was found that she undertook the work not on the basis of a common intention that he had bought the house for her, but on the understanding that she had the right to reside there and that there was a common intention to provide her with a secure home. The judge stated:

"I do not think that full effect would be given to the common intention by inferring no more than an irrevocable licence to occupy the house. I think the legal consequences that flow from the intention to be imputed to the parties was that Mr Ungurian held the house on trust to permit Mrs Lesnoff to reside in it during her life unless she consented to the sale and another property purchased for her in substitution."

The consequences of this finding were that she was the tenant for life under the Settled Land Act 1925 with the power to sell and have the benefit of the proceeds of sale during her life.

In this case, given the man's promise was not found to constitute any beneficial share in the property, it was still open to the court to find a licence by estoppel or a contractual licence since there was consideration in that the woman had given up her nationality, home and career in Poland. However, neither of these were considered appropriate and so the Settled Land Act provisions were deemed to have been invoked. It may be that this approach by the court was felt appropriate in the light of the unusual facts and that the reasoning in the decision will prove to be the exception rather than the rule.

12. Homelessness

If it has not been possible to preserve the home, the final remedy to explore where there are children or a vulnerable cohabitee who are now homeless, is the duty under Housing Act 1985 Part III to secure accommodation for those who are homeless, in priority need and not intentionally homeless.

The relevant provisions have already been considered in detail in Chapter 3. Where there are children or the homeless cohabitee is vulnerable within the meaning of the s 59 Housing Act 1985, there is likely to be a priority need. Where it has not proved possible to obtain a transfer of property order for the benefit of the child or other long term relief from the court, as a result of which the vulnerable cohabitee or family become homeless unintentionally, the local authority would owe them a duty to secure them accommodation in accordance with s 65 HA Act 1985. Where there are children who can reasonably be expected to reside with the applicant, there is always priority need for homelessness purposes. The local authority then has a duty to secure accommodation for the partner with whom the children are to remain. This is a good reason for many local authority and housing association landlords to consent to assignments of the tenancy of the rented family home even where this is specifically prohibited by the terms of the tenancy agreement, for the ultimate housing duty towards the parent with the children following breakdown of the relationship will fall to them in any event.

It remains to be seen whether local housing authorities will begin to insist, in non-violent cases, that non-tenant and non-owner cohabitees with the right to make an application for a transfer of property order for the benefit of the child, exercise that right before they will be considered homeless. It is to be stressed that in such cases, as the cohabitee has no right of occupation, it would have to provide temporary accommodation pending the outcome of the application as set out in Chapter 3. The homeless non-resident parent will not be owed any duty by the local housing authority unless he or she can show they are independently in priority need.

13. Personal property

With the advent of the "share owning democracy", an increase in the number of disputes between cohabitees in relation their personal property such as savings and shares is perhaps likely. Essentially the rules relating to the division of personal property of cohabitees on relationship breakdown are the same as for real property. The law of trusts can be used where the property is of sufficient value and it is alleged a non-legal owner is beneficially entitled to a share of the property.

Generally, anything owned before the relationship or purchased by one of the cohabitees during the relationship remains the property of that partner. Gifts remain the property of the donee. It seems that joint bank or building society accounts held by cohabitees and intended to be a common pool of funds will be deemed to be held as joint tenants in equity, regardless of any disproportion in the relative contributions, in the same way as is presumed in the case of a married couple (see *Bernard* v *Josephs* (above) and *Jones* v *Maynard* [1951] Ch 572). Severance of that joint tenancy by giving written notice to the other will result in the creation of a tenancy in common in equal shares of those monies. If the common pool presumption can be rebutted, by an express or implied contrary intention, then the funds will be held on resulting trust for the contributors in shares proportionate to their contributions. If there is a cohabitation contract or other written declaration which deals with the ownership of such funds this is likely to be conclusive.

Share ownership in joint names entails considerations similar to those relating to real property and discussed in relation to the family home. It seems that resulting trust principles are most appropriate here in the absence of any express declaration to the contrary.

As a matter of practical importance, it is always essential to alert the bank or building society of a dispute and, if appropriate, to alter the drawing arrangements to prevent the funds being drawn by the other party. Any dispute concerning personal property which is litigated by a legally aided client will again be subject of the legal aid statutory charge. Transfer and settlement of property orders can be sought where there are children as discussed above.

14. Proceedings under the Married Women's Property Act 1882 and the Matrimonial Proceedings and Property Act 1970

It is easy to overlook the possibility of proceedings under these two Acts when advising heterosexual cohabitees, as they are likely to be relevant in a minority of cases only. However, an application can be made under s 17 of the 1882 Act for a declaration as to the ownership of disputed property where the parties had an agreement to marry. The application must be made within three years of the termination of the agreement and may be particularly useful in relation to personal property since the proceedings are considered family proceedings in respect of which the first £2,500 of property recovered or preserved is exempt from the statutory charge where the litigant is legally aided. Section 37 of the 1970 Act provides that where a spouse (which includes a partner in couples with an agreement to marry) makes a substantial contribution in money or money's worth to the improvement of property that person is entitled to a beneficial share. This avoids the need to prove common intention under a resulting trust and may therefore be advantageous.

Conclusion

The law relating to the unmarried family is not set in any cohesive framework, or indeed, in any framework at all. The law is inconsistent in its treatment of unmarried cohabitees, sometimes treating them as if they were a married couple, and sometimes preferring to treat them as two quite unrelated individuals. In some rare situations, such as in the context of the Fatal Accidents Act 1976, heterosexual cohabitees are treated as a species apart. Cohabitees of the same sex, on the other hand, are not recognised as a unit at all by the law. Whilst the reforms relating to children of unmarried parents are to be welcomed, these children are probably still at a disadvantage in the context of financial relief on the breakdown of their parents' relationship, compared with children whose parents divorce; this is discussed in Chapter 8.

Many areas are in need of reform. The aim must be for a statutory framework which provides consistent treatment of cohabitees in all contexts, and encourages rather than discourages the unmarried family to make its own arrangements in advance of breakdown, as is already done in many other jurisdictions. It would be easy to specify that the provisions were to apply only to cohabitees who had lived together for a period of two years or more unless there were children of the relationship, in which case there seems no real reason why a time limit is needed. Some cohabitees may specifically not want special treatment as a cohabiting couple, and it should be possible to permit such couples to "opt out". Any developments in this direction are a long way off, but it would be relatively simple for the courts or Parliament to acknowledge the benefits of cohabitation contracts for couples both of the same and of different sexes. It is submitted that far from being contrary to public policy, given the expense to the public purse of litigation, simpler methods of resolution of disputes between former cohabitees is very much in the public interest.

Other major anomalies could also be addressed. A uniform treatment of cohabitees in tax and social security legislation is long overdue. An extension of bereavement damages to cohabitees under the Fatal Accidents Act 1976 is another simple and logical reform. Perhaps the most urgent is for consistent resolution of disputes relating to a tenancy of rented accommodation in which cohabitees have been living. As shown in Chapter 9, joint tenant cohabitees who are joint tenants but have no children, do not have a legal remedy. Even where there are children, depending on the nature of the tenancy, the court may still not be able to intervene. A simple answer would be to extend the relevant provisions of the Matrimonial Homes Act 1983 to cohabitees with children.

Bibliography

Arden, A: Homeless Persons: The Housing Act 1985 Part III, 3rd edition, LAG, 1988

Bainham, A: Children: The New Law, The Children Act 1989, Jordans, 1990

Barton, C: Cohabitation Contracts, Gower, 1985

Berkowits, B: The Family and the Rent Acts: Reflections on Law and Policy, Journal of Social Welfare Law, March 1982, pp 83-100

Bevan, HK: Child Law, Butterworth, 1989

Bond, DW: Simon's Taxes, 3rd edition, Butterworth, 1985

Bridge, J, Bridge, S and Luke, S: Blackstone's Guide to the Children Act 1989, Blackstone Press, 1990

Central Statistical Office: Social Trends 21, HMSO, 1991

Daniel, M: Spouses, Cohabitees, Their Home and Lenders, Family Law, November 1990, pp 445-447

Dyer, C and Berlins, M: Living Together, Hamlyn Paperbacks, 1981

Fricker, N: Committal for Contempt in the County Court, Family Law, July 1988, pp 232-253

Fricker, N: Injunctions and Undertakings: New County Court Forms and Rules, Family Law, April 1991, pp 143-155

Hayton, D: Equitable Rights of Cohabitees, The Conveyancer, Vol 54, 1990, pp 370-387

Hoath, D C: Public Housing Law, Sweet & Maxwell, 1989

Hoggett, BM and Pearl, DS: The Family, Law and Society, 2nd edition, Butterworth, 1987

Jackson, J: People who live together should put their affairs in order, Family Law, November 1990, pp 439-441

Law Commission: Fourteenth Annual Report, 1978-1979, Law Comm, No 97, HMSO 1979.

Law Commission: Reform of the Grounds of Divorce; the Field of Choice, Cmnd 3123, HMSO, 1966

Law Commission: Family Law Review of Child Law Guardianship and Custody, Law Comm No 172, 1988

Maidment, S: The Law's Response to Marital Violence in England and the USA (1977) 26 International and Comparative Law Quarterly, pp 403-444

Office of Population and Census Surveys, Social Survey Division: General Household Survey, 1988 No 18, HMSO 1990.

Office of Population and Census Surveys: Population Trends 63, Spring 1991, HMSO, 1991

Ogus and Barendt: The Law of Social Security, 3rd edition, Butterworth, 1988

Oliver, D: Why do people live together?, Journal of Social Welfare Law, July 1982, p 209-222

Pahl, J (ed): Private Violence and Public Policy. The Needs of Battered Women and the Response of Public Services, Routledge, 1985

Pahl, J: Police Response to Battered Women [1982] Journal of Social Welfare Law, pp 337-343

Parker, S: Cohabitees, 2nd edition, Kluwer Law Publishers, 1987

Parry, M: The Law Relating to Cohabitation, 2nd edition, Sweet & Maxwell, 1988

Pearce, N: Name-Changing: A Practical Guide, Fourmat Publishing, 1990

Pizzey, E: Scream Quietly or the Neighbours will hear, Penguin Books, 1974

Priest, J: Families Outside Marriage, Family Law, 1990

Rodgers, CP: Housing – the New Law, a Guide to the Housing Act 1988, Butterworth, 1989

Scottish Law Commission: The Effects of Cohabitation in Private Law, Discussion Paper No 86, 1990

Smith, PF: Evans and Smith: The Law of Landlord and Tenant, Butterworth, 1989

Sparkes, P: The Quantification of Beneficial Interests: Problems arising from Deposits, Mortgage Advances and Mortgage Instalments, Oxford Journal of Legal Studies, vol 11, no 1, Spring 1991, pp 39-62

Steiner, J: Textbook on EEC Law, 2nd edition, Blackstone, 1990

Thorton et al: The Unmarried Family, College of Law Lectures, College of Law, 1990.

Treitel: GH: The Law of Contract, 7th edition, Stevens, 1987

Ward,M and Zebedee J: Guide to the Community Charge, Institute of Housing, SHAC & CPAG Ltd, 1990

Weitzman: The Marriage Contract: Couples, Lovers and the Law, 1981

Wood, J: The Social Security Act 1990, the Clean Break Rejoined, Family Law, January 1991, pp 31-33

Index